T0339478

Internal Audit Leadership

With an emphasis on value creation and leadership, this book will help organizations around the globe to build stronger internal audit functions, highlighting the latest risks, including COVID-19, and the most cutting-edge tools to assess them.

As environmental risks grow in number and complexity, and organizational resources become more constrained, the need to maximize both efficiency and effectiveness in internal auditing (IA) has never been greater. International audit expert Patricia Kaim leverages nearly 30 years' experience to offer real-world solutions to a range of IA issues, including how to:

- audit key major areas, such as organizational culture, diversity and inclusion, fraud, blockchain and cyber risk
- design first-class continuous monitoring
- improve stakeholder management and add value to a range of auditing activities
- increase audit speed without compromising on quality.
- develop high-performing IA teams with high agility, emotional intelligence and morale.

Auditors, audit executives and quality assurance professionals in business and government will gain a new understanding of how to add value to their organizations, and a toolkit of best practices in IA design, management, analytics and more.

Patricia Kaim, CIA, CFE, CAMS, CFRIS and CCE, has over 26 years of experience in regulatory compliance, operational risk, information security and cyber technology, digital banking, data management, cryptocurrencies and business developments. She successfully drove change, managed complex projects regarding consumer banking and digital banking and led the internal audit transformation for several organizations including data analytics and innovation. She supervised large teams and complex projects over digital banking, consumer and branch banking (over 5,000 branches), asset management, capital markets, including third-party vendors, and SOX compliance. She has heavy experience working with examiners and regulators, and has had exposure to diverse cultures and the great opportunity to work in LATAM, Mexico, the United States and India.

Internal Audit Leadership

Elevating the Internal Audit Function
to Accelerate Value

Patricia Kaim

 Routledge
Taylor & Francis Group

NEW YORK AND LONDON

Designed cover image: Getty

First published 2024
by Routledge
605 Third Avenue, New York, NY 10158

and by Routledge
4 Park Square, Milton Park, Abingdon, Oxon, OX14 4RN

Routledge is an imprint of the Taylor & Francis Group, an informa business

© 2024 Patricia Kaim

The right of Patricia Kaim to be identified as author of this work has been asserted in accordance with sections 77 and 78 of the Copyright, Designs and Patents Act 1988.

Library of Congress Cataloging-in-Publication Data
Names: Kaim, Patricia, author.
Title: Internal audit leadership : elevating the internal audit function to accelerate value / Patricia Kaim.
Description: New York, NY : Routledge, 2024. | Includes bibliographical references and index.
Identifiers: LCCN 2023015766 (print) | LCCN 2023015767 (ebook) | ISBN 9781032557199 (hardback) | ISBN 9781032557168 (paperback) | ISBN 9781003431893 (ebook)
Subjects: LCSH: Auditing, Internal. | Leadership. | Value.
Classification: LCC HF5668.25 .K35 2024 (print) | LCC HF5668.25 (ebook) | DDC 657/.458—dc23/eng/20230427
LC record available at https://lccn.loc.gov/2023015766
LC ebook record available at https://lccn.loc.gov/2023015767

ISBN: 978-1-032-55719-9 (hbk)
ISBN: 978-1-032-55716-8 (pbk)
ISBN: 978-1-003-43189-3 (ebk)

DOI: 10.4324/9781003431893

Typeset in Optima
by Apex CoVantage, LLC

Contents

Acknowledgements

To my family . . . .
Never stop learning, and dreaming, never turn down an opportunity to gain additional experience, and never give up!!!

Introduction

During the pandemic, and specifically in March 2021, I decided to start drafting this new book. I realized how important it is to change how audits are handled; the pandemic has changed everything. The world will never be the same. I love auditing, consulting, developing high-performance teams, designing new continuous monitoring and innovative auditing tools and leveraging relevant data to identify relevant issues and mitigate risks.

I have over 26 years of experience in the financial sector, leading complex projects to simplify processes and procedures, improve customer experience and drive organizational change. I have strong international market experience in the United States, Uruguay, Mexico and India. I have been exposed to complex business environments, cultures and diverse challenges that helped me to develop more robust consulting, audit and management skills. I am focused on people as internal audit departments need to hire, develop and retain talent better.

I had the wonderful opportunity to audit local and global businesses, including retail branches (over 7,000 branches), consumer banking, digital banking, asset management, capital markets, treasury, insurance, fraud management processes, third-party vendors, models and operational risk management (ORM), among others. I can easily identify relevant risks, design, develop great data analytics tools and identify outstanding solutions to add more value to the board of directors and stakeholders.

Organizations need stronger IA functions and leadership practices; auditors must be more effective and efficient when constructing and completing risk assessments, conducting business monitoring activities and managing audit engagements. They need to identify smart audit scopes, complete audits faster or in 90 days, design and implement more continuous auditing tools and leverage relevant data (e.g. in audit engagements, including risk assessments, business monitoring activities and issue validation activities). Audit leaders must build stronger relationships with stakeholders and manage and motivate their audit teams too.

DOI: 10.4324/9781003431893-1

Organizations worldwide must focus on audit transformation, and COVID-19 has accelerated this. Financial institutions are embarking on digital banking; simplifying processes, procedures and products; and investing increasingly in technology to replace or enhance legacy systems, gain additional efficiencies, reduce costs and gain more market shares. Thus, IA departments need to innovate and transform the internal audit approach to add value over the full lifecycle of the business transformation. Audit leaders must engage better and earlier in the process, identify innovation opportunities to enhance risk assessment and business monitoring, and manage audit engagements by developing continuous auditing tools and leveraging more relevant data. We must be more flexible when assessing key risks and evaluating key controls. Audit leaders need to challenge audit teams to look outside the box to leverage key data, understand the business under review and the regulatory landscape, and to align the assurance activities to the areas of highest risks where the most value could be added.

Considering the business transformation, how can you modernize the IA audit function to add more value? Well, we are going to cover this in this book. However, the chief audit executive (CAE) can be a fantastic leader to engage in the business transformation; challenge the business; develop, retain and enhance the internal audit skills required; and encourage the development and usage of more data analytics tools. Although few IA departments have started this process, or others may believe they are already there, IA transformation is more than adding innovative technology tools or developing more data analytics tools. Data analytics is key during the entire year; we cannot add value if we are not using data to complete the audit testing, including risk assessments, business monitoring activities and issue validation activities.

I firmly believe that the majority of the IA departments have started a journey without taking a step back; what do they really want to accomplish in the short and long terms? How are they adding value to the organization? Are they considering the value approach? There is a long way before we can reach the IA modernization status or the world-class audit distinction. Different steps are needed; this is a work in progress that will require a compromised and disciplined approach to transform and improve the audit advisory and assurance activities.

We need to elevate the IA value proposition and take the IA role to the next level; COVID-19 has demonstrated that things can change in a second, so we need to be always ready and prepared. Digital-driven organizations have a competitive advantage and could serve customers better during complex events or scenarios. Those innovative IA functions are the ones that could make a lasting impact and differentiate them from others.

IA leadership goes together with innovative data analytics tools, process mining, robotic process automation, stronger IA methodologies, better audit management systems, effective and opportune monitoring tools and automated risk assessments, stronger audit teams that fully understand the business, and the right audit staff capacity and skills (e.g. communication, negotiation and presentation skills) including data analytics and technology skills. Innovation must be part of every auditor's DNA; we need to find the right talent and ensure auditors feel supported, challenged and encouraged to always look outside the box, fail and learn new things every day.

For IA departments and Compliance teams to build a great foundation and reputation and to add excellent value to the organization, they must understand and adapt quickly to the evolving and challenging environment. They must understand all high risks and have adequate capacity, analytical, technical and soft skills to deliver the best value to their stakeholders. For example, risk assessments need to be more detailed, flexible and specific to assess each risk driver. Auditors should update risk assessments multiple times during the year to identify emerging risks. Do you have robust risk assessments? Are you leveraging relevant data to assess key risk drivers (e.g. fraud, sales practices, operational, third-party vendors risk?). Data is underused; data analytics is a huge ingredient and can play an effective role in quantified risk assessments, continuous auditing and self-assurance activities.

Embarking on the IA transformation journey requires time, resources, significant effort, flexibility, transparency and support from the board of directors and stakeholders. This is not a straightforward process or only a one-time exercise: this is a continuous process that will require great expertise and dedication from a dedicated data analytics/innovation audit team and the entire IA department. Also, we need the right talent and leadership; we need people willing to transform or support a better IA strategy/vision to elevate the IA function even further. Are you genuinely adding value to your organization? Well, innovation will get you respect and a reputation in the business world. We will review these and additional great topics in the following chapters. Internal audit leadership matters.

Here we go . . .

Chapter 1

Effective Internal Audit Engagement

Internal auditors play a key role within the organization. Nowadays, companies must pay more attention to having a strong IA function considering the impact of operational, legal, reputational, compliance, fraud, technology and third-party vendors risk, among others. More companies are highly exposed to cybersecurity and more sophisticated fraud events, which require more effective audit testing and a value-added approach. Things are more complex nowadays, and data plays a key role too.

Internal auditors should not only focus on audits already scheduled or included in the annual audit plan. The audit plan must be flexible. Auditors need more continuous auditing tools and better data analytics tools, including more frequent and better interactions with key stakeholders. Auditors need to build stronger relationships with them throughout the year. They must understand the business, key risks, high-risk processes and key controls. Still, they must also be familiar with the business strategy, business objectives, challenges, key initiatives and emerging risks. Auditors need to add more value through audits and other relevant audit activities (e.g. business monitoring activities, issue validation activities, risk assessments, credible challenges provided to stakeholders during committee meetings and tollgate meetings). They also need to drive change, educate and challenge things proactively. Auditors should have a passion for driving change.

A typical auditor always follows specific procedures and guidelines to manage audit engagement. For example, an auditor sends (e.g. senior audit manager or audit manager to comply with the IA methodology) an intention to audit memo to express the intention to commence the audit in the next few weeks. After the planning ends, the senior audit manager must send an audit engagement memo (to the business head) that includes the final audit scope, key risk, key processes, audit team members and audit timeline. However, in this chapter, I would like to focus more on the daily activities auditors must accomplish to improve stakeholder engagement and provide more value to the business.

DOI: 10.4324/9781003431893-2

You may wonder, how can we accomplish that?

Through arduous work and dedication, learning the business, listening to your stakeholders, sharing your points of view, IA or business best practices. You can always raise your hand when there is a potential risk when conducting business monitoring activities or more relevant audits by either reviewing the involved processes in more detail or sharing timely and relevant findings. Stakeholders appreciate knowledgeable auditors and the ones that truly challenge the business to improve the control environment. Well, it is not easy to be an auditor as you need the discipline and courage to keep challenging the stakeholders even if they disagree initially with your critical findings.

Auditors should collaborate closely with them when a technology project is in progress, a new product is about to be released by management, and operational or fraud events are identified by the business, customers or another line of defence. I highly encourage the auditor's participation earlier to add more value to stakeholders. Auditors should assess the key risks, automated controls and open issues (if any) in advance; if concerns are identified earlier, the business will have enough time to fix or define new or additional corrective actions before technology and product releases.

I want to highlight the importance of having a preventive and continuous audit function for your organization or when you need to build one. Stakeholders have higher expectations regarding IA departments as the control environment is more complex, and criminal minds take advantage of weak controls. I would like to share the right ingredients that a good IA function should have or to improve to provide better value to its stakeholders:

- Talent acquisition, development and retention
- Stakeholders' engagement with first and second lines of defence
- IA quality assurance function
- Data analytics tools
- Innovation
- Business knowledge

Talent Acquisition, Development and Retention

IA departments need to identify the right talent and have the expertise to cover key risks (e.g. technology, third-party vendors, compliance, fraud, anti-money laundry, fiduciary, sales practices, model and cybersecurity), key processes and products, including regulatory requirements. Adequate and robust audit training regarding policies and procedures, regulatory requirements, IA methodology and key testing programmes developed by

IA subject matter experts (SMEs) (e.g. third-party vendors, data management, fraud management, sales practices, committee effectiveness, technology and compliance) are highly recommended. For example, mandatory training should be available and tracked for compliance purposes.

Auditors must also have additional certifications (e.g. Certified Internal Auditor [CIA], Certified Public Accountant [CPA], Certified Fraud Examiner [CFE] and Certified Information Security Auditor [CISA]). In addition, they need to have a balance between flexibility and firmness. It is not good to have weak auditors that are not strong enough to present complex issues or to manage difficult conversations with senior management. Although technical skills are important and requested in job postings, soft skills are also critical (e.g. analytical mindset, critical thinking, presentation and communication skills, project management, conflict management, stakeholder engagement, management and leadership skills) and more difficult to find or develop in the short term. For example, getting the right message across can be the difference between IA playing a reactive, assurance-based role or being a trustworthy business advisor – where the real value is delivered. Thus, companies need strong, sound and very professional auditors who keep their integrity, reputation and independence intact. Also, auditors need to be independent and objective always.

It is also important to understand the skills gaps. A skills gap assessment is highly recommended (at least annually) and must be refreshed at least quarterly. Additional co-sources or full-time employees could be hired to address the resource skill gaps, and new auditors invited (from other locations) to current or future audits. The guest reviewer programmes (which give high-performing employees from independent business units the opportunity to gain IA experience) could be another interesting option. The business will appreciate that as the guest reviewers can share their expertise (once back to the company) with the rest of their teams.

Organizations must invest in the IA function and find, develop and retain talent by offering audit members the best opportunities to fulfil their personal and professional skills. These new opportunities are highly valuable to IA personnel. Adequate training is essential to enhance auditors' technical and soft skills. Training should not be vague or basic; real case examples or robust case studies can facilitate the application of concepts learned. While working for an international bank, I delivered a particularly useful training (stakeholders' engagement) that I found fascinating and useful to improve auditors' soft skills. I had to travel to various locations to deliver the training and met different auditors who experienced challenges when presenting audit findings. Few auditors did not know how to build stronger relationships with their stakeholders. This training gave auditors the right tools to identify key stakeholders, develop stronger relationships and manage conflict when delivering a difficult message. Putting yourself in your stakeholder's shoes can make a dramatic difference. Soft skills are critical when managing stakeholder relationships, presenting and negotiating an issue and managing conflict.

Another critical point is that every communication channel requires a different strategy and style, whether with senior audit managers or audit committees. If you must deliver a complex issue to the business, it is common to find resistance or lack of acceptance by impacted stakeholders. However, auditors must be able to deliver the message appropriately, focusing on the facts, risks and consequences to the business or organization. Auditors must deliver the message and help the business to understand it.

IA departments sometimes suffer a high attrition rate due to a lack of leadership, robust IA methodology or technology tools, insufficient resources or support from the audit leadership team when issues are presented to senior management. Companies must retain and develop talent and give internal candidates better opportunities to develop their skills. Do you have a talent programme, or is your attrition rate too high? Well, you really have an extra challenge here if there is no adequate retention strategy. Human resources (HR) must be involved to ensure talent programmes are in place and audit team members are developed too.

Stakeholders' Engagement With All Lines of Defences

Managing and building relationships with the stakeholders take time and never end. It is a constant process that requires time from audit managers, audit directors and above to build good relationships and add more value. It is important to mention that auditors are responsible for conducting themselves, so their objectivity, integrity, confidentiality, independence and competency are not open to question.

The business needs to understand how important it is to collaborate closely with auditors to minimize potential risks. Auditors should not only show up when an audit engagement is about to start. However, they should meet business heads or their direct reports regularly to understand the business strategy, new products coming, emerging risks, new regulatory requirement's impact, customers' needs or complaints, key projects and initiatives. Audit teams must retain meeting minutes; all follow-up items identified through those meetings could be included in future business monitoring activities, issue validation activities or audits.

In addition, it is critical to building good relationships with the second line of defence (e.g. finance, compliance, legal and HR). A strong control environment requires strong first, second and third lines of defence. The first line of defence (business) must work with the second or third line of defence (IA). A weak second line of defence puts good pressure on IA teams to identify relevant risks and issues.

From my own experience, I have seen businesses moving from insufficient assurance or weak (audit report ratings) to a better rate by working very closely with compliance and IA teams. Open and transparent communication with IA teams is a plus. For example, before putting an issue into validation, IA teams should work closely with the business (one or two months in advance) to validate the sustainability of corrective actions or share feedback if corrective actions or issues are not ready for IA validation. Auditors must constantly interact with their stakeholders and engage with them earlier; transparency is key.

Effective stakeholder engagement often enhances business alignment and elevates IA's awareness, focusing on the most relevant risks. We need to improve risk assessments and business monitoring activities and develop better data analytics tools and continuous auditing tools to become more relevant to business objectives and strategies. We also need to build closer relationships with senior management, board of directors and chief executive officer (CEO) to understand their current needs, challenges, open issues and business strategy to increase our business knowledge, define smarter audit scopes and transparency and improve the IA's relevance to other operating functions.

Internal Audit Quality Assurance Function

Auditors must focus on the quality of work. We must inspire auditors worldwide to deliver high-quality work and promote high-quality standards. As an auditor and then an IA senior director, I have always emphasized high-quality communication with stakeholders and high-quality testing and documentation. Thus, an IA QA function is relevant to maintaining high-quality standards locally and globally if there is an international presence.

Not all organizations have a strong QA team which ensures that the IA methodology is used adequately and consistently across all IA teams. The QA team is also responsible for performing the quality reviews of work papers (e.g. risk assessments, issue validation and business monitoring activities) and developing or enhancing training materials based on observations identified through QA scorecards or reviews. QA scorecards are issued to provide recommendations or findings regarding the working papers reviews; issues may be raised to IA teams. Thus, it promotes a culture that rewards continuous improvement of the IA methodology and enhances the IA best practices.

An IA department that consistently delivers a high-quality service to the organization is recognized by the board of directors and senior management. Regulators constantly evaluate the IA function of financial institutions. A QA function continuously contributes to this objective, as well. Regulators can raise regulatory issues if certain areas or topics require enhancements or attention (e.g. inadequate risk coverage, risk assessments and business monitoring activities). After completing the selected reviews, the QA function could raise issues.

Of course, it is relevant to maintain good independence between the QA function and any other IA teams or CAE. The QA function has relevant regulator experience and can also contribute to developing IA teams and relationships with regulators. Frequent informal meetings with the QA team allow IA teams to quickly address any questions regarding IA methodology and coverage and, of course, help to build a stronger relationship with the QA team.

To build an effective QA function, it is relevant to have auditors with business knowledge and experience auditing the businesses under review. QA team should be able to challenge the audit teams. Rotation is highly recommended to build a stronger QA function, and allocating strong audit managers or senior audit managers to help the QA team could be an excellent option. These auditors will become more familiar with the IA methodology and benefit their teams when completing the temporary QA assignment.

How are you helping your business to understand the IA methodology? QA team could provide training to stakeholders to explain the IA methodology so they can understand an audit report, audit report rating, different audit phases (pre-planning, planning, fieldwork and reporting), how to write a corrective action and audit expectations during the audit engagements and issue validation activities. This training should be provided a few times every year to enhance their understanding of IA methodology and subsequent enhancements or changes.

Data Analytics Tools

Analytics is becoming more relevant for the IA function. Due to the complexity of businesses, emerging risks and fraud events, it is not possible to perform testing just based on a sample; we need to analyse the entire population. Auditors must leverage relevant data during audit engagements, risk assessments, business monitoring activities and issue validation activities. We cannot add relevant value to stakeholders if we do not use relevant data to identify trends, concerns and outliers, and to complete audit testing. Data analytics is under-utilized and more work is necessary to design and enhance data analytics tools and continuous auditing tools.

I have experienced the benefits of leveraging relevant data as listed here:

- *Complete the audit engagement faster*. For example, analysing data and trends can help auditors focus on what matters before starting the planning or fieldwork phase or during business monitoring activities. Target reviews can be identified earlier due to high operational losses in certain business areas (e.g. higher customer complaints, cash differences, refunds, fraud losses and sales practices) or when analysed in conjunction with other key data points (e.g. customer complaints, operational losses, fraud events, allegations and net promoter scores [customer's surveys or feedback]).

- *Perform cheaper and smarter audit engagements.* Fewer resources may be required to complete audits and issue validation activities when the right and relevant data analytics tools are utilized. However, auditors need to have data analytical skills to pull, analyse data queries and build stronger data analytics tools that could be leveraged during business monitoring activities and monthly or quarterly testing (continuous auditing tools). Auditors can identify issues earlier and topics for further review. Also, these data analytics tools provide cost savings (fewer resources and quicker audits or testing) and more impactful results in the long term. Once these automated tools are released, additional hours can be saved significantly, especially in the long term.

A data analytics team must be in place to have the right support during audits, risk assessments, business monitoring activities and issue validation activities. It is desirable to look for individuals with strong data analytics backgrounds and business knowledge to facilitate the definition of queries and data analysis. When I had to build the data analytics function for an organization, I hired auditors with strong analytical skills that could support the audit teams. I also asked my entire team to take the Analytics Academy training available and looked for external training too. I made this training mandatory, including myself. I brought external candidates too. Data analytics and innovation activities were a priority for my audit team so we could expand our horizons and audit better.

It is also relevant for the business to build the data analytics function to identify issues earlier. I have seen more organizations taking the lead on bringing additional resources to support the control functions and self-assurance activities for both the first and second lines of defence. There is a high demand for data analytics, and more IA job functions request this skill. Compliance programmes must be more flexible and innovative and incorporate best practices into their testing too.

Auditors must challenge the first and second lines of defence to leverage more data when selecting branches, reviewing key risks (e.g. sales practices, conduct risks, compliance, fraud, third-party vendors and operational risks), or when auditing their programmes (e.g. compliance programmes such as Enterprise Testing, Conduct Risk Reviews, Branch Oversight Programs, Wealth Management Testing and Mortgage Testing). No single function (second or third line) can be effective if there is insufficient data to complete testing or monitoring activities. We may be able to identify still a few concerns but not the relevant ones or even nothing. However, I am confident that your initial conclusions or observations can change dramatically (more impactful issues) when data is available and fully utilized.

However, one of the most notable obstacles in building a sustainable analytics capability for IA is changing the traditionalist mindset. Forward planning is critical and often requires a rethink of the IA methodology and testing approach to allow additional data analytics tools.

To build the data analytics function, IA leaders should consider at least the following:

- What skills are required (e.g. specific application software, data management expertise, presentation skills)?
- What software is necessary to pull and process the required data timely?
- Are there any licenses available for IA, or should we wait until assigned to the IA team?
- Does the laptop have the right capacity to pull and analyse the data?
- Who will be the single point of contact (SPOC) or the data analytics champion?
- Do you have system access to key applications?
- How should we document the data analytics testing to ensure consistency across all IA teams?
- What is the desirable organizational structure to support the data analytics strategy (e.g. a centralized function that will train and support all audit teams or one per audit team)?
- Are you using data or enough data during an audit engagement, risk assessments, business monitoring activities and issue validation activities? If not, why?

From my point of view, data analytics is more effective when all audit team members have analytics knowledge and do not depend on a few people to run queries or analyse data. This means your core IA professionals should have the right data analytics skills to perform the required testing. Audits highly focused on data analytics are more effective and can provide a greater impact on the organization. Soon, effective IA departments will integrate analytics as a core capability across their function and throughout the audit lifecycle. By acting now, IA leaders can take the lead on such an important topic and encourage the business to automate testing and use more data analytics tools to self-identify issues or enhance self-assurance activities. It is time to act now.

Stakeholders highly appreciate data analytical tools and more opportune findings, enabling auditors to position themselves more strategically within the organization. I would like to share a few benefits of using data analytics during audits, issue validation activities and business monitoring activities:

- Earlier identification of issues and better audit coverage.
- Smarter audit scopes to direct due to data analysis or trends identified.
- More relevant IA functions to the business and boards as more automated business monitoring activities can identify relevant and opportune issues throughout the year.
- Effective communication of issues through better data analytics dashboards, decks and audit reports on a monthly or quarterly basis.
- Closer relationship with stakeholders through continuous auditing, business monitoring activities, issue validation activities and audits.
- More credibility with our regulators as IA has better coverage and business oversight.

To build the right data analytics tools, the IA team must understand the complexities of systems to capture data and validate it for completeness and accuracy. Also, it is necessary to document the analysis performed and output, including additional testing, if required. For example, companies highly protect data, so obtaining business approval for extractions can be time-consuming and challenging. In the era of digitalization and business transformation (e.g. companies are modifying legacy systems and building better systems and applications), extracting and validating data integrity and completeness can be challenging.

Auditors need to use more extensive data to understand the business better, identify relevant business concerns or issues, and provide better audit coverage. Thus, it is important to build stronger relationships with stakeholders (first and second lines of defence, external auditors and regulators) to understand their needs, challenges and emerging risks. Auditors must provide more impactful audit results and add more value to the entire organization.

Also, auditors need to understand the business very well, the key risks and key control to develop better data analytics tools and continuous auditing tools. They must work with their business partners to identify the automated key controls and complete the design assessments. Typically, a multidisciplinary team will be engaged; strong auditors with strong business knowledge will help identify key controls and complete the design assessment while the data analytics team (also involved in the walkthroughs) will help them pull the required data. They will have to validate the completeness and accuracy of the data and potential exceptions once the tool is used at least once (before releasing the final product). The data analytics team will provide the data to the audit team to determine if it allows for adequate results or outputs. If positive feedback is received, the data analytics team will continue with the development phase until the tools are finalized, assessed and implemented by the audit team.

Innovation

IA leaders need to make innovation a centrepiece. We cannot continue testing using the traditional testing approach based on just a sample. For example, providing a good combination of data analytics tools or trend analysis by using the right technology to improve the business monitoring, risk assessments, issue validation activities and audit process and reporting are extremely important. Data is relevant in every audit phase and during issue validation activities.

One philosophy is to be the best for our stakeholders. So, how could you accomplish that without using relevant data? Auditors could improve things, especially considering key problems or challenges faced to improve things as listed here:

- Audits take longer than expected and sometimes take over one hundred days to publish an audit report.
- Audit scopes are not smart, so stakeholders think that audits are sometimes a waste of time. For example, auditors may not consider strategic, cultural or conduct risks or other relevant emerging risks when conducting audits. Auditors do not use enough data during pre-planning and planning activities to identify trends, concerns or outliers to facilitate the definition of the audit scope.
- Auditors only show up to conduct audits and are not involved with the business the entire year, so they lack business knowledge.
- Management does not recognize auditors as trusted advisors who could add value to the business.
- Stakeholders fear having a bad audit report rating.
- Auditors are not familiar with the business or do not have the right skills to review key risks such as technology, strategic risk, fraud, operational, compliance and cryptocurrency risk.
- Auditors do not use relevant data during planning such as operational losses, large fraud losses, complaints, allegations and transactional data to identify and finalize the audit scope leaving relevant key processes outside the audit scope. Another important thing is that auditors should use this data collectively and together to identify trends, outliers or additional concerns for further research or testing (e.g. sales practices, control breaks, potential collusion and excessive operational losses in certain branches or regions).

- The audit plan has so many audits that the business cannot manage all audits with all competing projects, priorities or reviews (second line of defence, self-assurance activities, franchise reviews, regulatory reviews).
- Audits are so manual that no data is leveraged due to the lack of audit resources, no data tools available and no access to the data. Information is under-utilized, or not enough hours are requested during the construction of the audit plan or refresh.
- The audit report is so long that it is not easy to digest all findings or recommendations.
- The customer's experience is not considered at all in the Process Risk and Controls (PRC), so audits are not focused on the customer's experience despite excessive customer complaints.
- The business process mapping (related to the PRCs) or the manager control assessments (MCAs) are still not mature, and auditors cannot place reliance on this to conduct audits. This is an important topic that I would like to expand on.

Why is an MCA not helpful in identifying better issues? Here are some potential reasons: business process mappings are outdated; key processes and key controls are not identified or inadequately rated; hand-offs are not clear; data analytics tools are underused for testing/monitoring purposes; self-assurance activities are vague or irrelevant; key stakeholders are not involved in end-to-end processes; business control teams do not have the right skills, capacity or data analytics tools to complete testing effectively; and relevant risks are not fully considered or fully mapped (e.g. compliance, fraud, cybersecurity and third-party vendors). Management may need to simplify processes, procedures and products to enhance the MCAs, design and implement more data analytics tools, and consider also best practices and an integrated approach.

Thus, how can audits be efficient and effective if the business does not know the key risks, key controls, handoffs and control owners? It will take audits longer than expected as the audit team, and the business will discover the controls together during the audit engagement or issue validation activities. How about key risks? How can companies minimize key risks, or can self-identify relevant issues if the MCA or PRC process is not mature at all? Well, it is going to be extremely difficult. Every organization constantly evolves, so the first line of defence should allocate sufficient resources and have better technology tools to regularly complete and update the MCA or PRC process. Continuous improvement is key; this is not a one-time exercise, so audit teams must audit this area diligently to add more value to the entire organization.

Thus, considering the aforementioned challenges, auditors need to be more flexible and innovative and provide better services to stakeholders to drive change. Auditors must challenge the business to ensure they are fully prepared for the audits or any other reviews (e.g. external auditors, regulators or additional franchise reviews); they also need to understand the key controls and have enough resource capacity and skills to finalize and update the PRCs and MCAs. How could you be the best for your stakeholders? How can you add more value to your stakeholders?

Here are a few ideas that could help:

- *Spend more time with your stakeholders.* Auditors need to work very closely with the business to understand current needs, concerns, challenges or any other potential risks that may impact the business goals, strategy, financial results or the company's reputation. Auditors can share their knowledge through regular meetings, committee meetings, working groups or additional training, among others. They should have monthly or quarterly meetings with key stakeholders, and the audit teams should be fully prepared for those meetings.
- *Use the agile approach to conduct audits or validate issues.* This is a more disciplinary approach to managing audit activities more efficiently and effectively. This does not substitute or replace the IA methodology. All audit phases can be conducted simultaneously by defining scrums meetings. It improves transparency with your stakeholders by sharing potential findings and pending information earlier. The main objective is to reduce the time invested during audits, issue validation activities and facilitate better communication between the audit team and the business.
- *Identify and automate audit testing (key controls) to enhance continuous auditing tools and business monitoring activities.* Auditors could build data analytics tools to easily identify trends, concerns and outliers regarding high-risk key processes (e.g. account opening and closing, regulatory requirements, user access, mandatory training, mandatory absence, customer wire transfers, customer complaints, refunds, operational losses and fraud losses). Quarterly continuous auditing or business monitoring reports could be available to highlight audit testing results, findings and corrective actions.
- *Analyse IA, self-identified and regulatory issues to identify trends, concerns or future thematic reviews.* Auditors need to identify trends, outliers or thematic problems (e.g. information security, third-party vendors, customer disclosures [across products, channels, portfolios], operational losses, fraud events and anti-money laundering [AML], among others). By identifying the root cause of thematic issues, auditors could identify more innovative audits, request smarter action plans and conduct a more holistic review or testing approach. This information could facilitate the audit planning and the definition of the audit scope; data is always relevant to defining a smart audit scope.

I highly encourage teams to analyse all IA issues, including issues raised by other IA teams, management self-identified and regulatory issues. Common themes are relevant (e.g. data management, third-party vendors, continuity of business, COB, system limitations regarding legacy systems [lack of automated or effective controls], manual processes or complex procedures that may require simplification, complaints management and resolution).

- *Focus on a smart audit scope.* Auditors need to spend more time pre-planning and planning activities to identify key business challenges and emerging and strategic risks. We should spend more time in these two audit phases to define a smarter audit scope; this is an enormous difference between an audit's success and failure. For example, an evaluation of the customer's journey, customer experience and an assessment of third-party vendors (business oversight and monitoring activities), fraud risk or strategic risk could represent the highest concerns (from a management standpoint) and may be relevant to include in the audit scope. The RCM should consist of high-risk processes, key risks and key controls mapped to all risk assessments (high-risk drivers). There should not be a disconnect between the RCM and the risk assessment for the auditable entity under review unless a valid reason is supported by the auditor's rationale (e.g. open issues and reliance on prior audits).

- *Automate risk assessments and business monitoring activities.* Auditors can pull data from key systems and applications or request it from the business. Audit testing results could be timely shared with your stakeholders. In addition, business monitoring reports can highlight new audit findings earlier; however, providing unrated business monitoring reports could facilitate communication with stakeholders and provide a better audit experience. You may be able to automate certain things or create additional continuous data analytics tools too (e.g. user access, mandatory training, mandatory absence, account opening and closing [customer's applications, signatures, consents, disclosures], operational losses, complaints data and fraud events).

Risk assessments must be flexible and detailed enough to understand key and emerging risks. If the risk assessments are not robust enough or detailed enough to assess key risk drivers (e.g. compliance, AML, model, liquidity, interest rate, technology, third-party vendors, operational and fraud risks) for an auditable entity, it will be more difficult to define a smarter audit scope and complete the audit on time. Risk assessments should not contain generic data or vague business metrics. Also, open issues should be allocated to each auditable entity; the more issues identified (by audit, regulators or the business), the higher the auditable risk, which will impact the audit frequency. Higher-risk areas deserve more frequent audits to comply with the IA methodology.

- *Develop smart audit reports.* Stakeholders will appreciate shorter audit reports but mainly timely audit reports. Auditors could automate the audit report process through the audit management system or other innovative tools. I honestly believe that audit reports should be shorter and easier to digest.
- *Develop smart audit committee decks.* Auditors could leverage technology to create simpler, shorter and more automated reports or decks. They could leverage certain key data points to populate certain sections of the reports (e.g. issue pipeline, audit plan status, key changes, concerns and thematic issues identified in audits).
- *Reduce time spent on issue validation activities.* IA teams could focus on validating the most complex issues, such as critical, high or moderate, and not spend too much time on low-rated issues. Thus, auditors will have additional time to build stakeholders' relationships; update risk assessments; understand the business concerns, challenges and priorities; and identify and monitor emerging risks. Auditors should cooperate with the business earlier; design assessments could be done when the issue/corrective action design is reported as complete but effectiveness testing once the sustainability period ends (controls have been implemented and have been working as intended for three or four months). Also, auditors need to leverage more data to validate corrective actions and open issues to save additional time.

Business Knowledge

The IA teams must know their business' and stakeholders' expectations well. The audit director and the chief audit director need to share the audit plan with the stakeholders to include their inputs and business direction. IA routinely considers the business strategies and objectives, regulatory and company policy requirements, industry and market information, and insights gained through participation in strategic discussions or key meetings.

Auditors must continue building relationships with all stakeholders, including the second line of defence. The latter could be assessed during audits or specific audits to cover only compliance programmes, as well. Auditors and senior management can improve the control environment by focusing on shared goals. Mutual respect, empathy and collaboration also enhance communication and produce better results in the long term.

They need to know their stakeholders through regular, timely, formal or informal meetings. A lack of shared knowledge does not help the communication and does not help auditors build stronger relationships with senior management. Informal meetings are also valid and could help build adequate trust, transparency, and reputation among stakeholders. Having an inventory of key meetings to assign roles and responsibilities (audit manager, senior managers and audit director) for attending each meeting, preparing the deck materials and developing meeting notes could be an excellent idea. This information, in conjunction with other data points and key management reports, is relevant to finalizing quarterly business monitoring activities for each auditable entity. The audit director or chief audit director should review the business monitoring memo or summary document quarterly. Business monitoring activities are important to keep risk assessments current.

The senior audit manager or audit director should review the meeting inventory regularly to add or remove others. It is important to ensure that all key meetings are conducted timely and that meeting minutes are retained in the audit management system. The QA team can periodically review or take a sample of business monitoring memos/documents to ensure that these activities are taking place. I like detailed business monitoring activities (one per auditable entity) as this will help auditors identify potential risks, topics or issues. If auditors identify issues during business monitoring activities, they must request management corrective actions to address the concerns.

Do you really know your stakeholders? Do you spend enough time with them? How often do you meet with key stakeholders? Do you have regular meetings? Is your input relevant during tollgate or committee meetings? If your answer to most of these questions is "no," I suggest investing more time with them. Business partners who truly engage with auditors can get more valuable input; auditors can add much more value to the business during those meetings and in preparation for future audits. Auditors who are really engaged with stakeholders can understand them better and gain additional knowledge in preparation for the audits.

Are you familiar with the three-line defence model? Well, I am going to cover this in the next chapter.

Chapter 2

Understanding the Three Lines of Defence Model

Ideally, all three lines of defence should exist in every organization, regardless of size or complexity. The boundaries among them are not always clear or, in a few cases, are not well defined or positioned in the organization. However, I have seen that the preferred approach is to have the three lines of defence in place as listed below:

- *The first line of defence:* It is the front-line staff and operational management responsible for assessing and managing the risks and controls. The systems, controls and tone at the top are crucial in anticipating, preventing and managing operational risks. For example, we could have the branch banking and branch oversight programmes, consumer lending, wealth management, insurance, retail businesses and asset management, including operations, among others. They offer products and services to customers. They are responsible for the MCAs and PRCs; they design and implement key controls to minimize risks. Thus, there should be adequate resource capacity and skills to implement key controls and complete oversight activities to comply with policies, procedures and regulatory requirements.
- *The second line of defence:* Independent from the first line of defence, it provides guidance and oversight compliance with policies, procedures, regulatory requirements and other risks to ensure that the business manages them. It includes ORM, compliance [compliance testing or enterprise testing and conducting risk reviews or inspections), controllership, finance, legal, financial control, ethics and HR functions, among others. They have the expertise and provide challenges to the business. Auditors need to assess these areas or departments to ensure they provide credible challenges to the business; their testing programmes or oversight activities are adequate to identify relevant risks.
- *The third line of defence (IA):* It is an independent assurance function on the entire governance, risk management and internal control framework,

DOI: 10.4324/9781003431893-3

including the way the first line and second line achieve risk management and control objectives. Establishing a professional and robust IA function should be a top priority and governance requirement for all organizations (smaller, larger or medium-sized); see figure 2.1.

IA provides independent and objective assurance of control environment, risk management and governance processes. Auditors must engage with stakeholders and review policies, procedures and regulatory requirements to ensure that key and well-designed controls are in place to minimize key risks.

This model interacts with local and global regulators and external auditors too. The first line of defence designs and implements key controls to minimize key risks. Thus, the tone at the top should be clear and focus on key controls and best practices to minimize potential risks. The quality of management, people and technology systems will enhance the control environment. Investors do not want to invest in weak companies or those with a bad reputation or a weak control environment. Companies cannot grow without a sound and sustainable control environment. The control environment is dynamic as companies must constantly adapt to economic, market and internal changes; management needs to identify and minimize emerging risks and resolve issues (IA, self-identified issues, regulatory issues) timely and effectively. Re-open or repeat issues impact management reputation, credibility, accountability and employee morale.

The first line of defence needs good support from the second and third lines. The second line must collaborate closely with other stakeholders and build good relationships with them. I have seen organizations where the compliance team did not have the right skills, capacity and data analytics tools to support the business. Companies started enhancing compliance testing programmes after IA and regulatory findings. This is a critical function for an organization; auditors need to review and challenge it.

However, the first line of defence has been the least well developed or qualified over the years, so big and global companies need to build stronger teams; this is also increasingly becoming so in mid-size and smaller ones. An organization needs to invest more in having the right control oversight functions (right skills, capacity and data analytics tools), developing additional monitoring tools, key management reports and self-assurance activities to identify relevant issues. They should not wait for the second or third line of defence to identify more complex issues.

IA's role is mostly detective and corrective; it requests business-specific corrective actions or suggests recommendations to minimize key risks. IA is not responsible for identifying all weaknesses or deficiencies. Auditors must conduct risk-based audits and focus on key risks, key controls and high-risk processes based on the audit scope agreed with management.

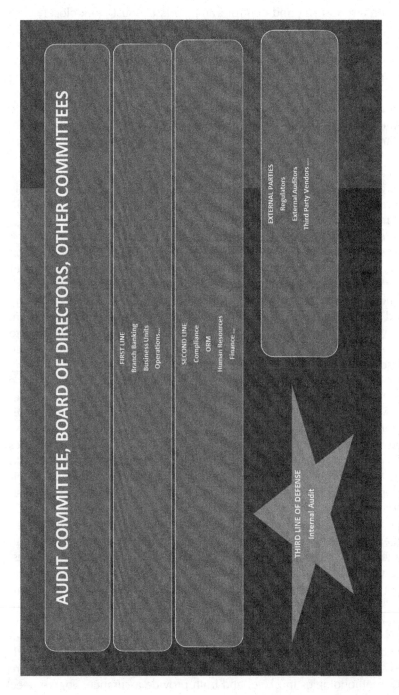

Figure 2.1 First, Second and Third Lines of Defence Interaction

To ensure a robust risk and control framework, IA must work closely with the first and second lines during the year. The model has a lot to offer if all lines of defence work together.

Auditors should be flexible with this model and not hide behind it. As every organization is different, there is no right way to coordinate them. The three lines of defence model can help an organization grow, strengthen and win. If auditors find a good observation, they need to raise their hand and not wait until an audit is complete. If you identify an issue in one region, you can share the observation further (e.g. global team, branch network and ATM network) to see if the business has a global concern or a more significant issue in other regions.

The advisory role is also particularly useful for stakeholders, so I highly encourage you to always look outside the box. Do not be afraid to try different things or audit differently. When you change how you look at things, the things you look at always change. You are not looking to create change for the sake of it. Ideally, you want your message or audit finding to be up to date, relevant and exciting. By taking a step back and re-evaluating your current audit testing approach or the way you are conducting the audit, business monitoring activities or the way you are interacting with the first and second lines of defence, you make more space for creativity and innovation.

I have always encouraged my audit teams to look outside the box, to figure out if key controls are well designed, if procedures are clear enough or reasonable to execute a particular control or transaction and to identify what can go wrong (e.g. controls not been executed as described in the procedure documents, no automated controls in place, lack of management oversight activities, no evidence of management's reviews or supervision and inconsistent activities in the branch network).

The internal and external auditors review the first and second lines of defence activities. I deeply recommend selecting additional audits to review the second line of defence to verify that the compliance or enterprise testing programmes are robust enough to identify relevant issues, testing performed can easily be reperformed by auditors, and work papers are clear enough to understand the observations identified. Another important thing: are they using relevant data to conduct testing, select retail or wealth management branches or identify sales practices? (e.g. operational losses, customer complaints, allegations, fraud, employee turnover, transactional data). If the answer is "no," how can this function add value to your organization? How do you know if the compliance testing team raises relevant issues? Are they reviewing the key risks and controls?

Let's go back to this model, this model is well known, but it is not close to being perfect. You may see an overlap between the independence compliance risk and IA functions in a few organizations. There are similar methodologies in place, and both provide assurance. So, we need better coordination and efficiencies among the three lines of defence to identify any potential gaps in coverage. For example, compliance testing teams should not focus too much on having similar or same audit testing approaches so we can coordinate efforts better. Otherwise, the business will not get the most from the second and third lines of defence. For example, suppose both teams use knowledge checks to review key processes in retail branches. In that case, issues will be similar (lack of banker's knowledge, unclear procedures, complex products or processes), but how do you know if employees' key controls are truly effective or executed consistently if no data is leveraged to complete the testing? There is a gap here.

We live in a digital era where customers use digital banking to purchase items online. Is your company, your second or third line of defence adapting to these customer needs? If not yet or they are in the process of, it is time to react; competition is fierce outside, and companies are investing more in technology solutions. IA departments must also invest (have the right skills, capacity and data analytics tools to perform business monitoring activities, issue validation activities, risk assessment and audit engagements) to enhance remote audit testing.

Thus, a strong three lines of defence model should be able to do the following:

- Utilize resources more efficiently to minimize duplication of activities; key risks and controls are identified, implemented, monitored effectively and issues are opened, tracked and resolved timely.
- Remove ambiguity by clarifying all roles and responsibilities so it is clear how this model works for anyone, including regulators. Senior management and governing bodies should communicate the expectation regarding how the information must be presented and shared and how to coordinate activities among them. Each line of defence should have policies, procedures and frameworks. For example, an IA charter clarifies its role in the organization regarding the IA function.
- Work together for the benefit of shareholders, customers and company reputation. What works well will depend on the organization's distinct risks and operational challenges.
- Create a risk ownership culture where everyone is responsible for raising hands, addressing issues timely and escalating concerns to senior management and the board of directors.
- Challenge without restrictions; new audit findings are identified, discussed and opened in the audit management system with management corrective. If you experience too much resistance from the first or second line of defence when good findings are raised, it is time to escalate further to the business head, other executives within the organization and the audit committee.

Audit executives must share information and coordinate activities with others. Thus, it is important to schedule regular meetings with external auditors or regulators to share the audit plan, testing scope and findings that may be relevant for their review. Audit directors and chief audit directors could schedule quarterly meetings with them to discuss organizational audit changes, issue validation activities, audit plan status, emerging risks or any other specific topics.

Each line of defence must be independent of the other; thus, the first line of defence will define and conduct monitoring activities over key controls identified in their PRCs, and a control group could be assigned to each business to perform independent testing (best practices), the compliance testing and IA teams should be risk-based and conducted annually based on their risk assessments. Coordinating these three approaches is relevant to minimize risks and ensure that the overall principal risks of the organizations are covered effectively to minimize any potential gaps.

An interesting new trend for global companies is the creation of the "Office of the Governance" that centralizes governance, risks and other activities such as issue management activities, third-party vendors oversight or other key relevant policies and procedures. However, sometimes it is unclear if this function is part of the first or second line of defence or if there is an overlap. It is important to have clear roles and responsibilities for each function to minimize duplication of efforts or lack of coverage.

I highly encourage having independent control teams to assess key controls and high-risk processes. I have seen organizations within business control directors (responsible for the PRC tool and self-assurance activities) who report to both the business head and the Office of the Governance, only to the Office of the Governance (if any) or to an independent centralized function. The management of the PRC testing should be 100% an independent function (centralized function) to ensure the effectiveness of self-assurance activities.

We also need to enhance the communication among the three lines of defence to work together for the best interest of shareholders and the organization. I highly encourage weekly or monthly meetings between Compliance and IA teams to share issues, concerns, new regulation approaches and testing plans. The same should apply between the first line of defence and the Compliance or IA team. All lines have a common goal so the organization can enhance the control environment. Each line should be truly responsible for encouraging discussions, scheduling meetings and motivating great cooperation among them.

I want to share the following best practices for a successful integrated three lines of defence model:

- Provide a clear definition of roles and responsibilities supported by appropriate policies, procedures or a charter. For example, IA should have an IA charter and a robust IA methodology document.

- Manage good coordination, communication and transparency of issues and concerns to assist all in accomplishing their goals. This could benefit from a centralized issue management system fully connected with IA and Compliance repositories or other systems; thus, any issues raised in audit or compliance testing reports will immediately feed the centralized issue management systems.
- Discuss compliance and audit plans with the first line of defence to get feedback and to minimize duplication of activities (second and third lines of defence). Are you reviewing similar processes or areas? Are you conducting a few audits or reviews at the same time? If you can coordinate efforts, the business will appreciate that, and you will minimize the challenges provided by the business.
- Define and streamline the responsibility for the exchange (and timing) of risk management information (including reports). Compliance and audit draft reports must be shared with the management before being published. Also, if you are working for a global organization, please involve the respective global teams, especially if issues are related to compliance, legal, AML, third-party vendors, data management and operational risks.
- Reinforce independence among them to avoid compromising their effectiveness. In situations with no three lines of defence, the governing body should be advised of the structure and its impact.
- Assign each risk (as defined within the organization) to a responsible owner in the relevant line of defence, such as business units, ORM and other corporate experts. Each risk and key control identified should have a senior manager owner who can take accountability for corrective actions.
- Reinforce the ORM culture through an effective communication strategy; the message from the top should be clear and support the other lines of defence even when identified issues point out significant management gaps.
- Define a standard language or methodology for identifying, evaluating, measuring and reporting risks. In addition, a standard protocol should define how findings or relevant topics are shared and discussed with senior management, audit committees and the board of directors. Information shared by the IA department should be clear and easy to digest by senior management. For example, standard decks could inform the management of key themes identified. Also, these key themes should impact some auditable entities.
- A robust governance risk and compliance (GRC) system support risk identification, assessment, monitoring, assurance and reporting. Also, responsible programme managers must be engaged in assessing high-risk areas, ranking key risks, key processes, probability of risk exposure and impact. Monitoring plans must address all risk areas; monitoring

plans should detail how compliance risks are reviewed on an ongoing basis.

- Have a centralized issue management system to track regulatory, self-identified and IA issues. For example, auditors could manage the issue pipeline better and will be able to identify any concerns earlier on.
- Implement a QA programme within the second line and third line of defence to ensure that the corresponding methodologies have been used adequately and consistently across teams, and an independent challenge is provided to ensure the quality of work delivered.
- Each line of defence must have adequate skills and capacity to meet their roles and responsibilities. This can be more difficult in the second and third lines of defence due to resource constraints.

IA must evaluate the oversight activities performed by the second line of defence and highlight any observations in the audit report. When auditors confirm the audit findings with management, they also need to assess if the second line of defence should have identified them. IA must assess if compliance, ORM and legal teams provide adequate oversight over the first line of defence. For example, if you identify that regulatory requirements have not been applied adequately or consistently across different states or procedures do not exist, you will need to challenge that. Is there a mechanism or process in place to identify, track and monitor any changes to regulatory requirements? You will need to have additional discussions with the compliance and legal departments, as they should have challenged the business. If there is a gap, it could be highlighted in the audit report (a new issue must be raised to the second line, or additional wording could be added in the executive summary).

In other instances, we need to assess compliance or enterprise testing programmes within the organizations; for example, does enterprise testing have a robust programme to audit the branch network or the compliance risk at the enterprise level? If you are auditing branch banking or consumer lending, you may need to add one or additional audits to cover the programme(s). Have you considered it during the audit plan refresh? Do you have any auditable entities, or do you need to add another one to ensure there is appropriate coverage? Are you working closely with your compliance SMEs to agree on the audit scope (e.g. account opening, closing, customer wire transfers and transaction monitoring)? Are all regulatory requirements mapped to your auditable entities, or did you consider all regulatory requirements in your risk assessments? How will you cover all regulatory requirements that impact branch banking, consumer lending and consumer banking in the long term?

IA functions must adapt to changes in the control environment and invest in technology solutions to create more data analytics tools. Innovative technologies can provide better opportunities to increase efficiencies and improve audit coverage by reviewing all transactions or improving continuous business monitoring activities. By adapting to the current environment, including timely consideration of current or new regulatory requirements or digital transformation, auditors could drive more changes through the three lines of defence model.

While the maturity of IA groups within individual organizations could vary, auditors can start identifying observations or sharing more ideas to encourage more innovation so the first and second lines can also innovate or leverage more data. Innovation should extend beyond coordination and communication; thus, having more continuous auditing or monitoring tools is a plus. We need to elevate engagement connections with first- and second-line stakeholders and drive the IA transformation to add more value to the entire organization.

If you are part of the first, second or third line of defence, I highly recommend providing feedback to other lines on how they can potentially add more value to your team and the entire organization. Be flexible when you use this model, and be open to receiving feedback from others. Let's move now to another exciting topic, how to add value to various stakeholders. Auditors who want to be trusted advisors must understand stakeholders' goals and concerns and ensure that all engagements focus on delivering better value.

Chapter 3

How to Add Value to the Organization

When you speak with auditors, they are convinced that adding value to the organization is a high priority. However, sometimes when you reach out to their stakeholders, there is a disconnect. Thus, having a clear definition of how to add value to an organization is not an easy step and requires constant working and effective communication and transparency with stakeholders and the board of directors.

We need to know and revisit the IA standards, which state that the IA function should add value to the organization. IA is an independent, objective, assurance and consulting activity that adds value to the organization and improves its operations. It helps an organization accomplish its objectives by bringing a systematic, disciplined approach to evaluating and improving the effectiveness of risk management, control and governance processes.

From my point of view, an organization is best served by a fully resourced and professionally competent IA staff that provides value-added services critical to the entire organization.

What are the main challenges faced by IA departments when selling this message?

- They are unclear on how to add value to stakeholders or keep saying, "I am an auditor that adds excellent value"; however, their stakeholders have a different view.
- They do not know how to deliver value or prioritize what is relevant for their stakeholders, or they do not know the business well. Auditors are unfamiliar with the current strategic projects; they do not meet with them often or are new to the organization. Audit departments that experience a high turnover can easily understand this point. To add value, it takes time to know your stakeholders, products, services and more.
- They are so focused on delivering the audit plan or other audit activities that they do not have time to spend with key stakeholders to understand their concerns, challenges, business objectives or priorities.

DOI: 10.4324/9781003431893-4

- Auditors do not know the business well and are typically not focused on business strategies or digital business transformation, key projects, products or customer journeys. Thus, the traditional audit scope may not be so relevant for stakeholders as the company is facing a new digital transformation or branch transformation. Still, auditors are not even participating in key leadership meetings or engaged in key initiatives. However, few auditors may say that "the audit must be conducted accordingly to the plan." What do you think about this approach? Well, you will not be adding too much value to the organization. Who challenged the automated controls? Are automated controls well-designed or considered to meet business needs?
- They do not ask for stakeholders' feedback regarding audits or issue validation activities. We need to get stakeholders' feedback if we want to improve and add value to the organization.
- Despite focusing on valuable activities, a portion of the audit work is to complete testing programmes not recognized as relevant (e.g. raising low-level issues or agreeing on bureaucratic action plans).

From my own experience, I have noticed that sometimes auditors are afraid or not accustomed to looking outside the box. We need to conduct audits differently; there are certain things that auditors can assess better. I have seen so many organizations focused on testing mandatory controls that it is difficult to provide more real value to the business. Branch reviews are completed only around mandatory controls (already agreed with Management) but remember, criminal minds always know the controls that do not work in your organization and can take advantage of that.

I sometimes hear that "it has been defined globally," so "we cannot change this as it was also agreed with our local regulators." I have sad news for you, you are not conducting smart audits and not identifying relevant or critical issues. If you have delivered too many effective audit reports, why do you feel you are providing excellent value to your stakeholders? If the control environment is changing too much, if the business has not even identified or does not know the key controls, if regulatory requirements have not been tested 100%, if there are too many manual controls in place and if your organization has a local and global presence or a big branch footprint, please re-assess how you are conducting your audits or if you have the right skills, capacity and data analytics tools to conduct audits, complete risk assessment, conduct business monitoring activities and validate issues.

Providing value is not just focusing on delivering the audit report timely or testing just mandatory controls. The value proposition or definition needs to evolve with the organization, emerging risks and regulatory risks, and with COVID-19 audit departments changed the audit testing approach.

For example, audits were immediately cancelled, and audit remote testing was conducted. Thus, auditors had to develop more data analytics tools to enhance remote testing by leveraging more data (e.g. operational losses, complaints data, large fraud losses, transactional data, key management reports, testing results conducted by the first or second line, video surveillance to evaluate activities in branches or ATMs). Thus, the first step is to define what value-added means for your stakeholders, including the board of directors.

We should never forget that the value added is given and recognized by our stakeholders and must be built constantly and diligently. The first approach is to ask all your stakeholders what they value and not. Considering the customer's experience, what do you think they value more? Well, I am a customer too, and when I go to a bank, I would like a quick and effective service. If I want a credit card, I want to open it fast so I can use it immediately. But, if I experience a fraud event, I want my credit card cancelled immediately when I contact the call centre or be able to block it on my Bank Mobile App or online. When auditors consider this approach, the audit scope will add more value to management. Do you assess the customer experience or journeys in any of your audits? If not, why? Is this not relevant for your stakeholders or customers?

Thus, the next step is to figure out how the organization is functioning and how the IA function is delivering better expectations. For example, if the organization wants to be the best for its customers, has it defined the customer's journeys related to account opening, account maintenance, closing, collections and claims/complaints? Are these journeys included in the PRCs or MCAs? If the answer is "no," IA could help by reviewing these processes during business monitoring activities or audits. Thus, auditors could challenge the business and request corrective actions to address the control gaps.

If you hope to add value to your organization, you must have a sound understanding of business strategy, objectives, key priorities and emerging risks. Thus, it is important to understand any IA skills gaps and act quickly to define a plan to address them. Your stakeholders need your expertise, and you can share your knowledge effectively or IA best practices during walk-throughs or critical meetings. There is never a perfect time to share feedback or challenge the business; do not miss an opportunity to add value.

You need to build trust among your stakeholders to succeed. Stakeholders will always seek your advice if your audit department has a good reputation. They will always want the best IA teams to review their businesses. If you do not have a good reputation, you must act quickly to start changing perceptions, rebuilding relationships and moving IA to the next level. Actively seek opportunities to build and maintain good relationships with individuals at all levels within the organization, both locally and globally. Auditors must develop their network within the organization.

During this process, it is relevant to maintain independence and challenge stakeholders to improve the processes and address the concerns identified. In addition, engage your stakeholders when defining the audit scope or when events occur at the organization by reviewing involved procedures in detail to complete the root cause analysis. Management is far more likely to support the audit work when auditors are involved earlier in the process and when they can see how the auditor's findings or recommendations contribute to the achievement of business strategies and goals.

Also, if there are key technology projects in progress, raise your hand to participate in risk committee or steering committee meetings or working groups; it is better to identify issues earlier than later. Your expertise is valuable for your stakeholders, so you can add even more value by managing closer relationships and sharing your points of view during this process. Do not wait until the next audit to raise concerns; stakeholders will not appreciate that. If you identify issues earlier, you can allow the business to address the concerns earlier; when the audit starts, you can focus on other relevant topics. Lead your audits and your team with transparency, do not assume that you know the business or how you could add value; always ask questions to get the additional information and clarify any doubts you may have.

For example, participating in critical last-minute assessments requested by senior management or the CEO is important to show the IA value. I remember one day when the CEO asked IA to review a key process involved in a business sale. The CEO trusted IA to check it. I quickly assigned a few resources to review key risks and key controls. Being a trusted advisor takes time and reasonable effort.

I always consider details when managing relationships with stakeholders and look outside the box. Chief audit directors and audit directors must deliver an excellent message to their IA teams to encourage them to add more value. You should encourage them to test areas not reviewed in detail before or to expand to other areas that are strategically important to the company's overall success (e.g. new distribution agreement, digital banking, core key initiatives), to use more technology and data to conduct audits or just an end-to-end review (e.g. account opening for deposit products or credit cards, wire transfers and ATMs audits). We also need more SMEs within the IA teams; they should be involved during the audit engagement, business monitoring activities, risk assessments and issue validation activities.

Knowing where the biggest risks are makes it easier for auditors to focus their efforts on the areas where the most value could be added. We need to audit differently, reduce non-value activities, focus on what really matters, such as customer experience, sales practices and regulatory compliance, and develop more analytical tools to conduct testing, business monitoring activities, issue validation activities or complete audits earlier (in 90 days). We need to conduct audits more efficiently and identify issues earlier (e.g. business monitoring activities, continuous auditing tools, data analytics tools and agile audits). However, sometimes IA teams are not ready to take the next step or to try something different due to a lack of audit capacity, skills or data analytics tools.

Auditors must be engaged with stakeholders through weekly, monthly or committee meetings or informal catch-up meetings. If you are a good auditor, stakeholders would like to spend time with you to figure out if you have any concerns. It is common to find high-performing auditors participating in critical global or oversight committees and tollgate meetings. Auditors must ask challenging questions regarding key risks (e.g. sales practices, third-party vendors and compliance risks), key processes, open issues and impact on new processes, procedures and products. Auditors must be engaged all the time.

I always recommend to my team to find excuses to meet stakeholders. And, if they need your point of view before implementing a process or launching a new product, always be available to share your feedback. You can be a good advisor without compromising your independence and objectivity. Be the best for your stakeholders, and ensure your goal is met and renewed constantly to exceed their expectations and to improve the impact and influence of the IA function.

Finally, do not forget to ask for feedback after participating in a committee meeting, audit or another task force. Stakeholders want to be heard, and they need to have an opportunity to share their views on how an audit could add more value. Please do not miss this opportunity to be the best for your stakeholder by asking what you can do better. They highly value the advisory work that IA can provide. Hearing what your stakeholders think will help establish a mutually beneficial relationship.

I recommend having face-to-face informal conversations to get their feedback, so they feel more comfortable and open to providing honest and valid input. If they respond quickly to your request, this is a good sign. Always remember that we need to be the best for our stakeholders and ask for feedback so we can drive more change.

I like having conversations with them and then asking for an email to document their feedback and any recommendations they may have after finalizing an audit. During this process, it is also important to share this feedback with your boss and your team to keep strengthening the work provided. For example, when I had a meeting with one stakeholder, she highlighted her appreciation for my team with passion as auditors had the right knowledge and experience and were very respectful to her team. She also mentioned the importance of the advisory work during the entire year to build a better control environment and support the business strategy. The close partnership and collaboration help her team to strengthen the MCA process and close issues more efficiently.

Within a few days after the stakeholder feedback meeting, provide a summary of the feedback to your audit team and include the steps required to address any concerns or areas of opportunity. Nothing works better for getting stakeholders engaged in giving feedback than when they feel they have been heard. You will have an action plan in place to act on their suggestions. You can always add more value when you put your stakeholders first and focus on building stronger relationships.

During this conversation, I noticed how important it was for the business to continue collaborating closely with my team to share the best practices and points of view to improve the control environment. We agreed to continue with the MCA sessions, I also allocated additional resources in the following few months in preparation for the future audit; we had bi-weekly meetings to review additional information, business priorities and concerns that helped us to define and share the preliminary audit scope earlier.

Lastly, be open to feedback and appreciate the time provided during this process. Understanding your stakeholder well and generating consensus is key to the success of any IA function. Stakeholders appreciate when we asked them for feedback to improve future audit engagements. Continued feedback is important across the entire organization to identify new synergies, improve relationships and improve the control environment. I see that we both auditors and stakeholders can continue learning and finding better ways to engage more efficiently.

Without any doubt, feedback is a tool for continued learning and motivation for any team. During these sessions, do not forget to provide feedback to your stakeholders because this is a mutually beneficial exercise. Please, walk in your stakeholders' shoes when delivering the message. Walking in our stakeholders' shoes is to work together and understand them to get the best outcome possible. Stakeholders also need to be prepared for the audits to facilitate audit engagement. Let's consider a few additional questions:

- Is the business always prepared for an audit?
- Are they truly familiar with key controls selected by the audit team?
- Were key stakeholders or process owners invited to the walkthroughs?
- Does the audit team need to go through multiple interactions with stakeholders to understand key controls?
- Did the business deliver the document requests quickly?
- Is a business manager involved in facilitating all deliverables to the audit team?

We need to conduct more effective audits, which will be the next topic to discuss.

Chapter 4

Conducting Effective Audits
Opportunities for Enhancement

The IA function is critical for an organization. Conducting timely and smart audits is highly desired by stakeholders, shareholders and regulators. Regulators always review IA methodology, audit plan, audit testing approach, audit findings, risk assessments, business monitoring activities, issue validation activities, resource capacity and skills and IA metrics, among others.

All auditors assigned to audits, risk assessments, business monitoring and issue validation activities should have a solid understanding of the business (e.g. organizational structure, business strategy, priorities, technology initiatives, key processes, key risks and key controls, regulatory requirements, policies and procedures), and the IA role to satisfy the board of directors, regulators and external auditor's expectations.

Most traditional auditors conduct audits in three phases – planning, fieldwork and reporting. The length of each phase can take at least three weeks, or fewer depending on the audit scope. However, I would like to add another phase, the pre-planning phase. Auditors need a disciplinary approach to complete the pre-planning activities. It includes tasks such as reviewing the risk assessment for the auditable entity, regulatory compliance requirements, resource capacity to complete the audit and issue validation activities (if any), and data analytics requirements, and scheduling preliminary meetings with stakeholders to define the preliminary audit scope, among others. The preliminary audit scope will be the foundation of more detailed audit planning and fieldwork.

During the pre-planning phase, it is relevant to invite the SMEs or other experts (e.g. compliance, AML, technology, operational and fraud risks) required for the audit engagement. The senior audit manager must ensure that the SME involvement is negotiated in advance or during the audit plan construction/refresh as hours may be required (from other IA teams). It is the responsibility of the audit lead (audit manager), controller (senior audit manager) or audit owner (audit director) to identify the SME expertise required.

DOI: 10.4324/9781003431893-5

Once the pre-planning meetings are finalized, the key business processes, risks and controls are identified and the preliminary audit scope can be documented. It is highly recommended to have a tollgate meeting (IA team and SMEs) to discuss the preliminary audit scope, testing approach, open issues or other concerns. Meeting minutes should be developed and retained in the audit management system as evidence of topics discussed, agreed upon or scoped out (related to high-risk processes not reviewed during the audit engagement). The rationale of decisions made must be well documented, as well.

IA should focus on the most critical and relevant areas. I highly recommend defining a smart audit scope that creates the maximum value for your stakeholders (e.g. customer's journey, key technology projects, new products or services, digital transformation or retail branch transformation) and considers their input (e.g. COVID-19 impact, emerging risks, new regulatory requirements, open issues and other current audits), as well. Thus, the auditor should identify pre-planning or planning phases that consumed excessive hours but did not add too much value or did not meet stakeholders' expectations. Then, auditors could enhance the old approach and implement a smarter one, a more agile one.

Stakeholders can easily highlight a few concerns listed here:

- Audit plan does not cover all critical areas, and key processes so there are still critical gaps in the audit coverage.
- Audits take longer than expected; some were completed over 100 days and the business wasted a lot of time creating new documents requested by auditors.
- Auditors do not have the right skills or business knowledge to audit the business.
- Stakeholders do not agree on the value added by IA.
- Too many audits were performed at the same time. The business team had to manage so many audits that it was hard for the business to focus on its own priorities.
- The business head did not know that the IA team was going to audit the business this year.
- Auditors always review the same area over and over but the audit reports had an effective rating during the last three years.
- Audit always finds low-rated issues or no new issues at all. Why do I have a negative audit report rating if only self-disclosed issues were included in the audit report? Is it bad to self-identify issues (issues identified by the business)?
- Audit failed an issue during the audit but the IA team never raised concerns before moving this issue into IA validation.

How can we contribute to resolving these concerns? Well, a good planning phase can facilitate the following:

- *Build stronger relationships with key stakeholders* (e.g. senior management, business head, compliance, ORM, legal and other IA team members) and engage them earlier in the process to understand areas, potential concerns or emerging risks. Auditors need to be flexible and emphatic about stakeholders' needs, and concerns and they need to coordinate audits in advance. Auditors should consider coaching stakeholders to be prepared for every audit as audits must be completed in 90 days.
- *Obtain cost savings.* Request only relevant and useful information: ensure that the information requested is already available; the business docs not need to spend additional time on developing it. If data queries are necessary, auditors need to figure out data requirements and request data in advance. Also auditors can also verify if they can pull the data directly (your data analytics team can help you in advance). Thus, auditors need to send out the preliminary document request list during the pre-planning or planning phases.

    The audit team could request the following: organization charts, key performance indicators (e.g. customer's complaints/claims, allegations, operational losses, customer satisfaction surveys), fraud losses, technology incidents, key regulatory reports, key policies and procedures, the delegation of authority matrix, PRC or MCA, annual risk assessment results, key EUCs or other key technology applications or models, key technology initiatives/projects, self-identified issues or other issues open (e.g. audits, compliance reviews or regulatory reviews, external audit findings), key general ledger accounts or SOX accounts, key management reports (e.g. transactional data, fraud losses, financial results) and self-assurance activities results.
- *Define a smarter audit scope.* Better data analytics tools are required and pre-planning meetings (as discussed earlier) with SMEs to agree on the audit scope. I highly recommend building a day-to-day delivery tracker during audits with forward-looking dates to ensure better discipline during the audit engagement.

    Auditors need to agree with management on the key risks and key controls included in the audit scope. It is important to encourage auditors to look at stakeholders from the perspective of what may add value to them. Are these key controls important to stakeholders, could these controls impact the customer's journey or improve customer experience?

    Discussions with management should be held once key risks and key controls are identified, and the RCM must be shared before starting the fieldwork phase. Transparency is key during this process and the agile approach could facilitate timely audit completion. Thus, I highly recommend including no more than 12 key controls in the RCM: if you include more, you will not finish your audit in 90 days. It is also relevant to determine what should be out of the audit scope; this must be well-documented, agreed with IA SMEs and documented in the audit management system. Meeting minutes should be always maintained (stakeholders or IA meetings) including the RCM approval (senior audit manager and audit director) and evidence that the RCM was shared and agreed upon with management.

- *Provide better assurance by using data analytics tools through business monitoring activities, risk assessments, issue validation activities and audit engagements.* Active participation of the data analytics team or a data champion to pull relevant data is key to completing these activities on time.

  Data analytics tools are important to identify trends (e.g. claims and complaints, allegations, operational losses, fees and commissions charged, refunds processed, user access, mandatory absence, mandatory training, data quality gaps regarding account opening or customer maintenance processes). It is relevant to continue working on ideas and continuous auditing tools to include other relevant key controls too (e.g. wire transfers, customer refunds, operational losses, customer complaints, customer authentication exceptions, customer disclosures not provided timely, customer signatures not obtained during the account opening process or wire transfers and third-party vendors risk assessments). These are great ideas; you could add excellent value to your stakeholders by developing these or more ideas too.

  Always, the auditor should encourage the business too to use more data analytics considering the characteristics of the business. Auditors could obtain data and information directly (when they have access to the systems) to improve the audit testing but they also need to validate the completeness and accuracy of data before using it. They should not place reliance on data without evaluating it. Documentation should be retained of testing performed during business monitoring activities, issue validation activities and audits.

  Regarding business monitoring activities, it is important to identify key processes, controls or metrics that could be also reviewed quarterly in preparation for audits (e.g. committee effectiveness, new products released in the branches or online banking, new customer promotions, operational losses, fraud events, claims and complaints, mandatory training, mandatory absence, user access, branch exceptions tracked (in general) or incomplete monthly/quarterly branch manager's certifications). I prefer more detailed business monitoring activities as auditors will be able to identify issues easier. Automated risk assessments are also desirable; risk assessments need to be flexible, and detailed enough to identify emerging risks. Data should always be leveraged during issue validation activities, especially for complex (critical and high-risk) issues. Thus, we need to focus more on innovation activities to identify new opportunities to facilitate audit activities.

- *Stakeholders should have a better understanding of IA methodology and the agile approach.* Announcing an audit engagement enables the IA team to begin effective communications with their key stakeholders and to familiarize them with the audit process. The intention to audit memo is the formal notification that the audit engagement will commence in a few weeks and the initial request for information.

  Auditors need to spend time with stakeholders to ensure they understand the audit phases, audit report rating, expectations and timing especially if audits must be completed in 90 days or earlier. If the agile approach is used, they need to provide additional details as additional and more frequent meetings will be requested.

- *Assign audit resources timely and better.* Manage the assignment considering the resources available and the audit scope. Audit leads (audit managers) and controllers (senior audit managers) need to continue reassessing things that arise during planning and fieldwork and adjust (audit testing or the audit scope) to ensure value-added audits are provided.

  There should be an independent support team that can track or monitor progress against the audit delivery plan across all local and global audits. I recommend delivering training to IA teams to manage the audit work more efficiently and monitoring key milestones for each phase on a daily or weekly basis. A disciplinary approach is always encouraged for both the IA team and stakeholders. Stakeholders may request one status meeting per week or more frequent meetings but always request their feedback to agree on the best approach. You can also request more frequent meetings when issues are identified or must be discussed further.

  The goal of the audit team is to deliver the audit on time (as a rule), clear roles and responsibilities are essential as all must work towards the same goal. When we agree with Management that the audit must be complete in 90 days and more value will be added, they will cooperate with the audit team. Set the tone and the example. Are your stakeholders committed to audit deadlines? If not, you need to work harder with your team and stakeholders to finalize the audit report just on time. Quality is a top priority and should never be compromised.

  I would like to highlight the output from the *pre-planning* activities:

- Skeleton audit planning memo (APM) (list of stakeholders, preliminary audit scope, key risks and key controls, self-identified issues and other open issues). Senior audit manager, audit director and IA SMEs should review this preliminary template to agree on the preliminary audit scope. Tollgate meetings could be held during the first or second week of planning (if you had a decent pre-planning phase).

- Total hours and the resource plan (IA team members and SMEs) to complete the audit engagement. These hours must be requested and agreed upon during the audit plan constructions and booked (in advance) in the resource scheduling tool (if any). The audit team must consider any potential schedule constraints that may impact the IA team and the auditee.
- Preliminary data trend analysis if data is available. This helps auditors identify any anomalies to target further testing and optimize future sample selections.
- Mandatory checklist that tracks roles and responsibilities for each team member during each audit phase.
- Tollgate meeting minutes (IA SMEs including the data analytics champion, audit manager, senior audit manager, audit director, chief audit director and other regional directors, if required).

It is important to reinforce a disciplinary approach to request meetings, supporting documentation, data queries and sampling evidence from the business during the audit and before moving to the fieldwork. The rules of the engagement should be defined and shared with the stakeholders to ensure the information requested is delivered to the audit within 48 or 60 hours.

- *Retain meeting minutes with key stakeholders.* Always, auditors should be able to identify relevant local and global stakeholders that would be beneficial for the definition of the audit scope or during the audit engagement.

As we discussed in this chapter, the sooner you reach out to the auditee, the better. The audit team must conduct face-to-face walkthroughs with the auditee to confirm preliminary key risks and the control design, key business objectives and strategies, and applicable company policies, procedures and regulatory requirements. A walkthrough is relevant if conducted with process owners or people familiar with the process. It may include a visit to business or third-party vendor facilities. You might request documents or records during the walkthrough. I highly recommend minimizing the number of people attending these meetings if they are not relevant to the key processes, and key controls being discussed. I have seen organizations spending too much time on meetings; 20 or 30 people are invited to a simple walkthrough just out of curiosity or because the meeting invite was forwarded to them. This could impact the audit timeline significantly, if not managed appropriately.

By leveraging detailed risk assessments, robust business monitoring activities, information obtained during the pre-planning activities, and an initial meeting with the auditee or business head, the auditor could have a clear understanding of the key business processes and key risks to include in the audit scope. The key risks and key controls will be documented in the risk and control matrix (RCM) (e.g. process name, key risks, key controls and description, risk rating [high, medium, low], manual or automated control, frequency, control preventive of detective, control owner, design effectiveness assessment (DEA) conclusion, operating effectiveness testing [OET] objective and conclusion) and must be shared with the business to agree on key risks and key controls before starting the fieldwork. If Management provides valid feedback due to a few inaccuracies noticed, the RCM must be adjusted accordingly. Auditors must also consider control design, gaps or mitigating factors to determine if the control system effectively mitigates risks. The senior audit manager and audit director should approve the RCM before commencing the audit fieldwork.

During the planning, auditors must finalize the APM which should be approved by the senior audit manager and audit director before sending the audit announcement memo (AAM) and starting the fieldwork. I highly recommend another tollgate meeting with SMEs, chief audit director to discuss any comments they may have regarding the final audit scope.

The APM should be clear to all IA team members and other SMEs; this will include the following:

- Key risks and key controls
- Final audit scope
- Technology dependencies in and out of the audit scope
- Resource allocation and budget across all testing areas
- Critical access to data and hand-offs
- Reliance on other IA work or audits
- Key political and economic information relevant to the business
- Key performance indicators (KPI), financial results
- Key management reports (if any) relevant to the audit scope
- Self-identified issues, compliance, IA and regulatory issues open that impact the audit scope
- Third-party vendor (at least critical and high) inventory, rating and assessment results
- Data analysis (e.g. complaints data, operational losses, fraud events, transactional data and allegations, among others)

The auditor must review the risk assessment(s) covered during the audit to ensure key risks and key processes are included in the audit scope or rationale provided for scoping out decisions (agreed with corresponding

SMEs and rationale documented in the audit management system). Audit planning now comprises 35% to 40% of the total budget. This is a critical phase where we can best influence audit results and provide more value to your stakeholders.

Let's move to the *audit fieldwork*. One way to ensure fieldwork success is to develop a fieldwork plan. The purpose of the fieldwork plan is to specifically lay out a detailed "who," "what" and "by when" plan for all team members assigned to the audit engagement or fieldwork testing. I have seen audit fieldwork not completed on time due to poor planning. It is common to encounter a few challenges as listed here:

- Business was not ready for the audit.
- Wrong data queries were requested or provided to the IA team.
- Majority of documentation requests took over 72 hours.
- Audit work papers were not completed timely.
- Management corrective actions were not delivered on time (over one week).
- Stakeholders continue discussing audit issues without reaching a formal agreement.

A successful audit process depends heavily on the project management skills of the audit manager and senior audit manager. A good audit discipline is critical; following the plan and managing against the milestones will allow the IA team to know the engagement status at any point in time to facilitate audit completion.

During the fieldwork, the auditors obtain and analyse programme data and information to conclude the operating effectiveness of controls following the audit testing agreed upon. Audit steps may include interviewing key personnel, taking a sampling of documents (e.g. customer's instructions, key management reports, committee decks, investment contracts, customer's applications), analysing secondary data sources and performing additional data analysis.

The effectiveness testing conclusion must be documented in the work papers, and the control should be rated as effective or ineffective. If the control is ineffective, the control is not operating as intended and does not mitigate the risk identified. The preliminary audit finding must the documented including the 5C:

- Concern (finding).
- Root cause (why the exception occurred). This helps Management to define smart action plans to address the concern.
- Consequence/impact (potential consequences if the concern is not addressed timely or adequately).

- Context (additional details of observations identified).
- Corrective actions to resolve the issues identified. These corrective actions must be tied to root cause analysis and provided by management.

The end of fieldwork means that the testing is complete, work papers are complete and the factual accuracy of issues and action plans have been agreed upon with Management. One of the most critical aspects of the post-fieldwork phase of the audit is communication with management and sharing the draft audit report before publishing the final audit report. Typically, once the fieldwork ends, the draft audit report is prepared and shared with Management to get input. In addition, it provides a final opportunity for the auditor to ensure she/he has a full and complete understanding of the issues presented. In addition, it is important to minimize the time between the completion of fieldwork and the issuance of the audit report which will impact the efficiency of the audit (within 30 days of fieldwork completion).

I would like to highlight the output from the fieldwork activities:

- Issues and action plans are agreed upon with Management and reviewed by SMEs, as well. Auditors should confirm with Management if the issues were already known by the business. Self-identified issues (only if opened in the business system of records) or repeat issues should be highlighted in the audit report (identified by the IA team).
- Work papers are reviewed by audit managers, senior audit managers and audit directors (sample). All work papers must be detailed enough to support the testing results, and testing approach, and must be understood and reperformed by an independent party.

If action plans are not provided timely by the business, escalation must occur. The audit director or chief audit director should have a conversation with the business head to ensure the audit report is delivered on time. Always keep in mind that an escalation is a useful tool during the audit engagement not only during the reporting phase. I highly recommend finishing the fieldwork as planned in the third week of fieldwork. Once, the draft report is cleared by the chief audit director, QA team or the IA review, it can be shared with the stakeholders before publication.

I would like to end this chapter summarizing the most critical points during the audit engagement:

- Focus on effective time management (checklist to track all required and defined tasks during an audit).
- Finalize and manage the resource plan effectively; the IA team should be accountable for each task assigned.

- Implement a more robust and disciplinary approach during pre-planning activities (it is better to start earlier just a few weeks in advance).
- Define a realistic audit coverage considering the resources available. The audit manager and senior audit manager should revisit the timing and activities left to complete the audit on time.
- Define realistic deadlines and objectives considering the audit scope, and resource capacity.
- Conduct tollgate meetings (pre-planning, planning, fieldwork) with IA team members and SMEs to confirm audit scope and discuss findings.
- Reinforce a disciplinary approach with IA team members and stakeholders to complete the audit on time (90 days).
- Define the rules of engagement and leverage the escalation process during the audit engagement, if required.
- Use more data analytics tools to enhance audit coverage and always look outside the box when finalizing the audit scope and audit testing plan. You can assess the same key controls over and over and still not find any issues, but the key is how you evaluate a key control. One day, I asked my new IA team to explain to me the key controls identified or assessed over relevant customer transactions. I assessed similar controls in other financial institutions and I always found issues. To my surprise when the conversation ended, I told my team that despite the fact they shared ten potential controls (all were convinced that they have been testing key controls during the last years): "I did not see any single key control there to minimize fraud risk." Thus, we had to modify and improve the continuous auditing tool later and we ended up finding a relevant issue that enhanced the control environment. I always go back to the same basic question, what could go wrong? Are you sure this is a key control? Are there any automated controls built into the system to minimize key risks?
- Build closer relationships with stakeholders and include their concerns, challenges or emerging risks in the risk-based audit plan, and audit scope to add value to the business, shareholders and customers.
- Always, request feedback from your stakeholders and provide feedback to IA team members after finishing the audit. This feedback is a valuable tool to improve the effectiveness and efficiencies of IA practices. Feedback can occur informally during the assignment or formally after the audit is complete (audit evaluation template). These surveys could be built into the audit management system and sent to stakeholders and audit team members.
- Improve risk assessments and business monitoring activities by leveraging more data analysis or data analytics tools to conduct trend analysis, identify concerns and outliers or evaluate key controls effectively. You

should not be able to complete audits in 90 days if you do not know the business well. Sorry, you can still publish audit reports, but you are taking too much risk if no single issue or relevant issues are raised during your audit.

I am always sceptical about "effective audit reports" considering all risks each organization is exposed to especially financial institutions. We do not live in a perfect environment; companies do not have a perfect control environment and sometimes no robust first, second or third line of defence. We cannot audit a business, area, product or project well if we do not have the business knowledge, skills and relevant data to complete the audit testing. Data analytics is critical to completing audits successfully but more importantly to adding value to your stakeholders.

- Innovate, innovate, innovate more every day . . . Yes, you can do it!

Chapter 5

The Business Monitoring Approach

Taking a Value Approach

Business or continuous monitoring activities should provide value to stakeholders and a quick assessment of the control environment by providing timely information regarding new regulatory requirements, emerging risks, management concerns or challenges regarding processes and new product launches, among others. Annually, hours should be allocated to business monitoring activities that give auditors a flavour of any risks or changes to the control environment related to their auditable entities. Once the business or continuous monitoring is completed at least quarterly, the risk assessment of each auditable entity may require updates or enhancements based on potential findings or concerns. A change in the risk assessment could impact the overall risk of the auditable entity; it may affect the audit plan, as the auditable entity should be reviewed earlier or later.

Business monitoring activities should be completed quarterly; I highly recommend one business monitoring memo or summary per auditable entity, which will facilitate future risk assessment updates. Detailed testing is not required, but the audit director or chief audit director may require specific testing based on new events or changes in the risk profile of the auditable entity. SMEs (e.g. compliance, AML, technology audit teams) may be consulted during this process. I highly recommend sharing the final business monitoring summary document, the business monitoring approach and conclusions with the SMEs, if necessary (e.g. changes to risk drivers).

A business monitoring plan (BMP) or approach is highly recommended, and it must be updated quarterly if required. The senior audit manager, audit director or chief audit director must approve the business monitoring planning memo and the final quarterly memo. The IA methodology should define who must approve these two documents. It could include at least the following information as listed here:

- High-level description of business area, project, product, end-to-end process, legal entity

DOI: 10.4324/9781003431893-6

- Transactional data analysis (e.g. sales, accounts opened or products offered [debit, credit cards, personal loans, mortgage loans, investments], products cancelled, wire transfers, ATMs, loss mitigation strategies) and conclusions
- Operational losses, fraud events, claims and complaints, allegations; data analysis to identify trends, concerns, outliers
- Assessment of key risks tied to risk assessment risk drivers
- List of stakeholders' meetings held (e.g. committee meeting, one-on-one meeting with business head and direct reports, business tollgate meetings)
- Issue pipeline status (e.g. second line of defence, IA, regulatory and self-disclosed issues) and challenges (e.g. past due issue, re-targets, reopens, repeat issues)
- Inputs from key management meeting decks or forums, Board's meeting minutes
- Third-party vendors analysis (e.g. inventory, risk assessments and risk ratings, contract changes, issues open, including customer's complaints)
- Key regulatory or management reports, including key metrics (KPI, service level agreements)
- Key general ledger accounts and corresponding trend analysis (revenues/expenses)
- Technology incident reports
- Changes in the business organization structure, strategy, products, services
- Changes in the company's policies, policies, regulatory requirements
- Management monitoring and testing results (e.g. self-assurance activities and mystery shopping testing results in the branch network)
- Input from the audit director, chief audit director, head of audit and SMEs
- Execution of data analytics tools (e.g. key controls, user access, mandatory training, customer complaints and refunds processed) and testing conclusions
- Audit plan changes (new audits added or cancelled) due to black swan events such as COVID-19 or others that impact auditable entities, current and future audits.
- Status of any key projects the business manages or any other concerns identified by auditors that require follow-up or testing

This list can be shorter or longer, but I am sharing here a few ideas that could be relevant to assessing the key risk drivers included in each risk assessment. I highly recommend business monitoring for each auditable entity. One single business monitoring document for all auditable entities will not help you keep your auditable entities current, and you may not be able to identify any relevant issues timely or during business monitoring activities.

The business monitoring activities should clearly articulate the work performed and align with the key risk drivers and the business monitoring planning document. Auditors can use the results of business monitoring activities to identify additional emerging risks, update risk assessments and facilitate future audit work, as certain key controls could be assessed earlier (data analytics tools). Issues could be raised during business monitoring activities. The business monitoring report could have a rating (e.g. an effective or not effective business monitoring report). However, when the report is not rated, it can be digested easily by senior management, specifically if high-rated issues are raised.

When business monitoring activities are performed manually, auditors will take more time to pull, read and analyse the data. Very sophisticated IA functions are putting more attention into developing more automated business monitoring tools. Auditors need to understand technology constraints and legacy systems to automate a few activities to pull the data directly. They need access to the data and proper skills to analyse data effectively. However, it is not always possible to automate a business monitoring analysis 100%. Still, if you can automate a few key controls for testing purposes, you can save additional hours in the future and during audits.

Auditors could get additional benefits by automating a few business monitoring activities as listed here:

- Evolve from a traditional or more static approach to a more dynamic and flexible approach based on continuous auditing results.
- Increase management awareness of the new and relevant issues; management could resolve or address them earlier.
- Increase confidence in the IA assessments and value-added.
- Reduce the hours allocated to business monitoring activities and future audits while increasing effectiveness through better data analytics tools and analysis. For example, auditors can assess key controls (e.g. unresolved customer complaints or untimely resolutions, customer refunds not processed timely, disclosures not provided during the account opening and wire transfers). They could also monitor and identify password sharing. The solution could easily identify it, notice it when used simultaneously but in separate locations or buildings, and other anomalies such as customers accessing their accounts from different computers or company computers.
- Raise the bar so additional self-assurance or second line of defence activities will have to enhance their current approach. Auditors must also challenge the first and second lines of defence as they need to leverage data for monitoring and testing purposes.

The more advanced IA functions have already started using data analytics, adding value to stakeholders. However, not all IA functions are prepared to take this step because they may not have the right skills, capacity, data access or equipment to run big queries. Thus, chief audit directors need to consider the benefits of utilizing data analytics during business monitoring, issue validation and audits. We need to invest more in the right technology solutions and bring additional resources who can take the lead and drive the IA transformation.

If new analytical tools are designed and developed to enhance business monitoring activities, they can also be shared with stakeholders. Auditors must bring data to the table and ensure stakeholders leverage data for monitoring and testing. Self-assurance activities must be robust to self-identify issues, as well.

The Value of a Continuous Auditing Programme

The objective of a continuous auditing programme is to increase audit efficiencies. It provides increased audit assurance for continuous testing of key relevant controls between audit cycles; it increases audit coverage by reviewing the entire population of transactions. It also helps to improve the control environment by providing more efficient audit reports that can be issued quicker after the automated testing is performed. Typically, an audit report takes over 90 days to be issued, but a quarterly continuous auditing report could take a month or be issued earlier. It also improves audit efficiencies as these controls could be scoped out in future audits as they have been assessed already.

Continuous auditing complements business monitoring activities. Business monitoring activities focus on business trend analysis and KPI trends to identify emerging risks or concerns but make it harder for auditors to identify issues if no detailed or robust activities are conducted. However, few key controls (high-risk) could be assessed by leveraging the entire population. If auditors identify exceptions, they will discuss all with management, agree on findings and request corrective actions.

Continuous auditing innovates how audits are conducted, impacting the amount of evidence analysed and the level of effort required. We should consider the following things to implement a continuous auditing approach:

- Engage the audit committee and senior management to understand the value added. We all need to be on the same page.
- Perform a resource skill assessment and capacity analysis to develop continuous auditing tools (e.g. regression, data mining, SQL and audit command language [ACL]). Co-sourcing could be an option; they could help define the ongoing auditing strategic plan and approach but may not be able to access data. The audit director and chief audit director must request additional hours and resources during the audit plan construction.

- Identify and prioritize areas to focus on and identify the continuous auditing tools that could add more value across all IA teams.
- Develop and maintain the technical skills required and enable the technology necessary to access, manipulate and analyse the data.
- Identify key information systems, data sources, key business processes and automated controls. In addition, auditors must request access to data and be capable of pulling, adjusting and organizing data across systems.
- Identify the right technology tools to purchase (e.g. appropriate laptops and analytics software tools). The data analytics team and other audit team members must have the right tools to pull and analyse relevant data.
- Verify data integrity and completeness before launching the tool. In addition, please monitor and evaluate the effectiveness of the continuous auditing output for a few months.
- Understand the nature of the test or analysis performed when reviewing exceptions identified.
- Ensure secure access to the continuous auditing tool or system to prevent unauthorized changes; change management controls should be in place.
- Train stakeholders on the benefits of relevant data analytics tools and encourage the adoption and support of more continuous auditing and monitoring tools. For example, auditors could also share the data analytics tools with senior management to enhance the control environment or self-assurance activities.

Continuous auditing should not be a short-term project but a long-term project, a commitment to a more effective testing and sophisticated approach. The benefits are real, but IA departments must invest heavily to develop and implement the right tools. Chief audit directors need to build the business case, identify the benefits and costs, and quantify them, if possible. A project plan should have key priorities based on project cost, benefits and risks, including key milestones. Consideration of required resources is relevant for successfully implementing a continuous auditing programme.

Planning a continuous auditing initiative should be a very interactive process that involves the steps listed here:

- Identify the need and relevance of each initiative.
- Allocate resources (involve business units, technology teams, data analytics team and key auditors familiar with the business).
- Establish clearly defined roles and responsibilities and a governance model that enables clear visibility into results and thematic trends. A governance framework should also address processes for approving all designs and deployment methods and developing standardized

documentation. These tools should be reviewed by the QA team and could be reviewed by regulators in the future.

- Define a project plan, including project timeline, key milestones and deliverables.
- Design and review the continuous auditing tool and reasonableness of exceptions identified.
- Test data for completeness and accuracy and ensure documentation is retained.
- Maintain adequate documentation of assumptions, data sources and implemented changes. It is important to have adequate change management protocols to track automated tool changes.
- Follow the plan but make adjustments as needed.
- Monitor performance, progress and refine as needed.
- Report testing results to senior management and obtain corrective actions or action plans for the findings identified.

A continuous auditing programme will change the audit approach, including the nature of evidence, timing and level of effort required by internal auditors. They could add excellent value to the organization as more data is leveraged. The chief audit director and head of audit will have to obtain the audit committee and senior management support to implement more continuous auditing solutions. They will have to get the budget approval to bring more resources that can drive this IA transformation. Innovation is key; all audit teams must provide innovative ideas to implement better solutions in the short term.

We really need to look outside the box and be more efficient when conducting remote audits. Data analytics is underused; we need to use more data during business monitoring activities, risk assessments, issue validation activities and of course, during the audit engagement. We should test most key controls listed in the RCM by leveraging data and assessing the entire population. Auditors should start moving away from sampling techniques and leverage more data to review the entire population in order to identify more relevant issues.

The IA function needs to evolve faster; we need more and better data and advanced technology solutions. If you really do not have the right technology tools, it is time to move forward. This is the only way to start adding more value to your stakeholders and drive organizational change. The IA departments are still struggling with resources, data and legacy systems, limiting their ability to deliver better audit solutions and reports. However, we must plan diligently to transform these challenges into opportunities to innovate more.

Let's move now to the risk assessment approach.

Chapter 6

Risk Assessment Approach

Taking a Value Approach

The audit risk assessment is critical to conducting effective and efficient audits. Risk assessments create efficiencies and add value to your stakeholders. Risk assessments must be flexible and detailed; relevant data must be used. You may wonder why it is so relevant to use data and why the IA department does not spend too much time on risk assessments or develop more effective ones. How may this impact the audit testing and audit results?

Here are a few potential reasons:

- They do not understand the relevance of having robust risk assessments when creating an audit plan or conducting audits.
- They do not have robust business monitoring activities to keep risk assessment relevant and current. Thus, they cannot identify issues during business monitoring activities.
- They review the same processes repeatedly and cannot identify relevant issues during audits.
- Key risks are not well known or identified. They are auditing on the surface.
- They do not know how to build a more detailed risk assessment as they do not leverage relevant data for each auditable entity. Using generic data is easier, but guess what? This approach does not add much value and could dramatically impact the construction of the audit plan.
- An automated risk assessment is not enough to guarantee the right output; you need better data. Generic data does not help you much (metrics are available at the corporate level, issues not mapped to the auditable entity, regulatory requirements not considered, operational losses or customer complaints data not available or even considered).
- The following risk drivers should be included in the risk assessment as listed here:

  - Regulatory/compliance
  - Culture

DOI: 10.4324/9781003431893-7

- Fiduciary
- AML
- Models
- Market
- Credit
- Pricing
- Interest rate
- Liquidity
- Operational
- Fraud management
- Sales practices
- Data management
- Third-party vendors
- Technology
- Continuity of Business
- Cybersecurity
- Conduct risk
- Climate change
- Accounting and reporting
- Policies and procedures
- Strategic
- Control environment (e.g. IA, compliance, regulatory and business self-identified, and emerging risks [e.g., black swan events]). The higher the number of open issues assigned to the auditable entity, the higher the score assigned to the control environment.
- Entity size. The entity size, key strategic initiatives, key products and services, employee turnover and other emerging risks are also relevant. For example, the higher the entity portfolio or size, the higher the risk.

Also, auditors should consider the following tips to construct stronger risk assessments:

- Auditors need to understand the business well to create auditable entities.
- It is important to assess and analyse the entity size, list of products and services, transactional data, financial results, key business initiatives, and priorities; understand the business strategy; and identify other relevant elements (e.g. models, third-party vendors, key technology and applications, and regulatory requirements).
- Also, they need to be familiar with key risks, processes and controls. They can leverage the PRCs and MCAs available, but this information needs to be accurate and complete.

- It is essential to use more data such as customer complaints, allegations, operational losses, fraud events, operational incidents and transactional data to assess the risk drivers better.
- They need to conclude on every risk driver, such as high, medium or low or even assign a score to comply with the IA methodology.
- Finally, finalize the risk assessment to get a final rating or score to determine the frequency of the audit.

The risk assessment procedures should include the following:

- Inquiries of management and appropriate individuals within the IA department (if such department exists) such as the audit director, head of audit and SMEs who could assist in identifying compliance, reputational, fraud and emerging risks, among others.

Here are a few questions that you could ask management:

- What are your main challenges?
- How has COVID-19 impacted your business strategies and resource capacity?
- What are the top business priorities for this year and next year?
- Have any key third-party vendor contracts changed?
- Have any key projects been delayed or put on hold by management? Why?

- Data analytics is relevant too (e.g. transactional data, financial results, customer complaints, allegations, operational losses, fraud losses, customer fees and refunds, accounts opened, closed, the volume of transactions processed in branches, through ATMs and online banking). Multiple-year comparisons of key numbers could be a good start to identify trends, concerns and outliers for further research and audit testing.
- Auditors should identify each auditable entity's key management reports for risk assessments and business monitoring activities.
- Identification of IA, regulatory, compliance and business self-identified issues that impact the auditable entity.

I prefer having an automated risk assessment; the key drivers (listed earlier) can be assessed timely by assigning a rating (high, medium or low or a score from 0 to 3). The rationale should be well-documented and supported by appropriate metrics allowing a third party to understand the score assigned. If changes are processed later, a clear explanation must be provided too. Once the risk assessment is finalized, the final score is automatically calculated (it defines when the audit should be conducted for each auditable entity) or selected by auditors (high, medium, low). For example, if a risk assessment is high, the audit must be conducted more frequently (at least annually or every 18 months based on your IA methodology).

Audit managers or senior audit managers can prepare risk assessments; however, the audit director and the chief audit director must approve all. Risk assessments must be flexible; auditors must update a few times during the year. I am not a big fan of static risk assessments; these are not useful in identifying emerging risks or concerns. They need to update all at least after completing an audit, issue validation activities and business monitoring activities, as required.

I want to share a few additional tips:

- Risk assessments cannot be static; auditors need to take the initiative to update often, especially when there are significant changes in the control environment, organizational structure changes, new regulations, policies and procedures, emerging risks or even when open issues are validated and closed by IA teams, regulators or new issues are raised.
- Audit managers, senior audit managers and audit directors should be able to update all risk assessments as needed. Locking every single risk assessment is not a clever idea. If potential changes in risk drivers impact the final risk assessment score, they may also affect the audit plan; thus, additional discussions will be necessary with the audit directors and chief audit directors.
- Auditors need to identify thematic issues as well (e.g. data management, change management, fraud management, MCA concerns, lack of automated controls, complex products and services, procedures, user access, sales practices and third-party vendors issues) and map all to corresponding auditable entities. This could facilitate the message delivered to senior management and the audit committee preparation. Management needs to be accountable for holistically, timely and effectively resolving these concerns to minimize additional risks.
- The rationale for each risk driver needs to be precise. It requires SME's approval (e.g. compliance/regulations, technology, fraud, third-party vendors, models), especially when risk is high or moderate or additional changes are required.
- Audit team members need to know each auditable entity very well. You could assign an auditable entity to an audit manager who will be responsible for business monitoring activities and future audits. If you have enough audit managers in your team, you could assign one or two auditable entities to each one and then rotate the assignment so all can learn other areas.

Auditors must be more prepared to assess the control environment and understand the business challenges and emerging risks. A robust risk assessment programme is a huge competitive advantage, as you can allocate resources to the highest areas and complete audits even earlier. Suppose you are familiar with key risks, controls, processes, regulatory requirements and key changes in the control environment. In that case, you can start working on the preliminary audit scope during business monitoring activities earlier. You can be more efficient during audits as auditors are familiar with the auditable entity under review.

In addition, auditors need to enhance risk assessments; however, they need to understand where they are; here are a few relevant questions that could help. It is important to answer the following questions honestly:

- What changes have been implemented in the business recently? Have these changes impacted any risk drivers?
- Have new business policies and procedures been created or updated? Did you update your risk assessments to reflect that?
- Has the business implemented or developed additional self-assurance activities or monitoring or exception reports to monitor new risks?
- Who is tracking the changes in policies and procedures documents? Does your risk assessment reflect this? How are you planning to review all business changes (e.g. business monitoring activities, future audits, issue validation activities and new data analytics tools)?
- Have you noticed increased customer complaints regarding new products, product features and revised procedures? Are there key reports available to track customer complaints, allegations, operational losses, fraud events, technology incidents (among others), and new key controls during black swan events (e.g. COVID-19)? Did the business address all customer complaints timely? Are you using these reports to assess the corresponding risk drivers? Why not?
- Have you leveraged any employee surveys?

Auditors must continuously assess how new black swan events may impact their auditable entities. Auditors need to evaluate if new auditable entities (to assess specific changes in the control environment) are required, and other audits must be conducted more frequently. Better business monitoring activities are needed to identify emerging risks (e.g. higher fraud events, online banking and ATM transactions, ACH transfers, cash differences, customer complaints and refunds).

We have learned a few things during the pandemic; auditors should leverage this pandemic as an opportunity to change their mindsets, adapt to the new reality and figure out other ways to complete risk assessments, enhance business monitoring activities and complete audits remotely. Most of the audit force is working remotely, and IA departments realized the importance of more advanced technology tools to add more value.

To accelerate audit value, we must invest more in data analytics tools, continuous auditing and advanced technology solutions.

Once the risk assessments are ready and approved, we are prepared to start the audit plan process. Make sure you complete all risk assessments in advance, as they will determine the frequency of each audit. Let's move to the audit plan construction.

Chapter 7

Defining the Audit Plan

Taking a Value Approach

The audit universe constantly changes due to new regulatory requirements, fraud events, market constraints, emerging risks, black swan events, new policies and procedures. Auditors need to be familiar with the control environment, key business strategic initiatives and technology projects, management challenges, changes in policies, procedures and regulatory requirements and high-risk issues (e.g. data management, fraud, compliance and third-party vendors). Companies face other risks, too, more organizational changes and business mergers and acquisitions; they go through their internal transformation (e.g. digital transformation, culture transformation, retail branch transformation and IA transformation). Change is a fact and occurs every single minute; thus, auditors need to be flexible to adapt quickly to this accelerated environment.

Effective internal audit resources no longer mean maintaining a world-class assurance programme that keeps the organization out of trouble. The IA function must add value through audits, business monitoring activities, continuous auditing tools and stakeholder interactions. The audit committee and senior management challenge IA teams; they need to "look outside the box" and answer the following questions: "Have you identified all critical risks? Have you covered all potential gaps?" Suppose new issues are identified (due to higher customer complaints, new or prior allegations, higher fraud losses or recent regulatory reviews) but not raised by IA teams. In that case, the IA QA team will conduct a postmortem review to understand the root cause (e.g. no prior audit engagements, incomplete audit scope, vague business monitoring activities and insufficient issue validation activities, among others). Auditors are under more scrutiny nowadays.

The construction of the annual audit plan requires time, and the audit teams must complete specific tasks before starting this process. For example, IA and senior audit managers need to review the audit universe, update risk assessments, create new auditable entities and combine or cancel others. Auditors cannot complete detailed risk assessments in two or three

DOI: 10.4324/9781003431893-8

weeks. If audit teams do not have enough time, they can complete them all but not with the quality required to assess the audit universe effectively. This could raise additional questions during IA QA or regulatory reviews. The more detailed, the better; however, the audit director and chief audit director will need to request extra hours and resources during the audit plan construction.

Auditors must update all risk assessments after completing audits, issue validation and business monitoring activities. We need more flexible risk assessments to adapt quickly to organizational changes and to identify emerging risks. Thus, the annual audit plan needs to be flexible too. This process will be much easier if you have a stronger business monitoring programme (one detailed business monitoring document per auditable entity), as your risk assessments will reflect reality.

Let's discuss a good example that involves retail branch banking. I want to define a potential audit plan. This will not be easy as you need to use more data the entire year (e.g. branch selection methodology, business monitoring activities, audit testing) and have the right skills and capacity to review the right thing. We do not need to check all branches, just a representative sample; however, we need a good branch selection methodology to focus on what matters.

Also, we could create different auditable entities that may require branch visits or remote testing. This concept applies to smaller or bigger branch networks (over 2,000 branches), but auditors should consider risk-based audits. However, we need to understand the key processes, key controls and key risks in a branch network (e.g. compliance, sales practices, thirdparty vendors, operation and conduct risk). It is also relevant to understand the branch oversight activities conducted by the first and second lines of defence, the business structure, key business priorities and initiatives, key products, services and the digital transformation if any (moving from the traditional branch model to smart branches which means digital branches, better technology and improved customer experience).

Data analytics will be truly relevant here to identify trends, concerns and outliers to conduct additional research and testing (e.g. customer complaints, allegations, operational losses, fraud losses, sales practices, transactional data and video surveillance). Auditors can select branches randomly, but it is better to have a branch selection methodology with key data points (e.g. operational losses, fraud losses, customer complaints and allegations, transactional data [e.g. financial data, the number of credit and debit cards opened, closed, accounts opened without being funded, accounts opened but closed in 60 days or never activated, customer wire transfers processed and branch employee turnover]). You could easily design a branch selection methodology with relevant data, automate it, and have a risk score for each retail branch. I highly recommend two or three branch review audits throughout the year, especially if you have different branch regions to cover. You need to assess what makes sense for your company (one annual risk-based branch review auditor, a few to cover other branch regions).

I highly recommend a risk-based approach to cover key risks and controls. Let's focus on key risks, processes and products to create a few potential auditable entities:

- Branches – Branches selected for testing (branch visits)
- Branches – Account opening and closing (credit and debit cards, personal loans, payroll)
- Branches – Account opening and closing for deposit products
- Branches – Account opening and maintenance for safe deposit products
- Branches – Branch cash controls
- Branches – Continuity of business
- Branches – ATM maintenance
- Branches – Customer complaints
- Branches – Customer wire transfers
- Branches – Operational losses
- Branches – Branch fraud management programme
- Branches – Key technology projects (if any)
- Branches – Key technology systems
- Branches – Sales practices (programme)
- Branches – Incentive programme
- Branches – Branch oversight activities (this could be a centralized team that visits branches to complete additional testing)
- Branches – Self-assurance activities conducted by the first line of defence, such as a mystery shopping programme (third-party vendor), trade surveillance alerts and additional testing over key processes (MCA process).
- Branches – Branch compliance testing programme, if any (second line of defence).
- Branches – Smart branch banking model

The audit universe will differ across the financial industry; this is just an example of key processes, products and services provided in a branch network and how we could create a few auditable entities. A financial institution could have a few smart branches or a more extensive network. Banks have invested in digital banking and digitalization and have reduced the number of branches across the globe. Customers are setting the trends, the competition is fierce, and banks must provide better services and products and remain more innovative and flexible to meet customers' needs. Auditors also need to review smart banking branches; an auditable entity to review all technology solutions, customer experience, communications and other initiatives to enhance and manage customer journeys may be required. The bank may not have too many or be in the process of identifying the customer journeys. However, auditors need to determine the best approach to cover smart branches, which could also expand the number of auditable entities.

Two important documents to consider: always review the current business organization chart and the business process mapping. The first one is valid to understand the business structure and to ensure you are not missing any critical areas. Auditors need to assess every organizational change and how it impacts the audit universe. The second is relevant because auditors must assign high-risk processes to each auditable entity to facilitate risk assessment construction. Also, each auditable entity should not have more than 10 or 12 processes; otherwise, completing audits in 90 days will be challenging. We may need to create a few auditable entities to cover all relevant processes related to account opening (deposit products, safe deposit products, credit cards, personal loans) listed earlier. Before using the business process mappings, please ensure it is complete and accurate to facilitate the auditable entity construction; otherwise, this will dramatically impact the completion of future audits.

Let's go back to the annual audit plan construction. We have all risk assessments for all auditable entities that will impact the frequency of audits. The primary purpose of the audit plan is to describe the audit work for the next four or five years, but it has other objectives as listed below:

- Set expectations with stakeholders of the value added by IA.
- Identify key themes, high-risk processes or other regulatory requirements (that require annual coverage).
- Assign the audit frequency based on the risk assessment results (at least one auditable entity per risk assessment).
- Determine the SME hours required for integrated audits (e.g. technology, compliance, AML fraud IA teams).
- Obtain budget approval from the audit committee (e.g. hours for each audit engagement, issue validation and business monitoring activities, risk assessments, data analytics support, innovation activities and potential advisory work, among others).
- Identify the skills required to develop additional data analytics and continuous auditing tools or to cover other risks. Audit and chief audit directors must provide corrective actions to address the resource gaps.
- Share the draft audit plan with stakeholders and IA SMEs before submitting it to the audit committee for approval.
- Stay relevant.

The annual audit plan development is based on a standardized risk assessment approach that measures key risks faced by the organization, including discussions with senior management and IA SMEs, an evaluation of prior audits or regulatory reviews and other potential audits (e.g. regulatory, divestiture and change audits). The audit universe is based on the historical knowledge and experience of the IA teams. They need to assess and understand the audit universe, which is the collection of all auditable entities. This is not a static exercise; it must be reviewed and refreshed a few times during the year to stay relevant.

Auditors need to divide the entire auditable universe into a few auditable entities, as listed further (see figure 7.1), and identify and complete all risk assessments. Each auditable entity should have a risk assessment with corresponding risk drivers (e.g. regulatory, compliance, AML, models, market, credit, pricing, interest rate, liquidity, operational, fraud, sales practices, data management, third-party vendors, technology, conduct risks, climate change, including IA, self-disclosed, compliance or regulatory issues that impact the entity). If you are not starting from scratch, you could begin with a roll forward of the prior year's audit plan considering the most recent risk assessments.

Once the risk assessment is complete, a risk rating assigned to each auditable entity will determine the frequency of a risk-based audit. For example, a high (H) overall risk rating will require auditors to conduct an audit at least annually, a medium-high (MH) every 24 months, a medium-low (ML) every 36 months and a low within 48 months. This is just an example as the IA methodology will describe the frequency required. The described frequency should start from the last audit report publication date.

For auditable entities with an insufficient assurance or a weak audit report (not effective audits), auditors need to complete audits earlier (within 18 months). Thus, auditors may need to cover all auditable entities within three years, with an additional focus on high-risk areas. For regulatory audits, the cycle is determined by the regulator (based on regulatory requirements). Also, it is critical to link the risk assessments to the annual audit plan and business priorities to add value to your stakeholders. Audit directors must work diligently with their IA teams to add value to their stakeholders, define smarter audit scopes and include a holistic review of key processes and risks (e.g. compliance, technology, fraud, third-party vendors, data management, cybersecurity and climate change).

During a risk assessment refresh, auditors can add new auditable entities, combine, or remove others due to new gaps, emerging risks, regulatory requirements, business strategies and black swan events. Once the audit plan is complete for the year and typically a four- or five-year plan is prepared too, the chief auditor director, head of audit, and the audit committee must approve it. This information should be available in the audit management system.

An audit plan refresh could be completed quarterly or more often to ensure that the annual audit plan remains appropriate and relevant. It is

Figure 7.1 Elements to Consider to Build the Annual Audit Plan – Value Approach

based on the IA understanding of key risks, key processes and emerging risks through periodic stakeholder interactions during business monitoring activities and one-on-one meetings. During the audit plan refresh, a timeline and data queries are shared in advance to facilitate the audit plan construction. It contains the local and global annual audit plans for each IA team; the teams will have to address any exceptions identified (e.g. cycle gaps, outdated risk assessments and suggested adjustments [e.g. new audits, revised budget hours]). Any changes to the approved audit plan require appropriate rationale and documentation.

During the audit plan refresh, audits can also be added, cancelled, postponed or accelerated within the year due to several circumstances (e.g. divesture audits, increase or decrease in the business risk profile, new technology initiatives [change project audits], new regulatory requirements, results of other activities such as operational incidents, fraud events and new allegations that may require retrospective reviews). The audit directors should share the proposed adjustments with chief audit directors (for approvals), so the audit committee can approve all adjustments later.

Regarding the moderation package (sent to the audit committee), top thematic drivers are highlighted (e.g. sales practices, business changes, customer complaints, regulatory requirements, digital transformation and branch transformation), emerging risks impacting the businesses (e.g. large fraud events, inadequate monitoring of third-party vendors, unethical events, high operational losses in specific areas such as cash management, customer wire transfers, ATMs, fraud events and new black swan events) and regulatory drivers (e.g. new regulatory requirements or concerns with open regulatory issues). In addition, it is important to add and cancel audits (e.g. divestitures, change projects and other organizational changes), including changes to audit hours, resource skills assessment and innovation strategies, if any.

The audit plan refresh should consider the impact on other hours (issue validation activities, business monitoring) as new activities could be added to the audit plan (e.g. retrospective review, new key technology, and business initiatives, black swan events and new regulatory requirements). It also includes the analysis and approval of hours required for current and recent audits (audit budget), including SME hours for integrated audits. Once the audit committee approves the revised audit plan, all changes must be reflected in the audit management system, including any changes to the audit budget or hours agreed with IA SMEs.

Auditors need to coordinate activities with others to ensure proper coverage and to minimize duplication of efforts. Creating auditable entities requires excellent business knowledge, interaction with stakeholders (the first and the second line of defence), and IA SMEs (e.g. finance, compliance, AML, risk, third-party vendors). Why is it important to discuss the audit plan with the compliance team or other IA teams? They also work on their audit plan, so resources must be allocated adequately and effectively across IA teams. We should not visit the same stakeholder twice or very often; we need to avoid duplication of efforts. Stakeholders should not be able to manage a few audits simultaneously. Audits need to be efficient; we also need more integrated audits (e.g. audits conducted with products, technology and compliance teams) that can cover the end-to-end processes; thus, more holistic reviews are desirable.

Auditable entities need to have the right size; otherwise, an audit will not be enough to cover all high-risk processes. An audit entity could be created considering a business unit, products, services provided to the entire organization (e.g. operations, collections, legal, fraud units), legal vehicles (when there are affiliated companies or subsidiaries), geographic location (e.g. branches and ATMs in different regions or sites), reporting line (e.g. data management and product management audits), end-to-end processes handled in a branch network (e.g. account opening, safe deposit boxes, customer complaints, continuity of business, customer wire transfers, operational losses, sales practices, fraud management and incentives) and other channels (e.g. digital banking, accounts opened online, fraud programme for online banking, mobile or Zelle).

During the annual review process, the chief audit director must document the approach followed to ensure adequate audit coverage. If auditors identify gaps in coverage (e.g. no sufficient auditable entities, no auditable entity to cover a regulatory requirement or high-risk processes and lack of coverage), auditors must address all in the short term. This exercise aims to ensure that all high-risk processes, key risks and controls, key technology applications, regulatory requirements and emerging risks are also considered in the annual audit plan. This analysis could include an analysis of the organization chart (tie audit entities to core business heads), PRCs, policies, procedures, regulatory requirements and key third-party vendors, among others.

Developing an annual or audit plan refresh is only a start – audit leaders need to focus on tactical execution to enhance the control environment and drive accelerated changes. They must consider the external environment, customer experience, channels and digital solutions. How are you considering the impact of black swan events such as the ongoing pandemic? The pandemic (COVID-19) significantly impacted the 2020 and 2021 audit plans.

Audit leaders must have adequate capacity to hire, develop and retain talents to deliver the audit plan. They must re-assess stakeholder value drivers through business monitoring activities, including the necessary skill sets. For example, with digital transformation, it is relevant to hire and develop and retain talent that will be able to review digital and cybersecurity risks.

Audit leaders need to invest in technology to develop more continuous auditing tools to improve efficiencies and demonstrate positive and valuable results to relevant stakeholders. During the pandemic, remote testing took over and auditors had to use more data and additional data analytics tools.

Auditors need to be challenged more by the board of directors on how to add more value to the organization, especially during black swan events. Several types of thematic audits can be executed during a pandemic, especially for financial institutions (e.g. customer complaints, customer journeys, key cash processes in a branch network, customer wire transfers, fraud management programmes including operational losses and large fraud events, key digital technology projects and solutions, key high-risk third-party vendors [e.g. contractual modifications, complaints, risk assessments scores and continuity of the business], MCA governance or MCA programme). Market conditions, cyberattacks, and digitalization bring even more sophisticated risks that companies need to respond to find long-term success quickly. Audit leaders need to have more flexible audit plans, which will require more frequent audit plan refreshes.

Always recruit leaders who can lead the IA transformation and have an open mind to look outside the box. If you find audit leaders enthusiastic about taking a value approach when defining the annual audit plan or conducting audits and challenging the IA teams, please support them fully. They will be able to lead the IA transformation successfully, improve the audit performance and accelerate the value-added proposition by leveraging more data analytics and developing more continuous auditing tools. Innovation is key nowadays and will be more relevant next year as remote work is not going away anytime soon.

Let's move to the analysis of resource capacity.

Chapter 8

Audit Plan Capacity and Allocation of Resources

IA is an independent, objective assurance and consulting activity that brings a systematic, disciplined approach to evaluating and improving the effectiveness of risk management, controls, and governance processes. To successfully manage the annual audit plan, the head of audit needs to ensure that all internal audit resources are sufficient and effectively allocated to the most critical assurance and advisory activities. IA needs to innovate and add more value to the entire organization.

Uniform distribution of resources across all audits ensures that no employee is underutilized or overutilized. Under-allocation of resources results in productivity issues. Over-allocation, on the other hand, can cause burnout, affect the quality of output and team morale, or, worst, increase the attrition rate. Determining the annual audit plan capacity is not easy and requires a good analysis during the annual audit plan discussions.

I highly recommend developing an informal resource model to estimate the resource capacity and hours required to complete the annual audit plan. This will require certain assumptions to complete audits and other activities (other hours). It is important to be careful with the other hours, such as the time needed to complete issue validation, business monitoring activities, risk assessments, committee decks and advisory work. The audit budget (hours required to complete audit engagements) is generally booked in the audit management system. Still, other hours may be tracked outside this system, making this process more difficult. We need to do our best to estimate these hours correctly; otherwise, you may not be able to request enough audit resources to complete the approved audit plan.

The audit resources necessary to deliver individual assignments will be driven by several factors as listed here:

- Geographic location of the business, branch banking network, ATMs, third-party vendors and transaction volume may require frequent audit visits, including consideration of local language needs and additional staff to meet tight deadlines.

DOI: 10.4324/9781003431893-9

- Complexity of businesses, units, products or services provided by financial institutions. For example, the operations department could be complex in a big financial institution due to manual controls and the number of services offered to other areas. The bank can have an extensive branch network, a few high-risk third-party vendors (e.g. ATMs, armoured services and record management), and several legacy systems that do not necessarily have well-designed key automated controls.
- Audit reliance on prior audit work completed within the last 12 months. This could reduce the size of the audit scope.
- Size and number of auditable entities. For example, more prominent auditable entities will require additional resources and hours to review all high-risk processes.
- Regulatory requests to review specific areas due to new emerging risks, regulatory requirements or black swan events.
- Key project initiatives led by the first line of defence (e.g. PRC mappings or PRC reviews, technology projects). Auditors should focus on the most relevant key projects and initiatives through business monitoring activities and change audits.
- Deep dive analysis of certain material events (e.g. large fraud events, technology incidents); IA will need to perform more detailed business monitoring activities or testing to analyse the control environment, root cause and management corrective actions.
- Committee deck preparation. It is important to estimate adequate hours here and understand the committee decks required per month or quarter as audit leaders invest decent time here.
- Business requests to update corrective actions, milestone corrective actions (if any) and new re-target dates for open issues.
- Pre-validation activities regarding open issues are important to minimize re-open issues; auditors need to be engaged with stakeholders to challenge them before moving issues or corrective actions into IA validation (e.g. IA, regulatory and business self-identified issues included in the issue pipeline).
- Last-minute administrative requests from other audit locations or IA teams (e.g. IA QA and operations teams)
- Development of more continuous auditing tools. This is one of the most important tasks to add more value to the organization. IA transformation is relevant to accelerate the value proposition; thus, additional hours are required to design and improve data analytics tools, continuous auditing tools, and business monitoring activities.

The CAE generally tries to balance assurance needs with resource capacity to provide reasonable assurance to the audit committee and senior management over the control environment. However, despite having conversations with audit leaders, I have sometimes experienced a lack of resources.

I have occasionally seen chief auditor directors who did not want to request additional resources due to bad assumptions, budget constraints, and a lack of understanding of the amount of time allocated to advisory activities.

However, the chief audit director needs to get additional resources when there is an evident lack of capacity and to explain to others (head of audit and audit committee) the impact on assurance activities, the IA team's morale, key business or IA initiatives. The audit committee can approve additional hours to meet the annual audit plan and to address additional changes to the prior approved audit plan.

To determine the resource capacity is important to consider the following:

- Develop a simple resource model or an automated excel spreadsheet to estimate the hours required for each audit engagement, issue validation activities, business monitoring activities, risk assessments, committee decks and advisory activities. The final budget must be approved every year by the audit committee.
- Identify the resources required based on the final budget and the number of hours available per individual (approximately 1,600 per individual after deducting annual holidays, vacation and training hours).
- Consider IA SME hours required for audit engagements and issue validation activities.
- Allocate resources to risk-based audits, business monitoring, issue validation activities and risk assessments considering the skills and business expertise required.
- Identify how resource shortfalls are resolved (e.g. co-sourcing, new hires and other IA teams).
- Ensure adequate discipline to manage the audit plan successfully.

Let's focus now on the resource capacity and a few assumptions to estimate this exercise accurately:

- *Number of hours required to validate an IA, regulatory, self-disclosed issue (identified by Management)*. Also, consider the complexity of the issue (critical [level 1], high [level 2], moderate [level 3] or low [level 4] risk). For example, we need 80 hours to validate a level 1 issue with two corrective actions (40 hours each). For level 2, 30 hours per corrective action (see Table 8.1), but we do not need to invest hours in low-level issues. I am assuming minimal risk regarding level 4 issues; thus, I will focus my resources on what matters.
- *Number of IA and regulatory issues will be opened during the year*. You could leverage historical data; this number does not need to be perfect, but at least you need to estimate additional hours. For example, if

Table 8.1 Few Assumptions to Calculate of the Resource Capacity

Issues/Issue Level	Corrective Actions	Hours		
Level 1	2	80		
Level 2	3	90	**Other Hours**	
Level 3	3	90	PRC Review	
Level 4	3	N/A	Continuous Auditing	
			Business Monitoring (BM)	
Regulatory Issues			Technology Initiatives	
Level 2	3	90		
			Re-open Rate	**10%–15%**
BM Activities			**#Auditable Entities**	**15**
Master Entity		140		
Child Entity		100		
RA Entities				
Hours		90		

the number of regulatory issues has been stable for the last three years (80 issues), you can estimate a similar number.

- *Budget for each audit engagement.* The audit scope is relevant to determining the correct hours (1,500 or 2,000). We must be reasonable here; if you are auditing the business for the first time and this is a high-risk auditable entity, it is reasonable to book more hours (two thousand). However, if this is the third time, a lower number is more reasonable (between 1,200 and 1,500 hours). For a lower risk-based audit, 800 or 1,000 hours is more appropriate.
- *Determine the FTEs* (full-time employees); divide the total estimated hours (for all audits and other hours) by 1,600 [hours provided by each full-time employee). Then, compare the current and required capacity to determine the resource gaps.

Chief audit directors will always challenge a significant increase in hours. When registering the audits in the audit management system, ensure each quarter looks good and audit engagements are booked across the years consistently (25% of audits published each quarter). Also, double-check if you are not booking any audits in the first quarter or booking too many audits in the last. Vacation time and holidays could impact 1Q and 4Q activities dramatically.

In addition, a skills gap analysis is required at least annually to identify the skills needed and potential resource gaps. The following ideas can assist you in developing the skills needed to complete the annual audit plan:

- Develop and deliver specific training to fill the skills gaps identified (e.g. model risk, data management, fraud management, third-party vendors, information security, data analytics and innovation, compliance and regulatory requirements, cybersecurity, cryptocurrencies, soft skills, writing skills, agile approach and IA methodology, among others). If training is not available, you could look for third-party vendors who can deliver advanced training. In order to develop the data analytic skills, my IA team had to take mandatory training (including myself). I also found a third-party vendor who helped us.
- Implement a mentoring programme to coach IA teams, especially soft skills, negotiation skills and stakeholder engagement.
- Allocate IA team members to other audits or transfer them temporarily to other IA teams to develop additional skills (e.g. technology, cybersecurity, change audits, and branch banking audits).
- Coach IA teams to take specific certifications (e.g. CIA, CFE and Certified Anti-money Laundering Specialist [CAMS]) to enhance their technical skills.
- Send team members overseas to participate in franchise reviews or international assignments, if possible.
- Implement a good talent programme to hire, develop and retain talent.

Encourage your team to gain at least two or more skills every year. Allocating resources to specific audits that need multiple skills allows them to sharpen their primary skill sets, and it will be an excellent opportunity to build new ones. They can also receive further training on acquired skills and the job; complex projects and additional exposure further help them to improve their soft skills.

Building an IA function is not an easy step. When I started working in Mexico City, I had to build a consumer banking audit team. It was difficult initially to identify the right resources due to language constraints as all candidates need to speak and write in English. Identifying the right resources took me a while, but I had to train them. In the beginning, I had to bring more co-sources (contractors) while I was hiring additional personnel.

If you decide to bring additional co-sources, you must consider the following:

- Have a procedure document in place to facilitate the onboarding process, so this process takes one week. Otherwise, this could significantly impact your audit plan.

- Manage the approved budget diligently to avoid surprises. The audit manager or senior audit management must approve all timesheets.
- Train them; they must learn the IA methodology, so they must take all mandatory training before starting the assignments (e.g. information security and IA methodology).
- Track all hours charged and paid to third-party vendors to ensure the accuracy and quality of work provided to IA teams. Audit supervision is relevant to ensure all contractual assignments meet IA expectations.
- Have an adequate third-party vendor contract with clear clauses regarding the quality of work, pricing, data confidentiality, dispute resolution, exit terms and ownership of working papers.

Innovation strategies and more utilization of analytics tools could improve efficiencies and accelerate value to your stakeholders. Also, continuous investment in the in-house IA department is required concerning training, recruitment strategies and technology tools. The most value-added approach is to provide value to stakeholders as efficiently as possible. Thus, the audit director and the chief audit director need to make appropriate decisions when allocating resources to meet the annual audit plan and add more value to the organization.

High staff turnover can significantly impact the quality of work and the audit deliverables. Numerous factors can cause a high attrition rate. Still, some can be eliminated by identifying the root cause (e.g. lack of resources and leadership, unclear messages from audit leaders, supervisory practices that focused only on punitive interactions that left workers with low morale and assignments that varied from day to day).

Considering that the advisory work is adding tremendous value, chief audit directors must encourage their teams to innovate and request additional hours to support these activities. Comparison between the advisory and assurance work can be a good indicator of the type of work provided or if there is adequate balance (that sometimes is not so visible with your stakeholder). Also, ensure sufficient transparency regarding the advisory work and proven evidence of value added to justify additional hours and facilitate the approval process.

In addition, if there are resource constraints, be clear about covered or uncovered risks in the working paper. When planning the audit, also be clear with stakeholders if a few risks are out of the audit scope. We need to maximize the hours spent, but resource constraints should not be an excuse to exclude relevant topics. However, resources should be reallocated to the most relevant areas (high-risk processes); this should be documented in the working papers.

To ensure adequate allocation of resources, a resource planning template may be helpful to manage the resources effectively. You could easily identify when there is over or under capacity. This template could help audit managers or senior audit managers to arrange the required resources at the right time and sequence. As different audit activities and audits are running in parallel, resource distribution is critical to ensure zero audit delays or issue validation activities.

Audit capacity planning is a multi-step approach to calculating and analysing the requirements and availability of resources. The following easy guide is particularly useful for designing a resource capacity planning template to manage the annual audit plan successfully:

- Consider audit planning, fieldwork, reporting phases, issue validation activities, business monitoring activities, risk assessments and continuous auditing efforts with a corresponding start, end date, and duration.
- Enlist the resources required for each task or audit (audit manager, senior audit manager, audit director, senior auditor and auditor).
- Calculate the number of FTEs required for each task or audit phase.
- Enlist the available capacity of each resource, including the budget available for each audit.
- Define each resource engagement's start date, end date and duration.
- Analyse the overlapping activities to resolve them and adjust them accordingly.
- Centralize all proposed changes to resource schedules. For example, the senior audit manager should at least submit resource changes.
- Finally, update the resource capacity regularly to resolve any concerns timely.

The senior audit manager and audit director must approve the resource allocation. If there is no automated tool available, a simple excel spreadsheet can help. An audit manager or senior audit manager could manage the schedule. For example, IA managers can meet weekly to discuss resource challenges or assignments. It can be time-consuming to keep this up to date, but it is important to manage all resources effectively.

When allocating resources to assignments (e.g. audits, issue validation activities, business monitoring and risk assessments), it is important to consider the following:

- Skills and expertise required to conduct the audit, issue validation and business monitoring activities.
- Number of resources required to meet the milestones, specifically when the IA team is conducting an audit for the first time or is a complex one.
- Allocation of resources to add value to your stakeholders.
- Distribution of the audit plan during the year to avoid starting it later or pushing assignments to the end of the year. The last one can easily

impact the audit quality and resource morale as they will experience pressure to finish everything before the year ends. I always try to book fewer audits towards the end of the last quarter to facilitate the annual audit plan completion.

- Business and audit priorities to define which ad-hoc assignments to take. You will experience new events not considered during the audit plan construction. Senior management may request an audit or a new fraud event triggers the audit. If the new resource request is over the resource budgeted, it puts at risk the completion of the audit plan. Thus, the audit team should complete a deep analysis before requesting additional resources; additional options could be available such as cancelling an audit, rescheduling it or moving it to the following year.
- Cost associated with each assignment. For example, if there are expense constraints to travel, audit directors need to assess how high-risk processes will be reviewed. Nowadays, auditors need to leverage more data and technology solutions to complete the walkthroughs and audit testing during remote work.
- The type of assignment recommended: a target audit, an end-to-end audit or enhanced business monitoring activities.
- Audit timing and resource schedule to ensure FTEs are also available to manage the audit requests and other relevant audit activities. Also, it is critical to agree with the stakeholders on the top priority assignments (typically the ones that add more value).

Additional changes will impact the approved annual audit plan during the year. A flexible audit plan is encouraged as it could be easily modified. Also, do not forget to agree with management on the annual audit plan and key milestones. If any constraints are identified during these meetings, please consider them carefully because business resources are necessary to complete audits successfully. If few audits are conducted simultaneously (e.g. audit engagements, compliance, regulatory or franchise reviews), raise your hand and ask the business if they have any concerns. For example, I have seen requests from management to move audits later due to recent audit results (issues raised in the last audit report). Thus, the business wanted to focus on open IA issues first.

Another important topic is to ensure that time spent on specific assignments or other activities is tracked, monitored, and booked in the audit management system. Audit hours approved are compared to hours booked annually. If the information is inaccurate, it will be more difficult to justify additional hours and get approvals from the audit committee.

Recruit leaders who focus on hiring, developing, retaining, and helping resources become more enthusiastic about the IA value proposition and people. The best IA departments hire future leaders who love learning, sharing, and developing team members. We need more people who care about others and are willing to coach, motivate and empower others. One of the most important things a leader can do is lead by example, share knowledge and support others by requesting the required resource capacity and skills.

An outstanding IA transformation will always require excellent audit leaders and stronger teams. Never forget people; they are your most valuable assets. True audit leaders listen to their teams carefully and passionately in an era of innovation, digitalization and digital assets. They support them with additional resources and motivate them to add more value. Always keep an open ear, always be available for your team, and you'll be boosting your team to produce more innovative ideas. People are intelligent; they'll know when they have a fantastic leader who cares and a leader that doesn't. You always go first if you want everyone else to be enthusiastic, committed and motivated. People follow great leaders, not bad bosses.

Let's move to issue validation activities.

Chapter 9

Issue Validation Activities
Taking a Value Approach

Auditors need to follow up on management action plans or corrective actions to address the internal audit issues (raised during audits or business monitoring activities), regulatory issues and business self-identified issues in audit reports. IA needs to evaluate the sustainability of new or revised key controls to minimize identified risks. One crucial element when reviewing these corrective actions is ensuring they have at least a sustainability period of three months after the control implementation. However, if a corrective management action takes over three months, auditors should request compensatory controls to minimize the identified risk.

Auditors need to monitor the issue pipeline to assign resources and complete the preliminary design assessment and the issue validation activities on time. Let's discuss a few critical challenges faced by auditors when issues are ready for IA validation:

- Management did not assign enough resources to address the issue on time.
- Management did not understand the information required to complete corrective actions.
- Inadequate management oversight activities to ensure corrective actions are delivered on time; thus, issues are not a top priority for management.
- Issue management team (first line of defence) has not performed robust testing to verify the sustainability of corrective actions.
- The business and IA team have not discussed progress made by the issue owner until the deadline approaches (issue or corrective action target date including the sustainability period).
- IA moves the issue into IA validation without performing a pre-assessment of the information received; thus, auditors could not provide timely feedback to management.
- The issue has eight or ten corrective actions but no key controls were identified (e.g. most corrective actions were around training, procedures

DOI: 10.4324/9781003431893-10

updates, and communication provided to customers or employees to address process changes). The corrective actions need to have a few key controls to address the root cause of the issue.

- IA puts the issue into validation even though the original concern was not fully fixed; management has not requested a new re-target date. Thus, the issue validation will fail, and the business may need to provide additional corrective actions or a new re-target date.
- IA and the business missed the deadline, and IA reached out to the business when the issue was already past due.
- The business has not confirmed issue closure with the IA team; however, IA started issue validation activities.
- Corrective actions backdated by the business; however, the business did not inform the IA team that the issues were completed two months ago. IA will have fewer days to complete the validation activities. This should not happen often; otherwise, the IA team needs to open an issue, and management must provide corrective actions to improve transparency regarding remediation actions.
- Insufficient IA resources to complete issue validation activities.
- IA resources are unfamiliar with issue validation activities and work paper documentation requirements, so extensive re-work is required before closing an issue (IA validation not completed on time).
- There is no issue validation framework to manage the issue validation pipeline. Issues are assigned to team members based on resource availability without considering the skills and expertise required. Test steps are not fully vetted and approved by senior audit manager or audit director.
- Data analytics is underused to validate a complex issue; however, data is required to validate this issue successfully, but the data analytics team does not have enough capacity to assist.
- Issue validation activities took longer than expected as the issue description and corrective actions were too vague to fully understand the key controls implemented by management. Auditors had to conduct an end-to-end review to identify the key controls.

So, how could we resolve these challenges together? Let's discuss a few alternative solutions:

- The resource capacity is important to successfully manage the issue pipeline (hours must be allocated to issue validation activities and resources booked in advance). This is an important audit activity; auditors can deliver value during pre-validation activities; thus, auditors need to book hours in advance.
- Data analytics requirements must be discussed with the data analytics team in advance. The senior audit manager and audit director must

review the testing approach and steps before starting any issue validation activities.

- An audit manager should monitor the issue pipeline weekly, especially when a few issues are due in the next two months. IA needs a good issue-reporting mechanism or a manual excel spreadsheet to manage the issue pipeline. Issues must be validated within a specific timeframe to comply with the IA methodology manual (30 days, level 1 [critical issue], 60 days, level 2 [high-risk issue] or 90 days, level 3 issues [moderate issue] or just 90, level 1, 2 and 3). I Highly recommend stronger issue management practices to complete issue validation activities on time or even earlier (within 60 days).

- Auditors need to schedule preliminary meetings with business owners (two or three months in advance) to clarify any questions regarding documentation requirements, audit expectations, and potential business or IA concerns.

- IA teams should have access to supporting documentation at least 30 days before issues or corrective actions are about to close. I highly recommend setting checking points to understand how issues are addressed and to clarify any questions Management may have. When I implemented this approach in a few organizations, I reduced the re-open rate to zero. Management appreciates this monitoring approach and the transparency gained. A closer relationship with stakeholders during issue validation activities saves time later by minimizing time invested in re-open reports.

- Auditors should verify during business monitoring activities and audits if management has enough resources to address all open issues. Issue management is relevant for the successful implementation of corrective actions. Senior management and the board would like more information about management concerns, challenges, and how issues are resolved. Management is accountable for providing relevant information to the IA teams and addressing corrective actions timely and effectively.

- Issue remediation activities are so important that performance metrics for business owners and senior management could be considered. When the business does not resolve corrective actions, re-targets are highly processed, and issue validation failures often show a lack of management oversight activities and accountability. Business leaders are responsible for resolving issues timely to improve the control environment.

- Corrective actions should be owned by a manager or above. When a more senior manager is responsible for corrective actions, there is a higher probability that the agreed corrective measures will be resolved timely and effectively.

- Issues should have no more than three or four corrective actions. Auditors must review and challenge management corrective actions to ensure key controls address the root cause identified. Corrective actions should not be a compilation of checklist steps irrelevant to the issue resolution. Management could combine a few corrective actions (same issue owner and timeline) to facilitate issue validation activities and documentation requirements, if possible.

- Adequate training for IA team members to ensure a standard approach (e.g. standard templates) is followed to complete issue validation activities and documentation requirements. The senior audit manager and audit director must review the working papers before closing the issues in the audit management system.

We need to be more efficient when validating issues. An issue validation should not end in a mini audit. Sometimes, we conduct deeper end-to-end analysis, and additional concerns arise. It is important to allocate time and resources to the most complex issues and focus on the corrective actions agreed with Management. Regarding level 4 or low-rated issues, it may be valuable not to perform any testing activities; management can easily close the issue(s) without requiring IA validation activities. Auditors can include the same topic or concern in future audits to verify that the issue was adequately addressed.

Of course, if new observations are identified during the issue validation activities, auditors would request additional corrective actions. If the root cause is different and related to a further concern, the IA team could raise a new issue with new corrective actions. However, if this finding is also related to the issue raised earlier, we may not be able to close the issue. I highly recommend paying attention to management's reaction when new observations are raised and how they will be resolved. If management is too worried about the issue closure and tries to minimize the new finding, this could be a red flag, so you may need to perform additional testing in this area.

If the corrective actions are delayed, the IA team needs to understand why this was not escalated to the IA team earlier. Management may wait until the last minute to disclose that the issue is still pending. This is not a good sign, and auditor leaders need to have additional conversations with senior management or escalate this further to the board. If the delay is reasonable (e.g. delays in a technology project or additional time required), Management will need to inform the IA team of the new re-target date. The business owner, business head, and others (based on the issue management framework) must approve all target dates. The IA will assess if the revised date is reasonable based on the information and rationale provided by the business. Some organizations may consider implementing issue vetting or tollgate meetings to discuss new re-targets or other concerns. Once the approvals and explanations are provided to the IA team, auditors must update the new retarget date in the audit management system.

An automated issue tracking mechanism (within the audit management system) helps manage the issue validation activities easier and to share timely feedback with stakeholders. Audit issues opened in the audit management system must interact with the corporate issue management tool, too; this could facilitate the following:

- Enhance the issue management methodology and monitoring activities by allowing consistency across IA teams (issue creation, issue rating, tracking, and monitoring activities).
- Improve the validation workflow. When management completes issues, auditors should get a notification that triggers the issue validation activities. If corrective actions are not addressed timely, auditors and business owners will be notified by email. Auditors should not start the validation activities when the business needs additional time or auditors are not comfortable with the actions taken. Auditors could send the issue back to Management by adding a few notes or comments in the audit management system (a retarget is required). In this case, I assume that auditors have not started any validation activities yet (the issue has not formally moved to validation).
- Develop an agile reporting tool that facilitates issue tracking and audit committee reporting. For example, issues are reportable anytime, and status will update timely as issues move through the remediation process (open, IA validation, closed and past due). Auditors can leverage this information when they need to prepare the audit committee deck or others.

If during audit assessment, the control is operating effectively, the issue can be risk mitigated and closed in the IA management system (IA issue) or regulatory system (regulatory issue). If recommendations are identified, it is also important to highlight that. To finalize the issue closure, issues require the respective senior audit manager and audit director approvals (IA issue) or audit director and chief audit director approvals (regulatory issue). Issue closure should not extend beyond the allowed timing to perform the issue validation activities.

IA is responsible for tracking all issues (e.g. IA, regulatory and self-disclosed issues included in the audit report) until resolution, and at a minimum, the audit committee deck should include the following information:

- High-risk areas associated with IA findings (e.g. critical, high-risk issues) or thematic findings (similar issues noticed during audits). Few thematic results could be related to data management, change management, third-party vendors (onboarding, contract agreements, monitoring activities, know your customer (KYC), AML, fraud management programmes, manual processes or complex products or services across bank channels (product simplification, customer disclosures, marketing materials) and MCA process. It is important to highlight this information in the deck to improve management accountability, improve holistic resolution, and create awareness of lessons learnt from past identified issues.

- Number of open IA issues from prior and current reporting periods and how these issues have impacted the control environment (downgrade or upgrade).
- High description of the highest priority issues, areas of impact, target dates, business owner, the status of management actions regarding current target dates, and potential concerns or challenges, including issue level or issue rating.
- Management metrics in terms of percentage of self-identified issues, on-time remediation activities, re-open rate, repeat issues or re-targets. These metrics are a good example of management accountability in addressing issues timely and effectively (pass the IA or regulatory validation).
- Number of issues closed from the prior and current reporting period.

The chief audit director and head of audit must approve the audit committee deck. Also, if there are thematic concerns (as listed earlier), the head of audit may need to escalate all to global committees or forums (to increase transparency, accountability and visibility).

Regulatory Issues

Once a regulatory letter is received, a multidisciplinary team should be responsible for analysing the letter and preparing the response to the regulators. If the observations are not clarified with the regulator, the business must provide corrective action plans to address the identified concerns.

Here are a few challenges faced by organizations when a regulatory review is announced and completed:

- Only specific personnel attend the regulatory meetings (e.g. Legal, IA QA teams, and IA Audit Head). However, we are missing an important topic here, and the business needs to be prepared for a regulatory review and understand the scope of the review. Thus, based on the regulatory review scope, key stakeholders familiar with the business under review should attend the key meetings.
- Management does not spend enough time building stronger relationships with local regulators. However, it is important to build good relationships with them by scheduling regular meetings (monthly or quarterly basis) to understand their concerns and leadership style and discuss other relevant topics (e.g. changes to the annual audit plan, issues raised

in prior or current audits, concerns with issue validation activities and resource capacity), among others.

- Regulatory requests not delivered on time and with the quality expected. It is important to provide accurate and complete information to minimize future issues (e.g. incomplete data queries or key management reports). A centralized team that coordinates all requests and ensures that everything is reviewed and approved before delivering this information could facilitate this process.
- Management response to initial observations is inaccurate or not focused on what the regulators are pointing out. It is important to involve key personnel during this process; otherwise, clarifying any questions or observations from the regulators will be more challenging.
- Corrective action plans not reviewed and discussed with the second and third lines of defence. IA must be involved in this process to validate all corrective actions or action plans. IA needs to play a key role here; otherwise, this could increase the re-open rate in the future.
- There is no automated system of records to identify, track and monitor all regulatory issues.
- Not all regulatory observations entered the regulatory system, so there is a gap between all regulatory letters received and the regulatory issue pipeline.
- Not all regulatory issues or requirements were met within the agreed-upon timeframe with regulators. The business needs to inform the regulator in advance if corrective actions are not resolved timely and provide a rationale.
- The business did not perform compliance and regulatory gap analysis, so the MCA or PRC does not include all regulatory requirements regarding key processes and monitoring controls to minimize the risk. Thus, the self-assurance activities are not robust enough to self-identify issues (first line of defence).
- Not all regulatory issues are validated timely by IA teams. In general, IA teams will have at least 90 days to complete the issue validation activities once the regulatory issues are complete. However, IA could complete issue validation activities earlier (60 days).

When regulatory observations are raised to the IA department, the same approach must be followed to ensure timely and proper responses are provided, including the corrective actions. The chief audit director, head of audit and IA QA team (this is a good practice) should review all responses and documentation provided to regulators.

The validation of a regulatory issue is more complex than an IA issue as the observations may be generic or not too much information was highlighted in the regulatory letter. The business may want to cover the end-to-end process and extend the corrective actions to minimize other potential risks. Is this the right approach? No, this is the main reason key stakeholders need to be involved in the discussions to understand the key concerns and identify the root cause(s) to provide proper corrective actions.

Regulators may request clarification if issues remain open for a prolonged period and if similar observations were identified by the second or third line of defence to highlight gaps in compliance or audit coverage. When issues remain open for more than six months, compensatory controls must be provided to mitigate the risk while the other automated or sophisticated solutions are in progress.

Regulators may conduct horizontal reviews of large banks regarding "Conduct and Culture" programmes, sales practices, incentive programmes, data management, fraud management programmes, third-party vendors, branch banking programme, AML programmes and other monitoring activities. Data management is key to monitoring activities and providing adequate information to senior management and the board. In addition, a stronger second line of defence functions is required, so many financial institutions are developing stronger compliance functions by enhancing their testing programmes and bringing additional resources.

Regulators are becoming more sophisticated with data analytics tools to assess the compliance programmes. The first, second and third lines of defence need to enhance data analytics capabilities to enhance monitoring and self-assurance activities and identify relevant issues faster. Innovation is relevant and essential to identify areas of concern, trends or outliers (e.g. fraud, operational losses, cybersecurity, AML, third-party vendors and other emerging risks). Also, the organization could identify potentially improper transactions or illegal activities by using more data analytics with a forensic lens.

Also, if you work for an organization or in the IA department, you don't want regulators to come in and find observations just by using data analytics tools with your data; you need to find the observations first. The same concept applies to the business; it needs to identify issues timely by leveraging additional data analytics tools. Remember, the information is available, but the data is often underused. We need to do a better job here; we need better tools to identify compliance and regulatory gaps and to better explain to the regulators how compliance and regulatory requirements are monitored effectively.

Issue Validation Working Papers

Issue validation is a key part of IA assurance work and is subject to third-party reviews; auditors must document issue validation activities to comply with IA quality standards. Auditors could design standard templates to complete testing activities and improve IA teams' consistency. When I review the working papers, I usually perform a detailed review to ensure all support the audit testing conclusions (design assessment and operating effectiveness testing).

The standard template could include the following sections:

- Issue description (audit, regulatory or self-identified issue), root cause, issue level, and corrective actions with corresponding due dates.
- Testing objective.
- DEA. The control design should be reviewed if the issue was raised due to a design failure. A walkthrough must confirm if the new control is designed to mitigate the risk. If the original issue was raised due to a failure in the operating effectiveness of the control, DEA is not required (if the design of the control did not change). I highly recommend developing a standard DEA template to facilitate the design assessment (e.g. control description, Who executes the control? Does experienced personnel execute the control? Is there a backup? Is there adequate segregation of duties? Is there a maker and a checker control in place? Can anyone surpass or avoid control? How is the control executed? Is there evidence of the control execution? Is the control sustainable?). Auditors should answer all these potential questions to conclude the design assessment.
- OET. The senior audit manager and the audit director must approve all test steps. Auditors need to identify key controls during the DEA and then evaluate all to confirm it the control is effective and has been operating effectively. Documentation should describe documents reviewed, data source, testing performed or exceptions identified by auditors. If management provides a key report, the auditor needs to review the report for completeness and accuracy and complete the test steps agreed upon (e.g. manager's approval, exceptions identified and resolved by management within the timeframe required).
- Sample rationale. The sample size should match the control frequency described in the IA methodology manual. However, auditors need to consider other data analytics requirements to validate the entire population and the effectiveness of the control. We should be able to use more data to complete the testing and move away from sampling techniques.
- Overall conclusion of both DEA and OET. Issue validation cannot be considered effective unless this conclusion is made at the overall issue level. Once the issue validation is complete (no exceptions identified), auditors can close the issue in the audit management system.

Suppose issues require specialized expertise (e.g. technology, compliance, fraud, third-party vendors, data management). In that case, the IA SMEs should also be involved in the validation process and the review of working papers.

The audit manager, senior audit manager and audit director must review issue validation working papers. The audit team could use standard documentation to complete these activities. This does not necessarily require the centralization of the issue validation activities but having a strong audit manager who can track monitor, and coordinate issue validation activities is extremely helpful. I am not a big fan of centralizing issue validation activities; IA teams need to collaborate closely with stakeholders as they can provide better value during issue monitoring and issue validation activities.

Auditors should map all audit issues raised to corresponding auditable entities as they may impact the control environment and audit assessments. They should monitor these issues frequently and add commentaries in the audit management system if concerns are identified. This information will feed subsequent audit committee decks or other materials to provide to senior management regularly.

COVID-19 Impact

COVID-19 changed the way issues are being validated. Auditors working remotely need to use more technology tools to conduct walkthroughs (zoom meetings, conference calls) – access and travel restrictions or reduced resource capacity impact how audits are executed. Auditors need to maintain an appropriate level of professional scepticism in validating issues and reviewing the evidence provided by management.

Auditors need to leverage more data to assess the effectiveness of controls. If you are auditing retail branches, you may not be able to visit branches during a pandemic or visit a smaller number. Things can still be reviewed if you need to assess the effectiveness of branch opening and closure procedures or if bankers follow mandatory COVID-19 guidance. How can you assess this? You could schedule call interviews with bankers over the phone, leverage video surveillance to complete the testing, and evaluate the effectiveness of self-assurance or monitoring activities conducted by the first line of defence. Also, you could leverage data to review and validate certain transactions processed in branches (e.g. customer wire transfers, cash transactions such as check deposits or withdrawals, fees charged, operational losses, customer refunds processed and customer complaints) and verify customer's presence or even transactions processed before or after business hours (e.g. video surveillance). How about monitoring transactions in temporarily closed branches? You could use data here too.

Here are a few additional useful tips:

- Discuss the testing approach with the senior audit manager and audit director. This is especially important to ensure an adequate testing strategy. The audit director usually has reliable, professional experience and can add value when discussing the testing steps with auditors.
- Assess the reliability of the audit evidence provided by management, such as scanned reports or other relevant scanned evidence, controls not executed timely (unreconciled cash items in branches or high cash differences, operational losses, large fraud events, customer complaints, sales practices and other KPIs or business metrics).
- Assess the audit testing approach to complete issue validation activities (e.g. more data analytics tools or data analysis to identify concerns, outliers or other trends).
- Manage and document scope limitations, if any. For example, during the pandemic, auditors may not be able to visit branches or go to third-party vendor locations. Thus, auditors need to document any scope limitations and explain how things will be reviewed in the future.
- What could go wrong from a financial reporting or operational perspective? What are you missing? Always keep this question in the back of your mind when completing DEA and OET. Key controls may have changed to meet customers' needs, and IA may need to review temporary controls during audits or business monitoring activities. For example, new audits can be added to the annual audit plan to review these controls, revised procedure documents. Increased technology, AML, cybersecurity, compliance and fraud risks are relevant in future audits.
- Identify and assess emerging risks such as continuity of business, cyber security, large fraud losses, and non-compliance with regulatory requirements or accounting rules. Is there a clear understanding of capital requirements and cash flow requirements?
- Maximize the use of technology when conducting testing. Encourage team members to connect through zoom meetings, especially when conducting walkthroughs.
- Challenge management when they point out that procedures or controls have not been impacted or changed, knowing that many people are working remotely or transferred to other areas to provide temporary support to other teams (e.g. collection centres, call centres and ATM maintenance). What has changed during the pandemic or since the last audit? Are the business tracking and monitoring all changes implemented? Are all procedure documents available to all employees?
- Increase audit supervision or implement tollgate issue discussions to brainstorm the testing approach. Involve IA SMEs, if needed. The senior

audit manager and audit director must review all working papers before issuing the audit reports or completing issue validation activities.

- Welcome IA QA reviews as they can provide a unique perspective and honest feedback to enhance documentation requirements.
- Leverage more and independent data to validate completeness and accuracy of data provided to IA (e.g. customer's signatures against IDs on file, the reasonableness of transactions processed such as wire transfers processed in 20 seconds, structured transactions processed for the same customer, higher volume of transactions processed before or after business hours, higher operational losses due to control breaks, ATM failures, fraud events and higher cash differences). Auditors can look at large amounts of data and relationships, filter data to identify trends and outliers, and focus on higher-risk transactions to improve audit testing or sample selection. Thus, the data quality is relevant to performing better data analysis and relevant audit testing.

These tips can also be considered during audit engagements, business monitoring activities, risk assessments and to develop more continuous auditing tools.

Issue Validation Hub

The pandemic and the rise in homeworking have caused companies to re-evaluate the role of expensive city centre offices. One idea gaining popularity among IA departments is the hub model, where companies can operate from multiple regional offices; a centralized model to gain additional efficiencies and reduce costs. IA departments are leveraging the hub concept and hiring personnel in other countries to manage the issue validation pipeline.

To implement this successfully is important to define the framework across different regions and rules of engagement with proper and opportune audit supervision. It is also relevant to have adequate reporting mechanisms to track all issues and manage the issue pipeline successfully. Depending on the issue volume, a senior audit manager and strong audit managers must be assigned to coordinate the efforts. Additional resources should be allocated based on the required audit skills and data analytics support.

Before implementing this approach, it is important to engage stakeholders timely to get their support and to identify an SPOC to manage all audit requests. Also, additional training should be delivered to IA teams regarding the hub framework and expectations to facilitate the issue validation activities (e.g. documentation requirements and how to manage different time zones), the inclusion of local regulatory requirements and lessons learnt to accelerate the value added to the business.

Chapter 10

Audit Working Papers and Detailed Review

Audit documentation is a critical element of audit quality as evidence of the work done by auditors. The documentation must stand independently and allow another person to reach the same conclusions. Workload demands are the biggest challenges faced in completing effective and timely audit documentation. When pressed for time, auditors may fail to document the work performed, testing completed, and conclusions reached, leading to incomplete working papers, tons of comments provided by audit managers and above, and potential deficiencies noted during peer reviews.

Working papers must be prepared to provide the principal support for audit findings. For example, during planning, the following documentation must be developed and retained:

- Background documentation
- Business priorities and objectives
- Audit announcement memo
- Kick-off meeting deck and meeting minutes
- Audit planning document
- Documentation request list, for example, the business can provide hard copies or electronic forms to support audit testing
- Vendor management and technology considerations
- Business process mappings for the area under review
- IA team and budget assigned to the audit
- Audit work programme (testing steps)
- Design assessment testing (walkthroughs)
- Flow charts
- Policies and procedures
- RCM (key risk and key controls to be included in the audit scope)
- data analytics requirements

Auditors should use standardized working papers to facilitate the audit documentation, covering the nature, extent, and timing of audit testing

DOI: 10.4324/9781003431893-11

procedures conducted, including testing results, among others. Do not keep unnecessary documents on file. For example, test evidence must be retained to support the exceptions and to allow re-performance of audit testing procedures. If you cannot reach the same conclusions, the evidence requires enhancements.

Also, all supporting documentation for design testing must be retained to evidence the walkthrough conducted, the transaction reviewed (test of one transaction from beginning to end), and the design assessment completed. The reliability of the evidence is also another key factor to consider; external evidence is more reliable than internal evidence (e.g. bank statements and confirmations from external parties), and written or independent evidence is more reliable than inquiry-only evidence.

Auditors must validate any reports or queries provided by Management. If you have access to the system, pull the information directly or see how the business pulls the information. Auditors must review the completeness and accuracy of data before conducting effectiveness testing. Documentation should be clear enough to understand testing conducted by auditors. Data queries or reports provided by the business must be reconciled to the system of records or reports from which they were obtained.

All working papers must include at least the following information:

- Name of the audit
- Auditor's name
- Reviewer's name
- Control description and frequency of the control
- Period of testing
- Date completed
- Testing objective
- Data source
- Sampling approach, population, if applicable
- Test steps, if applicable
- Testing results
- Exceptions identified
- Conclusions
- Tick marks definition
- Scope limitations
- Additional audit procedures performed in response to significant exceptions noted

An electronic audit documentation software will automatically take care of most of this. Automating the documentation allows the auditor to focus on the aspects that cannot be automated because they require professional judgement. This can improve efficiency and reduce the likelihood of errors. Applying the best practices can give auditors more time to focus on aspects of the audit process that require their critical thinking skills.

The objective of the working paper must be linked to specific control objectives in the RCM. When reviewing the working papers, ensure consistency across all working documents. For example, the control description listed in the RCM, walkthrough, and effectiveness testing must match, including the conclusions reached or exceptions identified. The reviewer should return the working paper to address comments if these elements do not link together. Scope limitations must be documented and used to highlight areas or procedures that will not be covered.

Let's focus for a moment on the sampling approach and population. It is important to describe the data source, and the number of occurrences within the population, sample technique (e.g. judgemental and random), frequency of the control (to determine the sample size required), sample size (based on the IA methodology) and sample selection.

All exceptions noted in the working papers must be well described, including the conclusion reached, such as "Based on the testing performed, no exceptions were noted," or exceptions, such as 3/10 reconciliations were not signed by the checker and several reconciling items have not been resolved." An explanation must be provided if there is a justified reason to execute a control differently (e.g. the checker/approver was on vacation or sick, so a different person had authorization limits). You need to understand why the exceptions occurred, and the root cause so that management's corrective actions will effectively minimize the risk.

Auditors should use standardized tick marks to avoid unnecessary repetition in the working papers. A tick mark is a little symbol indicating a task that the auditor completed. Keep tick marks simple, so it is easy to understand conclusions when reviewing work papers (e.g. # agreed to the system of records [General Ledger as of April 22, 2022] and recalculated by audit on April 22, 2022, and no exceptions noted). Another example, "x," can indicate an error and √ demonstrate satisfaction with the attribute. Also, it would help if you were specific with the data source and date.

Eliminating unnecessary business documentation in the file boosts efficiency, as well. Draft documents must be removed from the audit database. Only final working papers must be archived in the audit management system. Required personnel must review and sign off all the working papers to comply with the IA methodology. Before closing the audit management system, the audit manager and senior audit manager should verify that review notes are cleared and removed. Also, be sure to double-check cross-referencing among working papers. Ensure there is no Personal Identifiable Information (PII) in any excel files or queries attached (e.g. social security numbers, driver's license numbers, financial or medical records and biometrics). This data requires stricter handling guidelines because of the increased risk to an individual if the information is compromised.

Auditors in the field sometimes decide to catch up with documentation later. Documentation is more likely to be accurate if it is completed sooner rather than later. I highly recommend completing the working papers once the testing procedure is completed to minimize re-work and ensure the accuracy of the information obtained. This also applies to the review process; audit directors and senior audit managers must review all planning documentation before moving to the fieldwork phase and all fieldwork working papers before moving to the reporting phase.

Great working papers also improve efficiency in future audits or regulatory reviews. By documenting appropriately, the auditors are helping future audit teams avoid duplication of efforts or facilitating reliance on their work. With adequate documentation, less time should be spent addressing comments, questions, and concerns during working papers or regulatory reviews.

Let's move now to another important topic: detailed reviews. I am detailed-oriented; I perform detailed reviews and provide review comments to my team. The working paper review should be done throughout and during all audit phases (e.g. planning, fieldwork and reporting).

The audit working papers should be reviewed by senior audit managers and audit directors. When performing a detailed review, please consider the following tips:

- Ensure the testing programme was executed, the testing objectives were met and key risks and controls were assessed without bias based on the documented facts.
- Make sure all pieces fit together and look for consistency among different working papers (e.g. risk assessment for the auditable entity, audit plan, RCM, walkthroughs, DEA, OET, issues identified and audit report conclusions). Electronic working papers facilitate cross-referencing with hyperlinks. Each working paper should be referenced to be found easily.
- All high risks identified in the risk assessment are included in the audit scope. If high-risk processes are not included, a rationale must be provided, IA SME approval should be obtained and evidence retained in the working papers and audit management system. The reviewer should reconcile the key risks and processes (listed in the audit planning memo, audit scope and RCM) to the ones listed in the risk assessments.
- Determine if certain things must be escalated to the audit director or above or should have been escalated to audit director or above (during the secondary review).

- Ensure senior audit managers and audit directors perform the detailed review. Also, the audit director must be engaged during the audit and planning phase to approve the audit scope, audit planning memo and RCM.
- Ensure all working papers include signoffs. It should be signed by the person who prepares it so any future queries can be directed to that person. It should be signed and dated by any person who reviews it (first and secondary review).
- Working papers stand on their own.
- All working papers must support the detailed findings in the audit report.
- It is neat and legible. Make sure your writing is grammatically correct. Documentation that contains grammar errors reduces credibility. As most computers have spell-check functions, always use them. Complex words or technical jargon should be avoided; however, be sure to define these terms if necessary.
- It should fully state the year/period end (e.g. July 20, 2023) so that the working paper is not confused with documentation belonging to a different year/period.
- See the "big picture" to ensure that you are not missing additional testing and how the working papers support the issues identified or conclusions reached.
- Watch the level of details provided, too little or too much, and provide comments or questions, if necessary.
- Ensure the sample size complies with the IA methodology and sampling attributes are well documented.
- Ensure that important calculations are verified.
- Abbreviations and acronyms are spelled before abbreviations, so the reader understands the meaning.
- The audit file contains adequate supporting documentation and meeting notes of stakeholders' discussions.
- If referenced to another working paper, the complete reference must be provided, and ensure that the auditor documents the work performed to place reliance on prior work. No reliance should be placed on testing that was conducted over 12 months.

Ask yourself the following questions when reviewing each working paper:

- Do you understand how the control is executed?
- Is the control description clear?
- Does it make sense?
- Is the working paper or report provided by management authentic?
- Are the exceptions well documented?
- Do you understand the issue impact?
- Can you re-perform the test and reach the same conclusions?

- Is the working paper easy to follow?
- Does the sampling size match the sample size required per IA methodology?
- Are there any compensating controls in the area or other areas that minimize the identified risk?
- Can you group the audit issues that have common root causes?
- Are the management corrective actions targeting the root cause agreed?
- Is the issue rating rationale robust enough to justify the issue rating?
- Have you covered the key risks and processes to advance the audit?
- Have you assessed or identified a key control that minimizes the risk identified?

I share constructive feedback with the audit team when I review the working papers. I usually ask the audit manager or senior audit manager to schedule a call to discuss my feedback. It is important to consider the best way to deliver your feedback (e.g. detailed written comments, discussion only or both). Avoid fixing the working paper yourself as you do not have the full context and did not attend all meetings with stakeholders. I prefer face-to-face working paper reviews, the preparer can easily answer all my questions, which minimizes the re-work, and time invested in clearing comments.

Training should be provided to the IA teams to enhance the audit documentation and to ensure compliance with the IA methodology. I highly recommend developing standard templates to document the audit announcement memo, audit engagement memo, audit planning memo, risk assessment, business monitoring activities, walkthroughs, issue validation activities, DEA and OET. An audit management system can take care of this too.

Technology allows auditors to be more efficient when testing through data analytics and extractions. Innovation has become an important topic nowadays; audit leaders want to innovate more, deliver more value to stakeholders, minimize the time invested in audits, reduce audit hours, spend less time on the road and develop more continuous auditing tools, among others. They want to be more efficient when developing and reviewing working papers or preparing audit reports.

Thus, through an organized and innovative approach, auditors could deliver higher quality audits more efficiently and complete working papers earlier (following the standardized approach or electronic forms), which means more flexibility to leverage more data analytics tools to identify trends, and outliers or to better assess each key control. Technology plays a key role in our profession in facilitating the completion of audits and documentation requirements. However, no matter how technology evolves, we will always need to build strong relationships with our stakeholders. I will be discussing this topic in the next chapter.

Chapter 11

How to Manage the Stakeholder Relationship?

For any audit function to succeed, auditors must take care of stakeholders. Building strong relationships with them takes time and a well-thought-out action plan. It can be a slow process at the beginning. Identifying your key stakeholders is important to manage them more effectively. A stakeholder is an individual group of people who have an interest in an organization, people or groups inside or outside the organization (e.g. shareholders, senior management, board of directors, regulators, internal audit teams, external auditors, customers and third-party vendors).

To be an effective and influential audit leader, you must build and maintain strong relationships the entire year. To drive change, you must be involved in key business initiatives, projects, forums and committee meetings to build trust, reputation and respect. Audit leaders need to have a seat at the table. True audit leaders need to pull up a chair and sit at the table; do not wait until you get a formal invite; be visible and actively seek out opportunities to drive change and share your point of view. This relationship could start with senior management when you see, interact with or meet them. It takes a few seconds to cause the first impression, lasting forever. I want to share a few tips to have a positive first impression:

- dress well; dress for success. Your image educates others on how you want to be approached. Dressing appropriately minimizes unnecessary distractions so others can focus on the conversation and your message to minimize additional distractions.
- Keep eye contact and smile to send a good message during the interaction.
- Shake hands when you introduce yourself in person.
- Say your name or the name of your department slowly.
- Keep a good posture (arms, hands, and legs uncrossed) to show that you are open to the conversation and fully transparent.
- Be careful with your sense of humour; if you are not good with that, please avoid it.

DOI: 10.4324/9781003431893-12

- Seek the opinion of others; ask open-ended questions to start the conversation.
- Make your online presence respectable and impactful, and share your talent and unique perspective.
- Project a high energy level. I want to spend time here. Your energy level matters and you need to focus on this daily. I am a Reiki Master, and I understand the power of your energy and how important it is for you to have a good balance and health. A good energy level starts with eating healthy, exercising regularly, drinking enough water and sleeping well. Still, it can be impacted by interacting with others, not organizing well your day. We always need to pay attention to our energy level. We can attract good things when our energy is high, and it can also improve interaction with others.

Once you identify your stakeholders, you need to analyse them. Would you like to manage a few stakeholders more closely? You may want to keep others just informed about relevant things. The important phases of a stakeholder analysis are listed here, and auditors need to conduct this exercise effectively to build, maintain, and enhance stakeholder relationships as described next:

- *Identify your key stakeholders.* Do it by considering your auditable entities, audit engagements or current or future interactions with internal or external stakeholders.
- *Identify their needs.* It is highly recommended that you record these needs in a document as part of your annual assessment; this document should be flexible so you can adjust accordingly throughout the year. Audits can be added or removed from the annual audit plan; business and audit changes constantly occur. You will have to consider the latest changes and assess how all will impact the approved audit plan.
- *Analyse how your stakeholders can impact your audit activities.* Stakeholders must support your annual audit plan or initiatives (e.g. continuous auditing tools, data analytics tools, automated risk assessments or audit reports and monitoring activities). Who are your key stakeholders? Who can support these audit initiatives better? Are they familiar with these initiatives?
- *Assess the level of influence that your stakeholders have.* This will allow you to be more objective when conducting this analysis and defining the best strategy to manage this relationship more effectively. For example, if the influence and interest of your stakeholders are low (e.g. Finance, HR and other IA teams), you would like to monitor these relationships. Still, you may not need to schedule frequent meetings. However, if the interest of stakeholders is high (e.g. IA SMEs, IA QA team, compliance

and legal teams) but the influence is low, you could schedule additional meetings to keep them informed (e.g. quarterly). If stakeholders' interest and influence are strong (Business Head and their direct reports) because you audit them, you will need to schedule more frequent meetings (e.g. monthly meetings).

- *Define the IA value proposition.* You will have to provide this information to your stakeholders to understand the IA role, value-added, and other relevant audit activities. Why would you like to meet them often? Why are you requesting time on their calendars? Time is sensitive, and not all have enough capacity to deal with several auditors if auditors do not understand the business needs. You will have to define your value proposition, gain business knowledge, have clear audit expectations and goals, and bring value during the introductory and regular meetings.
- Identify the results of your stakeholder analysis and define a *smart plan.* how will you approach them or interact with them? Just focus on a few actions to manage each relationship successfully.
- *Evaluate your progress* (at least every quarter). So you can update your initial analysis and strategic plan. How will you know if you are making progress or managing the relationship effectively? Are you requesting feedback after finishing an audit? Are you receiving positive feedback?

Proper communication is key to building trust and enhancing stakeholders' engagement. Effective communication involves great engagement, transparency, responsiveness, availability, commitment, cooperation, and reputation among stakeholders. Communication is important as there needs to be an important exchange of information between auditors and stakeholders, and they need to trust auditors. If they do not trust auditors, they will not be able to see the IA value proposition or support auditors during audit engagements or other audit activities. They will be fewer opportunities to provide advice or drive change.

The role of IA will continue to evolve to manage higher expectations from key stakeholders. IA needs to do a better job detecting emerging risks, assessing the control environment, reviewing key business or technology initiatives. IA must continue investing in talent acquisition, development and retention to gain key skills. Many audit departments during the pandemic experienced high staff turnover, reduced budgets which may have impacted the value delivered to stakeholders. IA also needs to focus on data analytics and innovation ideas to provide more value to the organization by sharing best practices, assessing key processes and risks more effectively, and on sustained profit enhancements, product simplification and process improvements. IA could add excellent value here, so IA transformation is key; auditor leaders must move away from auditing traditional audits and add more value to the organization. They may need to increase the budgets to bring additional experts and hire desired talent (e.g. technology, cyber-security, third-party vendors, compliance/regulatory, fraud, governance and culture, and digital assets) and improve technology tools (e.g. data analytics, data management software, robotic process automation and artificial intelligence software).

Below are a few tips you can use to both build and improve healthy relationships:

- Be aware of first impressions and non-verbal communication (e.g. tone of voice, body language [posture, gestures, eye contact, appearance and body movements]). First impressions matter! Good posture will impact the conversation and your message.
- Be yourself – be natural.
- Be agile; do not wait until the last minute to share issues or concerns. Focus on innovation, data analytics and audit forward. Audit issues should be communicated timely. Management action plans must be developed early to promote timely report issuance and address concerns even faster.
- Be positive; no matter how difficult the conversation could be, remain calm and confident during the conversation. Keep the meeting positive by highlighting positive observations during the audit (e.g. stakeholders' engagement and support or additional improvements noted since the last audit) and positive feedback (progress made since the previous audit or issues raised passed IA validation activities).
- Be open, honest and accountable.
- Listen to your stakeholders; be active (listen with a purpose or attend with a pen) and avoid audit jargon. Use non-verbal behaviour (eye contact, smiling). Also, understand others' points of view before trying to get them to understand yours. Have an open mind; always have the big picture in mind; listen to suggestions, questions and concerns; and always thank people for their input and feedback. Another important tip (before closing the meeting or call) is to rephrase what they have mentioned in a way that you are trying to understand their points of view.
- Be aware of cultural differences, for example, in non-verbal communication.
- Set a good example; build trust, transparency and respect. Share your talent!
- Schedule periodic touch-base sessions. Regular meetings keep you and your stakeholders on the same page; you can easily identify emerging risks or potential issues or challenges before they even arise. Keep the communication channel always open so they can easily contact you. You need to be available for your stakeholders too.

- Prepare yourself, read, and have an agenda or a presentation deck (know your audience, structure your presentation, prepare a deck and be familiar with it, and prepare yourself for the meeting by practising it). Please focus on the audience and keep it simple. If you have a deck, send it in advance.
- Do not get sucked into a big debate; scheduling another meeting or call to follow up or answer additional questions is okay. Learn when you need to cut the conversation.

All these topics matter even more when you are on a video or phone call. Wear appropriate clothing, be aware of your video settings, mute your microphone whenever you are not speaking, and avoid any distractions or objects on your back. Also, always investigate the camera instead of looking at yourself talking on the computer screen. It will help others feel like you are 100% present.

Negotiating Critical Audit Conversations

Conflict is not something you need to avoid at all costs. Conflict can sometimes be the best way to drive change. Auditors need to be ready and prepared to challenge things. Occasionally, you will have to deal with complex or difficult conversations. It is important to use the tips mentioned earlier. There is a simple issue that you can quickly resolve; do not get emotional or take things personally. Difficult conversations are necessary, especially when critical issues are presented to senior management.

If you oversee a meeting, how do you manage it, or how do you restore peace? How can you ensure these conflicts do not harm your reputation or team morale? Let's ask yourself the following questions first and write down your answers:

- How do you turn the conflict into a positive force to enhance the control environment or to help your stakeholder to understand the issue impact?
- How can you help those involved in the conversation cooperate when an initial agreement is impossible?
- How can you manage the tone of the conversation as an audit manager, a senior audit manager or an audit director?
- How do you know when to cut the conversation or take a break?

Then, how can you identify difficult conversations?

- Lack of agreement on issues or concerns, issue impact or issue rating.
- Escalation is required as an agreement cannot be reached during the meeting.

- Defensiveness.
- Body language such as voice is raised, eyes rolling, arms folded or pointed fingers.
- Still sucked in the first bullet and unable to move to the next topic.
- Need to stop the conversation and have a break right now.
- Few people start exiting the room.

Well, if this happens, we need to resolve this situation as soon as possible, and this is not healthy for anyone. I had difficult conversations with stakeholders in the past. Still, I tried to put myself in their shoes, understand their perspectives and find a mutual interest or purpose (e.g. minimizing business risks, improving customer experience and satisfying regulatory requirements). Auditors need to influence others, listen carefully to the other person, adjust the message to reach an agreement and learn how to negotiate and reach an agreement. If a break is required to reconvene, take it. It will benefit both sides.

Please pay attention to their gestures and postures. If they feel frustrated or if your team keeps pushing the stakeholder without listening, it is time for a break. You know that the conversation is not going anywhere. When a conflict arises in a meeting, audit leaders need to take control; encourage people to provide additional information to clarify what they are thinking.

One important thing is to know the facts, prepare before the meeting, and pull materials and information obtained as the audience may challenge things that happened during the audit. Know yourself and your IA team well enough so that you are aware of concerns that may exist among people – and have a strategy to deal with different operating styles. Your stakeholders could find excuses and more excuses to avoid accepting the issue. Then, you can share your perspective and consider others. We demonstrate respect by asking them to share their perspectives too.

Another important thing is to quantify the impact. For example, there was a control break, but the stakeholder did not believe it would have a significant reputation risk as he had not seen material operational losses. After explaining the issue in detail, the auditor reinforced the issue impact and key benefits of addressing this concern. Also, the auditor analysed complaints data and operational losses, noticing a material amount within the testing period. The business could not debate whether an agreement was reached. I asked the team to get this information ready for the meeting.

If an agreement is not reached, summarize the main topics or concerns discussed and arrange a specific meeting to address the issue later. Always be open to reviewing additional information if required or helping to clarify the initial concern. Always ask, "Is there anything else I should know"? Also, ask yourself during the meeting: how do your stakeholders feel when you listen or change the approach?

Be professional and calm, and always listen and show respect. These are the primary techniques I use when managing difficult conversations. When people challenge too much, this could be a sign that you need to look deeper into the concern or area under discussion. Remember, stakeholders sometimes could be hard to manage because they have something to hide. But sometimes, there is a valid reason, and we must be fully aware and open to reviewing additional information.

How to Deal With Different Operating Styles?

You must know yourself and your stakeholder's style to manage the relationship and meetings successfully. Did you know that 90% of a professional football player's preparation happens in the classroom and film room rather than on the practice field? I learnt this from my brother, who was a professional soccer player. He spent hours in front of the TV before every game to study the other team and even after the game to learn from his mistakes. He knows in a penalty how each player would manage the ball. If we do not learn from our mistakes and expand upon what we are doing at a high level, we will not be able to succeed. Imagine if you try to understand or identify your stakeholder operating style and learn from your own mistakes.

We must observe their behaviour when discussing issues, presenting topics, when others challenge them or how they approach a task. In football and life in general, preparation is everything; everything counts. The difference in how and what we perceive things creates our different personalities. There are four types of perceptions, each resulting in different personalities.

There are no right or wrong personalities or styles; it is important to understand your stakeholders' styles to manage relationships better. Use the following information to think about your behaviour and how you will have to adapt better your approach to managing stakeholders' behaviour.

There are people that are more results-oriented, and love to be in charge. If they understand the benefits, they make quick decisions. They are very focused on results and productivity and want to meet deadlines. They need information that helps them to make quick decisions. They are efficient and independent. They must learn to listen more. To manage this personality, you need to consider the following: indicate the results first, do not waste their time so go to the point; be brief, ask questions that are relevant to the context, highlight the practicality of your idea and how it can give quick results, demonstrate your experience and show commitment to get things done.

There are others that are more people-oriented. They try to build consensus and reach an agreement. This type of personality does not like conflict and tries to please the majority. When dealing with them, be informal, support their feelings, ask questions that are not threatening, and do not force them to respond quickly. They need to process the facts and invest time before reaching an agreement and considering others' points of view. They rely more on intuition and the emotional impression of people. They can sometimes be defensive or overreactive. They do not respond well to conflict. To manage these stakeholders, you need to consider the following: smaller talks or face-to-face talks are better, support their feelings, show commitment by collaborating with them and show how your idea could impact others (e.g. customer experience, employee morale, process improvement and product simplification) and how others will react to enhancements in the control environment.

Detail-oriented people are more factual-oriented, challenge discussions, show their points of view, and need additional evidence or details to decide. They are well-organized and less tolerant of lack of clarity or decisions made on emotions. They greatly help in executing a logical, detailed, and organized project. They see the past, present and future as equally important. To manage them, you need to consider the following: organize your presentation or meeting, be always prepared; be precise, ask questions, do not rush them to decide, demonstrate your detailed knowledge and support their perspectives, if possible; listen to them carefully.

There are others that focus on the big picture, and do not like too many details. They are creative, and they always think outside the box. They always have valuable ideas, so you can always get their points of view and are ready to help. To manage this personality, you need to consider the following: ask for their opinions, do not impose things, support their ideas, demonstrate your creativity too, emphasize future value when presenting ideas or concerns, stress uniqueness as they love innovative ideas and provide additional time before deciding. You will need to spend more time with them or adjust your style if you are more analytical. They are future-oriented, and they drive change.

When you become aware of people's different personalities and styles, you can adapt your behaviour to suit your interaction better. Also, employ other areas of emotional intelligence such as social awareness and get curious about what the other person is saying. Look to your empathy and compassion, pause, and consider what might be happening with the other person and why they cannot buy the issue or concern. What are they saying? Is this new to the IA team? How can you manage that? After the meeting, always review what went well and wrong to identify what you could have done better. Learn from it and share with your team the lessons learnt.

I want to share a few additional tips before concluding this chapter:

- Be always prepared to get additional challenges from business, especially when relevant issues are discussed.

- Be ready to push back; anticipate challenges considering the nature and impact of issues discussed and the operating style of your stakeholders.
- Do not wait until the last meeting to share issues; stakeholders want to know your concerns earlier to ensure you have the right players at the table. Leverage the agile approach.
- Be patient, calm, honest and professional.
- Make sure you have sold the risk and impact before requesting the corrective actions. Also, it is important to identify the root cause to facilitate the discussion and to ensure that the business will provide adequate corrective actions to minimize the risk.
- Pay attention to body language and respond to it.
- Preparation is key before any meetings with stakeholders. Be prepared to provide additional examples, evidence of exceptions identified, testing done and other details, if requested.
- Ensure key players are invited to the meeting but minimize the number of people attending critical meetings, especially when issues are discussed. Who is your audience? Who is attending? Why are they attending?
- Control your state of mind; do not be defensive or raise your voice even if others are reacting improperly.
- Avoid giving mixing signals. This could impact your relationship. Use your self-awareness skills to identify your emotions and decide what or not to express them.
- Have an open-door policy to manage stakeholders' relationships and requests better.
- If you cannot agree, it is time to apply more self-awareness and social awareness skills until you reach a deal. If you get too frustrated, this is not good, and you must ask yourself why. Why? until you get it.
- Listen, listen and listen.

If you can build good relationships with your stakeholders, they will keep you in mind, reach out to you, and trust your perspectives and feedback. Audits should not be painful for stakeholders and IA teams. Your stakeholders may be able to help and support you better if you genuinely take the time to know them and build stronger relationships.

In the following chapter, I will share important tips for conducting smart audit engagements. Here we go.

Chapter 12

Tips for Planning a Smart Audit

The greatest challenge audit teams face when planning an audit is identifying a smart audit scope and focusing on high-risk processes. How can you add more value to your stakeholders? How can you identify more emerging risks in this volatile environment? How can you finish audits earlier? Auditors faced more challenges with remote work during the pandemic due to staff competencies and capacity, staff retention, budget cuts, audit inefficiencies and insufficient data analytics tools or technology solutions to complete testing or identify new risks. Thus, audit leaders must focus on more efficiencies, leverage more data analytics and have better technology tools while still delivering quality and relevant audit work.

IA departments face challenges due to resource constraints, higher turnover, and in some cases, a lack of understanding of the business, which is very evident to stakeholders. They may not trust auditors as they focus on conducting and completing audits on time rather than adding more value to the organization. Audit leaders must collaborate with stakeholders to understand the business, organization's strategy, key technology, business initiatives and challenges and respond to new and emerging risks. IA departments need to invest more in talent acquisition and retention. Annual audit plans must be flexible to adapt quickly to this evolving and challenging environment. Auditors must drive change, provide value and offer advice and feedback on thematic issues and concerns beyond assurance activities.

We cannot use the old approach, audit the same key processes and controls, or leverage the same audit programme or standard checklists over and over. Things have changed, and the IA teams need to evolve faster. We need more experts driving audits and data analytics if we want to add more value. Auditors must collect, review and analyse information and data before finalizing the audit scope during the planning phase. Thus, auditors must establish a positive relationship with their stakeholders to get their input, feedback and full support during the audit.

DOI: 10.4324/9781003431893-13

The following questions should be answered during the pre-planning/ planning phase:

- Is it relevant to conduct the audit now? Let's review one example. A bank is restructuring an area, key job positions are still open, and a new leader will arrive in a month. These changes were recently announced but unavailable during the audit plan construction. Thus, auditors could assess this situation during business monitoring activities as the new business may require additional time to define key business strategies and objectives and redefine business priorities. This is a good example that happens very often; I highly recommend auditors to be alert and re-assess each case before kicking off an audit. Auditors may be able to justify moving an audit later and get approval from the chief audit director and audit committee. A sound rationale should be provided with additional steps to monitor the recent changes before starting or scheduling an audit.
- What are the key risks and key processes included in the audit scope?
- Have you noticed any major changes recently or after the last audit?
- Are there any open issues that impact the preliminary audit scope?
- Has management self-identified issues and addressed all or a few before the scheduled audit? Is it better to plan an audit once these issues are closed?
- What are the business objectives, strategies and key priorities? Did the pandemic impact business strategies and financial results?
- What are the key systems, applications, databases and models? Is there a dataflow diagram to understand data inputs and outputs?
- Have all hand-offs been identified and considered (may involve other key areas or departments outside the preliminary audit scope)?
- What changes have been implemented during the pandemic or black swan events? Has the business team been stable? What's the staff attrition rate?
- What are the key compliance and regulatory requirements? Have all key policies, procedures and regulatory requirements been identified in the MCAs or in the business process mappings, PRCs?
- Are there any regulatory issues or self-disclosed issues? What is the aging?
- Did the SLD (e.g. compliance and risk management) review this area? Are there any open issues? Does the SLD have a robust programme to check this area?
- What percentage of the revenue does the business generate? And how many transactions are being processed, including monetary volume?
- What are the revenues, expenses and operational losses trends in the last three years?

- What are the key products, services and channels?
- Are there any customer complaints? Is this trending down or up? Why?
- Are there any large fraud events?
- Are there any unethical events or allegations?
- Are there any key third-party vendors (critical, high)? What services or processes are outsourced?
- Are there any relevant technology projects that may impact key processes or controls within the audit scope? Has the business conducted any risk assessments or evaluations over key projects?
- Are there any relevant key management reports to identify trends and outliers to leverage during business monitoring activities (e.g. sales practices, operational losses, cash differences in branches or ATMs, the volume of customer complaints, fees or refunds processed and large fraud losses)?
- Are there any key SOX controls involved? What are the testing results? Are there any open issues or concerns regarding SOX testing?
- Are any key EUCs impacting the financial statements or SOX accounts?
- Does the business have process flows, policies and procedures, and mature MCAs or PRCs?
- How effective are the self-assurance activities (first line of defence)?

These are a few questions to start the dialogue, but you will have more questions to ask as you move forward. You also need to balance the amount of information requested and reviewed, as you can ask for a lot of information when it is unnecessary. One important tip here is to check the document request list to minimize the number of documents and information requested. You may have access to certain information too. The business should not spend time developing new documentation for key control upon request; the information must be available. This means the control is not in place so there is a control design issue.

Auditors need to request additional information in advance during the pre-planning phase, such as:

- Organizational chart.
- Key policies and procedures.
- PRCs or MCAs, if available.
- All self-disclosed issues for the area, business or processes under review, including regulatory issues.
- Dataflow diagrams and key EUCs.
- Access request to key applications to pull data directly; this could save time as auditors will need data during planning and fieldwork. If this does not work, they must request all data queries to perform the trend analysis, sample selection, and further testing.

- Key management report (e.g. financial, operational, transactional data, operational incident reports and resolution), including management assessments or self-assurance activities results.
- Operational losses, customer complaints, refunds and allegations.
- Large fraud events that impacted the business to identify control breaks to include in the audit scope.
- SOX flowcharts, key controls reviewed, and findings.
- General ledger accounts reconciled by the business, if any.
- List of key third-party vendors, contracts agreements, risk assessments, SLAs, monitoring activities and testing results, customer complaints and open issues (if any).

An internal pre-planning meeting is highly recommended to understand the high-risk processes, the audit objective, and the next steps, including the preliminary document request list. This meeting will help the IA team to identify any additional SMEs and skills needed. Meeting minutes should be retained in the working papers, as well. A tollgate meeting (audit director, chief audit director, and SMEs [e.g. technology, compliance, third-party vendors, AML, finance, fraud and data analytics team]) to discuss the preliminary audit scope. Once all walkthroughs are complete, this initial audit scope will be adjusted during the planning phase.

The pre-planning meeting is a fantastic opportunity for the IA teams to freely discuss the key risks, concerns, open issues and local regulatory requirements. An agenda or skeleton audit plan memo (e.g. key business risks, key processes, open issues [IA, regulatory and business self-identified issues], a summary of key regulatory requirements, policies and procedures, data analytics requirements, preliminary audit scope and risk assessment) should be shared in advance. Meeting minutes should be retained in the working papers and archived in the audit management system.

Performing an audit based on internal information is especially important. Still, auditors need to be familiar with the key policies, procedures, regulatory requirements and IA leading best practices, leverage the work of others (if possible), request SME feedback, understand the large fraud events, operational losses, customer complaints or other data analytics trends, among others.

Tips to Gain Efficiencies During the Planning Phase

It is important to consider a few tips to gain extra efficiencies during the planning phase:

- Schedule a kick-off meeting with the business before starting the detailed audit planning.

- Set up the meeting in advance and share an agenda and deck before this meeting.
- Identify the key stakeholders who must attend this meeting and ensure relevant personnel will be available to conduct walkthroughs or support auditors during the audit.
- Ask the company to present the businesses, organizational structures, business objectives, strategies and key priorities.
- Provide additional details regarding the IA methodology, audit planning, fieldwork, reporting phases, audit objectives, preliminary audit scope and audit timeline.
- Be prepared to leverage the time allocated to this meeting effectively.
- Identify management's current concerns and challenges and request feedback to incorporate any other relevant topics during the meeting. Prepare for asking relevant questions during this meeting regarding the pandemic and other technology incidents, key organizational changes, or new business initiatives. Be always well prepared; this demonstrates that the IA team has business knowledge and is familiar with key initiatives and leading best practices, among others.
- Request an SPOC to coordinate the audit requests, walkthroughs, and the weekly status meeting to discuss potential findings and audit progress. Evaluate how the requested information will be provided to the IA team; using web-based document portals to exchange documents is common.
- Review and submit the preliminary document request list during the preplanning activities through SharePoint Sites. Monitor each request daily to ensure that all requests are delivered on time. I recommend having a tracker with key information (e.g. date sent, date received, pending information) to highlight the ones requiring additional follow-up or further escalation. This could facilitate the discussions with the SPOC.
- Schedule an internal audit tollgate session (with SMEs) before scheduling the formal kick-off meeting to discuss the preliminary audit scope and next steps. For example, invite the data analytics team to understand the data inputs, outputs, potential testing approach, and the possibility of reviewing the entire population. This team should be involved during the pre-planning meetings and through the audit to provide better support and value.
- Review all prior audit reports and working papers to determine if specific processes (not reviewed before) must be included in the audit scope.
- Review the business strategy and key technology plans.
- Ensure that the IA team will be available during the audit, considering vacation time and other priorities.
- Draft a high-level process flow or leverage the ones provided by the business to understand the key controls. If you can identify a few control gaps, you will be able to ask the right questions during walkthroughs.

- Be agile and ensure transparency with your stakeholders to avoid any surprises. During the weekly status meetings, potential issues and audit progress can be discussed to minimize confusion and improve efficiencies. When scheduling meetings or walkthroughs, it is also important to consider the time zones and locations.
- Validate draft narratives, flowcharts and RCM with business owners. Auditors should share and discuss the RCM with key stakeholders before moving to fieldwork, document their feedback and make any necessary changes.
- Work with the SPOC to ensure key personnel attends the walkthroughs to minimize the number of people attending each meeting. Also, always conduct walkthroughs with process owners; they have the business knowledge and they are familiar with key controls.
- Select the right sample size to comply with the IA methodology; always leverage data as this is particularly key to completing more effective testing and identifying more relevant issues.
- Talk to SLD to understand testing programmes, oversight activities (e.g. compliance, legal, finance, HR, fraud investigations) and open issues.
- Monitor the audit budget weekly to ensure the IA team charges all hours spent. If additional topics must be added, always assess the budget implications and impact on key audit milestones (e.g. end of fieldwork phase, audit report publication date).
- Consider the weeks required per audit phase to complete audits in 90 days. The audit manager needs to monitor the budget and key deliverables to minimize delays.
- Develop and retain meeting minutes for all key meetings, highlighting any agreements or feedback from stakeholders, SMEs, follow-up requests and questions that must be addressed.
- Review all working papers during the planning and before moving to fieldwork. For example, the audit planning memo and RCM should be reviewed and approved by the audit director before fieldwork starts.

Auditors must identify any critical areas or key processes associated with potential fraud risk to include in the audit scope and RCM. Obtain data to confirm that any significant operational losses or fraud events have occurred (independent testing verification is better). Be always careful with those areas or people within the organization that manage cash, process a high volume of transactions, handle customer wire transfers, process payments to third-party vendors and have access to the GL to book operational losses, customer refunds or other journal entries especially when managing customer's transactions or requests. Adequate segregation of duties is important to minimize potential fraud events or collusion (maker and checker control must be in place).

Key Metrics to Track During the Planning Phase

Key audit metrics must be monitored effectively to ensure timely completion, such as:

- Announcement memo sent on time (X weeks before planning phase start date).
- Planning phase completed in X weeks as planned (Yes or No).
- RCM completed before moving to the fieldwork phase.
- Data analytics leveraged during planning (Yes or No).
- High-risk processes and areas (tied to the risk assessment) covered in this audit? (Yes or No). If "No", has proper rationale been documented and agreed upon with SMEs?
- Can you advance the audit (only if all key risks and processes are included in the audit scope)?

Tips to Gain Efficiencies During the Audit Fieldwork Phase

Let´s consider a few additional tips to gain further efficiencies during the fieldwork phase:

- Communicate with management timely and effectively to avoid any surprises. Schedule a weekly status meeting to share potential issues, fieldwork status, and potential delays, if any. Avoid rescheduling or cancelling these meetings, as this is not a good sign. If there are any delays in the information requested, the business needs to understand that some key audit milestones may be impacted. Be clear and escalate further if significant delays are happening and not resolved timely.
- Complete and document all walkthroughs before moving to fieldwork; otherwise, this could significantly impact this new phase.
- Share and discuss the RCM with the business process owner before starting the fieldwork. The audit scope must be agreed upon with the business before sending the engagement letter (before starting the fieldwork). The engagement letter should include the key risks, audit scope and exclusions, audit timeline and the IA team, among others.
- Complete the audit programme and testing approach during the planning; audit director must approve it before moving to fieldwork.
- Complete the audit planning memo, too, and this should include the entity description, high risks and processes (mapped to the risk assessment under consideration), systems and applications, third-party vendors, audit scope and out-of-scope areas, regulatory requirements, open

issues (IA issues, regulatory and self-identified issues), IA team, timeline and budget, data analytics analysis or testing. The audit director must approve it before starting the fieldwork phase.

- Review all complex, new areas or changes in key processes in detail as they will require additional time and effort. More findings will require further vetting and discussions that could significantly impact the key audit milestones. Be agile here too.
- Understand the root cause of issues, and challenge management if corrective actions are not effective or sufficient to minimize the risks identified.
- Understand the SLD role and insufficient oversight activities regarding the audit scope and issues raised by the IA team. For example, an auditor needs to assess if an issue should be raised to the SLD (Compliance team). For example, IA noticed no compliance with few regulatory requirements and a lack of oversight activities by SLD. IA needs to raise an issue and discuss it with management, Compliance, and Legal teams.
- Keep an audit log of all changes made to testing programmes and audit scope, and reconcile all with the most recent risk assessment, audit planning memo, RCM and issue analysis. Also, verify that no single testing has been missed. For example, sometimes auditors need to expand testing activities when noticing a few exceptions and forget to update all working papers.
- Review all working papers before moving to the report phase to minimize any surprises or additional exceptions not discussed with management. There should be a primary and secondary review (senior audit manager and auditor director). Clearing up all comments that arose while reviewing the working papers is beneficial.
- Organize and upload all working papers in the audit management system and ensure that IA team members deliver all working papers timely and accurately. It is also important to ensure consistency across all working papers (standardize their format and flow) so they describe the key risk, control description, audit testing approach, testing results and exceptions identified.
- Avoid having the same IA team auditing the business, as we always need fresh eyes. Keep an expert auditor who has strong business knowledge but try to rotate other personnel, as well.
- Implement a disciplinary approach during the audit and set clear and realistic deadlines and expectations (e.g. request sample size before moving to fieldwork and data queries during the pre-planning phase to effectively analyse data and escalate further if requests are not provided on time).

Key Metrics to Track During the Fieldwork Phase

Key audit metrics must be monitored effectively to ensure timely completion, such as:

- Audit engagement memo sent on time (before the fieldwork start date).
- Fieldwork phase completed in X weeks as planned (Yes or No).
- Data analytics leveraged during fieldwork (Yes or No).
- Weekly status meetings scheduled with management? (Yes or No).
- Budget to actual hours spent on planning and fieldwork.

Tips to Gain Efficiencies During the Audit Reporting Phase

Let's consider a few additional tips to gain further efficiencies during the audit reporting phase:

- Auditors exposed to relevant organizations know that the audit report template varies. Each organization has its idiosyncrasies regarding presentation format. New audit directors and chief audit directors need to get familiar with it. When considering a new design or a revised version, please share with management and audit committee to get their input. Management needs to understand the audit report format. The report template, structure and wording can easily impact the effectiveness of an audit report.

An audit report should be a living document created during the audit engagement. An excellent audit report communicates the audit objectives, scope, issues and management corrective actions and timelines. It must have a concise executive summary to engage readers early by presenting the most relevant information first (executive summary). The auditor should follow the standard template available to ensure consistency across IA teams.

This section will cover a few tips for writing effective audit reports. I wouldn't say I like extensive audit reports, as the reader can easily lose and miss the audit message, primarily when several observations are raised. Auditors should be trained on how to write effective audit reports, and I would like to share a few tips that could help:

- The executive summary should be of one to two pages. Consider the best way to summarize why the audit was conducted (e.g. annual audit, fraud investigation, target review and continuous audit), including the auditable entity or business unit, audit scope, timeframe (limit the audit scope to one or two sentences or use bullets in case you have at least six list elements), audit report rating, issues and issue ratings. Also, highlight the controls that worked well or did not fail the audit testing.

- Issue details will be included in the following pages. The audit scope should align with the audit planning memo, RCM, risk assessment and other working papers.
- Make sure the writing is clear, constructive and appropriate in tone; avoid confusing words, jargon or technical words. Eliminate unnecessary words in the executive summary that do not add value or information to the reader.
- Use a number or percentage to describe a fact or materiality of the issue, if possible.
- Ensure all numbers or percentages tie back to audit evidence and all working papers, especially when trying to quantify the materiality of an issue.
- Include the critical-, high-, moderate- and low-risk-level issues in the issue section and ensure this includes the five elements as a concern, cause, consequence, context and corrective action plans with due dates as listed here:
  - The concern describes a control breakdown.
  - The cause provides the reason for the control breakdown; we need to ask, "why did that happen?" a few times until we figure out the actual root cause (e.g. manual or not automated, resource or system constraints, lack of guidance, no policies or procedures in place, untrained staff, and no back-up).
  - The root cause is related to the final "why." Why did it go wrong?
  - The consequence refers to the severity of the concern and what could happen if not addressed (e.g. reputational risk, compliance risk, higher operational or fraud losses). "Not having adequate guidance when opening customer accounts could lead to reputational and compliance risk."
  - The context provides additional details regarding the exceptions identified during the audit testing; it helps readers understand the concerns and consequences. Only include relevant information; limit the context to what the reader needs to know (e.g. 25 of 40 wires were not approved by management, and three customers were not screened adequately).
  - Regarding corrective actions, ensure all address the root cause and minimize the risk identified. Avoid a milestone corrective action (final corrective actions to be provided in the future after completing a business analysis) or corrective actions over three or six months (unless compensatory controls are also provided by management). Corrective actions must resolve the concern and the root causes identified.

The time assigned should be sufficient to demonstrate that the new controls are sustainable and operating effectively. In general, the frequency of the new controls determines the length of the sustainability period requested by the business. The issues should be discussed during the fieldwork or earlier (once identified), so all issues should be known by management before sharing the draft audit report.

Once the issue memo is shared, the business will have "X" days to provide the corrective actions (typically seven days). This timeline should be discussed with management during the planning kickoff meeting and reemphasized during the status meetings.

In certain circumstances, auditors need to request management to look back to identify additional exceptions or resolve similar ones outside the audit testing period. For example, the audit identified duplicate payments regarding third-party providers in 2020, and the IA team may want to verify that no duplicate additional payments were processed in prior years. Also, ensure there is an issue owner (manager or above) who will be responsible for addressing the concerns timely to comply with the issue target date.

- Have an issue rating scale that management understands to facilitate the issue discussions. Management needs to know that a high risk rating indicates that corrective actions are significant to address the concerns; mitigating controls must be in place while the other corrective actions are in progress.
- Add other open issues that impact the audit scope, including progress made by management. Also, the final audit rating should be impacted by pending audit issues, self-identified issues and regulatory issues.
- Analyse all exceptions and root causes to assess if they can be combined to facilitate the discussions and subsequent IA issue validation activities.
- Confirm no audit repeat issues; otherwise, auditors must highlight this in the executive summary and issue description section. Repeated issues will impact harder the audit report rating.
- Add the audit period and provide key statistics and metrics regarding the auditable entity under review in the background section/executive summary, if applicable.
- Check spelling and grammar mistakes even when working on the draft audit report. Use Microsoft Word or Google Docs spell check tools.
- Avoid any colour references in the report or tables. I do not personally like this, as this adds confusion. However, use tables or graphs only to summarize or highlight key trends or relevant data.
- Remove indirect recommendations (such as "Management should consider . . . or implement. . . ."). Replace with direct language regarding corrective actions.
- Write all audit observations worthily to facilitate the preparation so you can cut and paste the information from working papers in the audit

report. This concept also applies when writing the audit objective, scope and business background in the planning memo document or in the audit management system.

- The audit database must be closed after publishing the audit reports to ensure compliance with IA requirements (within three or six days). Here are a few tips for completing the audit folder faster:

  - Ensure all working papers are reviewed, signed off, and all coaching notes have been addressed and removed.
  - Verify that all reportable issues and rating rationale are documented and match the final audit report.
  - Attach the final audit report to the working papers.
  - Validate that the key milestone dates are accurate and complete and include a sustainability period.
  - Review the audit budget and explain all differences over 10–20%.
  - If the audit database is not completed on time, provide a rationale.
  - Review the audit log, identify all changes processed, and ensure that the supporting documentation and working papers have been updated accordingly to minimize or avoid any discrepancies.
  - Review all non-reportable issues, immaterial observations or concerns agreed with management, audit director and chief audit directors; all must have a detailed rationale and the corresponding approvals (senior audit manager, audit director and SMEs).
  - Lock the audit database after completing all required steps listed earlier.

The audit manager and senior audit manager need to provide timely feedback to the audit team. Performance evaluation should be provided for all auditors after the fieldwork is complete. Feedback should be provided informally during the audit engagement and formalized before the audit report publication date, if possible. In addition, the risk assessments (or the auditable entities reviewed) must be updated after the audit database closure (within the next 30/45 days) and completion of issue validation activities (it may require a few updates during the year due to the volume of issues identified).

Key Metrics to Track During the Reporting Phase

Key metrics must be monitored effectively to ensure timely completion, such as:

- Report completed within 30 days after finalizing fieldwork.
- Final audit report issued timely.
- Number of issues raised, including audit report rating trending.
- Number of repeat issues.

- Number of re-opened issues.
- Number of issues closed by the agreed due date.
- Number of open high-rated issues (% of high-risk issues).
- Number of issues identified by management.
- Number of key processes that failed IA testing.

In the following chapters, I will cover another exciting and relevant topic: data analytics and continuous auditing to execute more effective audit testing and facilitate the identification of new emerging risks and relevant issues. Here we go.

Chapter 13

Data Analytics Tools and Continuous Auditing

In recent years, data analytics has strongly impacted how auditing departments collect, validate, and analyse data for monitoring key controls and audit testing purposes. The traditional audit tests the control design and operating effectiveness based on a sample of transactions. However, with data analytics tools, auditors can review the entire population of transactions and find more impactful issues.

Data analytics play a key role in fraud prevention, detection and investigations and should also be a key ingredient for a holistic fraud risk management programme. It is also essential to conduct a smart audit; auditors need to leverage more data during the entire audit engagement and before starting a new one to identify red flags and unknown emerging risks (e.g. risk assessments, business monitoring, and issue validation activities). When working remotely, auditors need more data to complete relevant audit testing and the business to make better decisions (e.g. launch a new product or promotion, simplify products or services, close certain branches or locations, cut the business in specific regions or countries).

A better and more continuous analysis could be provided to the business. Issues not identified before can be easily identified by discovering and analysing relevant trends, anomalies, patterns and outliers; identifying the root cause; and selecting the most effective testing approach. I would like to highlight a few additional benefits when using data analytics tools:

- Enhances the effectiveness and efficiency of audit engagements (e.g. pre-planning, planning and fieldwork phases). For example, audits can be planned earlier when identifying considerable risk areas (e.g. higher operational losses, no checker controls to approve third-party invoices, higher teller's decisions/exceptions processed without manager's approvals, excessive refunds or structure transactions for a customer). Also, by leveraging more relevant data analytics during planning, auditors can select larger or specific samples based on anomalies and patterns. It can also be leveraged to conduct tests of details and substantive testing.

DOI: 10.4324/9781003431893-14

- Enhances business monitoring activities that could be automated to analyse more relevant data or evaluate key controls. For example, data can be analysed to identify trends, patterns or outliers (e.g. operational losses, customer complaints data, fraud events, allegations, sales practices and customer refunds). Also, data analytics tools to evaluate key controls (e.g. mandatory training, mandatory absence, customer authentication and disclosure requirements during account opening, and user access) could be developed.
- Improves risk assessments by automating key risk drivers and leveraging specific data points (e.g. entity size [revenues, expenses, products, services and additional transactional data relevant to the auditable entity], employee turnover, KPIs, operational losses, fraud events, customer complaints, refunds, allegations, technology incidents and open issues). Also, data is critical to select additional locations for further testing, such as third-party vendor locations, retail banking branches (branch risk score), wealth management offices (risk score) and ATMs.
- Facilitates the early detection of potential fraud events and errors (e.g. duplicate payments to third-party vendors, multiple customer refunds for the same customer, numerous loan applications with the same phone and address).
- Identifies and interprets relationships among key data points. For example, we could identify specific sales practice concerns that may require additional testing by reviewing key data points (e.g. operational losses, customer complaints and allegations).
- Reduces costs associated with auditing and business monitoring activities.
- Provides management with a higher level of operational assurance and coverage. It also helps auditors assess and evaluate the business's continuous monitoring tools or self-assurance activities.
- Enables auditors to identify new and emerging risks, prioritize high-risk areas and processes, and better allocate audit resources. This could facilitate the inclusion of additional audits in the audit plan, as well.
- Adds more value to your stakeholders as a higher volume of issues could be identified faster (e.g. a higher number of exceptions processed by employees, higher volume of customer wire transfers in cross-border locations or operational losses in certain retail branches or ATM locations, and higher volume of unresolved customer complaints).
- Provides stronger data support to justify the issue risk rating. For example, a finding can be more impactful and much stronger when reviewing the entire population (e.g. identified approximately 40% exceptions in the loan approval process).

On the other hand, continuous auditing is defined as the automated performance of an audit on a more frequent basis to review specific key controls or data points. This will allow auditors to understand the execution of key controls, rules and exceptions. If exceptions are identified, they are communicated to the business more frequently. The frequency of the continuous auditing tools will depend on the inherent risk related to the business, area or product under review. For example, for higher risks areas, this should be conducted more frequently.

While the application of data analytics by internal auditors has certain benefits, some IA departments are still struggling to find the resources or to understand how to obtain access to the data. Data is underused. Sometimes the data analytics team needs to go through so many layers of approvals to get access to systems that could be a nice nightmare or could have serious problems transferring data into a usable format.

Auditors must understand the technology systems to pull data and feel comfortable with data quality. They must have access to the data, understand the organization's data management system (e.g. IT applications and infrastructure, security) and underlying dataflow, and have the right knowledge and the most effective data analytics tool. This can be a big challenge if not planned carefully.

We need to develop more analytical tools to assess the control environment effectively. However, building these tools is challenging without the right resource capacity, budget and technology tools. We need to follow a realistic approach to figure out where to focus first, design, validate and implement new additional continuous auditing tools. This process has seven steps; here is a suggested approach:

- Identify the scope and plan.
- Obtain and validate the data.
- Analyse the data output.
- Interpret the results.
- Communicate the results.
- Document the tool design and maintenance requirements.
- Maintain the tool.

Identify the Scope and Plan

The audit team needs to determine the key risks and controls, the costs vs. benefits, and the value-added. Auditors need to understand the business processes, key risks and controls to identify the best ideas to focus on. The CAE should concentrate on those areas that can add excellent value to stakeholders and IA teams. Auditors need to be able to prove or provide success stories of how continuous auditing has enhanced the control environment.

If management has continuous monitoring tools, auditors do not need to focus on the same topics. They could validate those tools for completeness and accuracy and conclude on the effectiveness of tools in identifying relevant issues. Has management identified any relevant matters? Also, auditors could validate the tool design, assumptions, change management process and other key reports. Before designing ideas, auditors should figure out what is already available to use their resources more effectively.

Here are a few additional questions to ask yourself:

- What is your audit objective?
- Is there a deep concern with this process or area?
- Do you want to monitor potential fraud events, compliance with policies and procedures or regulatory requirements?
- Can you save additional hours by building this continuous auditing tool?
- Can you provide higher assurance?
- Can you facilitate the branch selection by having a branch risk score?
- Can you enhance business monitoring activities?
- Are you familiar with the key controls? Are these automated controls?
- Do you understand the relevant data sources and requirements?
- Are you able to identify areas susceptible to potential fraud schemes?

Also, auditors need to understand the business, key risks, and control, especially the automated ones. They need to work with their business partners (e.g. data owners and IT department) to identify the key automated controls to complete the design assessment, including the identification of the system, applications, data sources, data storage, data format and other requirements. Typically, a multidisciplinary team will be engaged; strong auditors with strong business knowledge will help to identify key controls and complete the design assessment while the data analytics team (also involved in the walkthroughs) pulls the required data. The audit team will have to design the plan to accomplish different steps, including the resource plan and timeline, hours required, and key deliverables per phase.

Key deliverables: project timeline, data analytics requirements document and walkthroughs, among others.

Obtain and Validate the Data

This step can be a challenge for specific organizations considering the legacy IT systems, management's unwillingness to provide access to data, or management's misunderstanding of the audit purpose and goals. Auditors need to resolve these challenges first; this phase could be one of the most complex ones, so be cautious when estimating the efforts. Additional meetings may be required to identify the data owner or who will be able to provide access. Gaining access in a usable format can be challenging too. Thus, auditors need to work with data owners to negotiate access rights and to have audit technology tools compatible with the organization's IT environment. Timely access to the data will facilitate the data extractions, identification of exceptions, analysis of trends, patterns, anomalies and the follow-up of flagged transactions.

Once the data is obtained, the data analytics team needs to clean the data by eliminating duplicate data or identifying any gaps; they also need to ensure completeness and accuracy of data. They need to validate the integrity of the data by performing additional tests such as edit checks, tying to other data sources, comparing to key reports, and reasonability checks. Most software programmes can fix anomalies very easily.

Key deliverables: data requests, list of anomalies or gaps to follow up with data owners, data analysis with initial exceptions or concerns.

Analyse the Data Output

During this phase, we need to interpret the results, develop the test scripts, execute the analysis and validate with supporting documentation (e.g. wire transfer forms, invoices, and customer consent). Here are a few questions:

- Does this make sense?
- Are the key controls working as intended?
- Is there a violation of policies and procedures?
- Is this a control override?
- Do we need to revisit our understanding of key controls described by management during the walkthroughs?
- Do we need to pull the query again?

Once the audit testing is finalized and all auditor's questions addressed by the business, auditors should be able to confirm if an actual exception exists. Auditors need to document the testing results. This is not a straightforward process; sometimes, we need to have additional meetings to understand the data output, so this process is very dynamic.

Key deliverables: documented testing approach and testing results.

Interpret the Results and Communicate to Management

This step is crucial to truly identify the data concerns or exceptions that must be shared later with management. Data visualization can be a fantastic tool for identifying trends and patterns. Auditors need to summarize the testing results against original analytic objectives (key controls identified) and prepare the deck to share with management. I highly recommend highlighting the control failures, common themes, anomalies, patterns, exceptions identified and their impact. Some useful tools are Excel, ACL and statistical analysis system (SAS). Data visualization software such as Tableau and Power BI can help you to understand and communicate data.

Key deliverables are an interpretation of testing results, a summary of exceptions and supporting documentation such as test scripts and queries, and a presentation deck.

Document the Tool Design and Maintenance Requirements

It is important to agree with the audit director and above when the tool will be implemented and how often it will be used. The frequency will depend on the risk associated with the area, business or key processes under review or regulatory requirements. For example, automated risk assessments could be conducted quarterly, and continuous business activities or auditing could be performed monthly or quarterly. Having a tool champion is relevant for tool maintenance and for supporting data extraction in the future.

Another essential element to consider is tracking all changes made to the automated tool; we should expect additional enhancements as testing progresses and other changes occur in a controlled environment. Change management processes must include user access restrictions to minimize the risk of unauthorized changes to assumptions, parameters or thresholds. The CAE should be responsible for assessing the effectiveness of the tool periodically, as well.

Key deliverables: finalize the data analytics documentation regarding data requirements, data extraction, data source, data queries, repository, testing approach and testing results. Obtain approval from data analytics SME and audit director.

After implementing the tool and discussing it with management, the auditor must conclude if an issue should be raised. This could happen even during the design phase. Identifying a new finding may require additional testing, such as other interviews and documentation reviews. This happened to me a few times; this is the main reason we are building something to add more value to our stakeholders.

Leveraging data is so critical for the IA function that more resources must be allocated to these activities sooner than later. Designing a new tool could take at least three months. It is not a straightforward process; proper planning and oversight activities to accomplish the key milestones and deliverables are extremely important. In addition, auditors must constantly assess the utility of each tool and identify opportunities for enhancements. This should be a dynamic process considering that the control environment is subject to changes, new risks can emerge, new controls can be implemented and new regulatory requirements can be released.

Continuous Auditing Strategies and Objectives

Data analytics is becoming more important for the audit function and will be dramatically relevant in the coming years. Audit leaders must define data analytics strategies and objectives for the IA departments and teams. They need a sharp vision for how data analytics or continuous auditing could support the IA function, add more value to their business partners, enhance testing efficiencies and effectiveness, provide more continuous monitoring and auditing tools and enhance the team's skills. They also need to get senior management support and inform the audit committee how and when the results will be reported. Senior management must understand the value IA can bring to the table and how exceptions (if any) will be shared, including audit expectations to address the identified findings.

I see more IA departments hiring chief audit directors or audit directors for Data Analytics and Innovation who will drive the new data analytics strategy, vision, and mission to build advanced audit tools and solutions. They also need to increase business awareness of the relevance of data for decision-making, monitoring, and self-assurance activities. They need to educate stakeholders and take the lead to drive changes. IA needs to review the high-risk business processes and key reports, challenge the first and second lines of defence to leverage more data analytics, and enhance self-assurance activities. Thus, these new roles are critical for successfully implementing a sustainable data analytics strategy. Innovative chief audit directors and audit directors need to inspire, motivate their audit teams and the business and drive the IA transformation by developing better tools and implementing IA best practices (e.g. defining a data analytics framework, improving efficiencies, enhancing business monitoring activities, risk assessments, gaining additional synergies by conducting more holistic and integrated audits, and completing the audits in 90 days).

Chief audit directors and audit directors need to consider four important ingredients to implement a successful and sustainable data analytics strategy: resources, budget, technology tools, and model engagement across IA teams and business partners. Once the IA strategy and vision are clear, estimating the resources required to build the data analytics team and enhance the staff's skills is important. Here are a few additional questions for audit leaders:

- Do you have enough resources to meet the data analytics objectives in the next two or three years?
- Have you assessed the skills gaps? What do your survey results show in terms of data analytics skills?
- Do you need to hire more data analytics experts? Can you bring external resources?
- Can you provide additional data analytics training? Do you know how?

- Is a data analytics academy already available in the organization to improve staff skills?
- Do you have the right software to pull and analyse the data or the most suitable for the short- and long-term goals?
- Have you shared the data analytics strategy or plan with senior management and the audit committee? Do you have their support?
- Do you have any additional challenges or concerns?
- Do you have a clear road map to meet the IA goals?
- Have you considered data analytics goals for your team as part of the performance goals?
- How can you add more value to your stakeholders during business monitoring, issue validation, and audit engagements by leveraging more relevant data?

I am giving you here few ideas that could be relevant to build the data analytics strategic plan and future stage. The data analytics team will need the right capacity and a strong knowledge of the organization's systems, underlying systems, assumptions generating the transactions being analysed and business risks. Suppose auditors do not understand the data before being reported. In that case, they will be concluding inadequately on exceptions identified, and this could add much frustration to the process and additional delays.

I have experienced different roles in my career where I had to build a data analytics team from scratch by training the entire team and bringing data analytics SMEs to do the heavy lifting. I completed skills gap assessments and determined the capacity required to meet the short- and long-term goals. It was not a centralized function; I managed the data analytics team. Also, I have experienced centralized teams that supported other IA teams; it can also be good for knowledge sharing and expanding the skill sets; however, it must be carefully planned to ensure adequate support. There is no unique approach; audit leaders must decide the best one to meet the IA needs.

The CAE may want to increase the hours allocated to data analytics, define an internal goal to ensure at least 60% of audits use data for testing purposes or increase the number of continuous auditing engagements. CAEs may have multiple priorities, but not enough resources and budget to accomplish this, so proper planning is key. However, data analytics should not be cut or compromised. I highly recommend designing a road map to track key priorities, audit milestones, and deliverables; this should cover three to five years. As IA and business priorities can change, the road map must be very flexible to adapt to new circumstances quickly; however, any changes to the approved plan should be communicated immediately to the audit committee and stakeholders.

The CAE needs supporters starting from the audit committee, key stake-holders, IT departments and SLD, and all must work together to drive change and support each other. The audit committee needs to buy the budget esti-mates to bring additional resources and technology tools as it must be clear how data analytics will impact the audit approach and help other depart-ments and the entire organization to achieve its goals (e.g. product and process simplification, improved customer experience, digital transforma-tion). IA needs to consider business priorities and determine the best way to improve efficiencies and effectiveness while auditing. Creativity, innova-tion and critical thinking are key relevant skills we need to look for when recruiting new candidates. They need to join the audit team to bring new and refreshed ideas and support the data analytics goals.

It is especially important to select the best technology to accomplish these goals. There are few data analytics tools, such as Microsoft Excel, ACL, Microsoft Access, SAS, computer-assisted audit techniques (CAATS). Data visualization software such as Tableau and Power BI can help you to understand and communicate data. There is no single tool; auditors typi-cally leverage a few tools that must be compatible with enterprise systems. This is not an easy step, and auditors need to explore the options available or used by other departments; these could be expanded to IA, too, and it could be only a matter of expanding the license. I highly recommend hav-ing an inventory of all applications, systems, and analytical tools used by other departments. This could save time and money while figuring out the investment required.

I would like to share now few examples that can help you to enhance business monitoring activities in a financial institution:

- User access analysis to verify employee profiles follow roles and respon-sibilities. This could help identify possible toxic combinations that may lead to potential fraud events.
- Mandatory training available for each area to validate compliance with training deadlines.
- Operational losses analysis to identify areas of concern, trends and pat-terns for further research and testing. This could also be converted to a continuous auditing solution (e.g. identify authorization levels and appro-priate booking, cost allocation to business centres and adequate support-ing documentation, maker and checker controls are in place to comply with the delegation of authority limits or thresholds requirements).
- Customer complaints analysis to identify trends, anomalies and com-mon patterns across products, channels, and business areas, and timely resolution to comply with complaints management requirements. We could leverage this data further to identify fraud, sales practice and noncompliance with policies, procedures and regulatory requirements.

Also, we could consider all customer complaints or comments provided by customers online (e.g. company website, LinkedIn, Facebook and Instagram) to identify additional concerns for further testing.

- Customer refunds analysis to identify trends, common patterns across products, channels and rationale provided by employees to ensure compliance with the refund policy requirements. All refunds should be processed under a maker (preparer) and checker control (could be a manager or above) with proper oversight by management. Adequate segregation of duties is relevant to minimize potential fraud or sales practice risks.
- Credit memo posts analysis. Bankers can book credit memos to advance cash to consumers when depositing a check. The policies and procedures must be clear that this must be used when specific criteria are met under a maker and checker control (e.g. threshold limits, number of entries per customer per day, the rationale that must be entered in the system (by a bank employee) to request this transaction). If this process is manual, it will be more difficult to ensure consistency across the branch network (with higher number of branches). This could be an exciting area for further research and analysis if the financial institution allows this.
- Payment analysis. For example, include payments made to terminated employees and potential overtime abuses, including rehiring employees terminated due to fraud or performance issues across the enterprise or different legal entities. This could also apply to third-party vendors. Does the company track all third parties that do not pass the due diligence process or were terminated? Does the company ensure that those employees or third-party vendors are not hired or re-hired later?

To build this vision, additional resources and energy will be spent, but we will be able to see different results and efficiencies in the long term. As listed earlier, additional data analytics tools can be developed to enhance business monitoring activities. You may find other examples, including other continuous auditing tools to develop (e.g. dormant accounts, payments to third-party vendors, employee expenses account opening [e.g. debit and credit cards, and customer wire transfers]). Proper notification systems should be in place to provide feedback to stakeholders on emerging risks, exceptions or anomalies identified.

Let's focus on the continuous auditing tools listed earlier to identify additional red flags:

- Dormant Accounts

  - Identify all dormant accounts that should meet the criteria and check if all have been flagged as dormant.
  - Identify dormant accounts moved to active status and then to dormant in a brief period just to process a few transactions.

- Check demographic changes on dormant accounts (e.g. customer's address, phone numbers and new beneficiaries) were processed under maker and checker controls. For a sample, confirm with supporting documentation.
- Check significant withdrawals, and confirm maker and checker controls were in place before moving to active status (key control) or processing any transactions.
- Cross-check new addresses to employee addresses.

- Accounts Payable to Third-Party Vendors

  - Verify if each invoice is processed under a maker and checker control (key control).
  - Verify if invoices over a certain amount were approved in compliance with a delegation of authority limit.
  - Check duplicate payments (red flag).
  - Verify if payments were processed only for known third-party vendors that provided services to the organization.
  - Verify that invoices processed for each vendor match vendor name, address, phone number, and same bank account, and all match with vendor profile and contract agreement.
  - Review the sequence of check numbers for gaps in vendor information, lack of proper approvals or potential red flags (consecutive checks are always noted).
  - Verify that no payments were made to terminated third-party vendors (red flag).

- Employee Travel Expenses

  - Verify that all travel expenses were approved under a maker and checker control (key control).
  - Identify expenses not associated with travel expenses charged during weekends, holidays, vacations or in other countries not allowed to travel per policy requirements (red flag).
  - Identify duplicate reimbursements processed to the same employees (red flag).
  - Identify expenses not in compliance with the authorized expense policy (e.g. expenditures in entertainment or gifts).
  - Analyse excessive expenses in specific categories (e.g. lunch and dinners).

- Account Opening (Debit and Credit Cards)

  - Identify that all customer applications were approved under maker and checker control to ensure adequate segregation of duties (key control).

- Verify that all customers received the disclosures, signed off the consent form, and were authenticated by bankers if opened in a retail branch (key controls).
- Identify accounts with the same phone number, address, email, PO Box numbers or branch addresses (red flag).
- Identify multiple applications for debit and credit cards opened for the same customer (red flags)
- Identify accounts opened outside branch hours (red flag).
- Identify accounts with missing information (e.g. missing signatures, mandatory key data).
- Identify accounts that have not been funded for over 30 and 60 days (red flag).
- Identify all exceptions processed (e.g. the customer is not present when accounts were opened, no address verification was done, and negative credit score).
- Accounts opened without customer IDs, unauthorized or expired IDs (red flag).

- Customer Wire Transfers

  - Analyse all wires processed under maker and checker controls to comply with policy and procedures requirements (e.g. maker does not report directly to checker or checker has a higher level than the maker [key control]).
  - Identify wire transactions processed outside branch hours (red flag).
  - Identify structuring; suspicious wire transactions for same customers under 10,000 (red flag).
  - Verify that the screening was completed and that all banker's decisions were documented, including exceptions approved by the checker.
  - Analyse wires processed in 20 or 30 seconds; does this make sense? Have all steps followed (e.g. screening, customer authentication, customer disclosures, maker, and checker's approvals) to comply with the procedure requirements?
  - Verify customer's authentication requirements, and match signatures on wire forms to IDs on file. Also, identify missing signatures or lack of customer authentication [red flag].
  - Identify if transactions were processed over the phone or in the branches; select a sample and verify against supporting documentation requirements.
  - Look for a high volume of wires from one customer (large or frequent wire transfers) and confirm if those customers were in branches by looking at video surveillance.

Data analytics will be constantly enhanced in the following years with innovative technologies, new IA and regulatory requirements, and new IA priorities. Organizations and audit leaders need to change how audits are conducted; we need more data analytics experts; over 60% of auditors should be able to understand data and leverage data during planning and fieldwork. I will predict smaller IA departments with higher data analytics skills to add more value. The auditor should leverage more data analytics to understand trends and patterns, identify anomalies and relationships among data in order to identify potential fraud with third-party vendors, employees, and customer behaviour. We also need better reports and dashboards to facilitate business monitoring activities. Organizations will continue their innovation processes, increase automation, and digital mechanisms to serve customers.

Having IA departments with over 1,000 will not be justifiable if data analytics teams only count for 5% or 10%, the IA department will be under scrutiny, and board needs to challenge chief audit directors more to enhance data analytics across the department quickly. The composition of IA teams must change. We need quicker (90 days) and faster audits, which can only be attained by speeding up data and training resources and bringing in new SMEs and experts. Quality cannot be compromised but only enhanced constantly to add more value to stakeholders. Auditors must improve their data analytics skills and keep up with innovative technology. The time is now; IA modernization is key for the success of this profession, and we need to take further steps to elevate the audit role in an organization.

Chief audit directors need to elevate the IA role and take faster steps to build a stronger data analytics function that will benefit the entire organization and drive even deeper changes that will support the business. Data analytics is key to any world-class IA department. The data analytics transformation is not only about technology but also about changing 100% of the way we conduct audits; it requires stronger leaders who can translate their vision into actions. Awareness is important; communication is key; you can only reach the destination by driving the boat with determination, knowledge, proper equipment, and guidance. Storms cannot be avoided, but you must always be prepared to navigate safely and through unpredictable weather.

Digital work brings new challenges where auditors must dig deeper into understanding data, correlations, and key data relationships to identify issues sooner – communicating the why of the data analytics transformation is more important than the how. We must create a culture of IA innovation across the entire IA department where continuous improvements, ideas, and flexibility are common patterns. Still, all is required to get to the point we need. IA departments need to be better, and they need to meet the demand of the future. Technology and innovation will change how, where and when we execute audits.

My best advice is to innovate more to complete audits faster and provide outstanding value to your stakeholders. Leverage more data to drive change in your organization. As you think about your goals for this year or next, consider the relevance of data and how you can work with others to enhance everything you are working on right now, from risk assessments to audit execution. Data analytics is crucial in risk assessments, business monitoring, issue validation and audit engagements. Fraud and cybersecurity risks continue to grow, and the sophistication and complexity of incidents and events. We need better tools and data to identify red flags that may have previously gone undetected for years. The time is now.

Let's move to another important topic: complete audits in 90 days.

Chapter 14

How to Complete Audits in 90 Days?

I want to introduce a good concept: the completion of audits in 90 days. We need to complete audits faster to add more value to our stakeholders. Going through an audit is like climbing Everest. Why? You can always find obstacles, but most importantly, you need to learn technical climbing skills, be ready for any risks and be strong enough to manage challenges (e.g. fear, harsh weather, falling rocks, lack of oxygen). You must know yourself deeply to manage strange feelings; sometimes, you may want to return or give up; however, you must move on and be ready to try new ways to reach the top. The trip can take longer than expected, but when you reach the top and see the horizon, you will feel exhausted and happier, and thanks to God, it is all over. That feeling will change everything; yes, you accomplished your goal.

Before moving to this topic, let's think for a minute about how you can respond to the following questions:

- Do you feel that your audit process takes longer than it should?
- Why can't IA teams complete audits in 90 days?
- What would you like to improve to be more efficient and effective during audit engagements?
- Are you frustrated with any audit(s), or are your stakeholders frustrated with the IA team?
- Why do you not like to conduct audits anymore?
- Do you think that you have picked the right profession?

Please write your answers in a paper to discuss later with your team. After reading this chapter, you will learn additional tips that helped me through my audits. Following simple audit efficiency tips can help you finish audits earlier, which could be less painful for your audit team and stakeholders. Let's focus on the challenges first so we can cover them later.

DOI: 10.4324/9781003431893-15

Here are a few challenges that auditors may face:

- They may be a lack of resources and skills to audit the area.
- Audit plan hours have been reduced significantly, but there are still many activities to be accomplished on time; auditors must manage different activities during the audit (e.g. work on a couple of audits or validate a few complex issues, so the time allocated to the audit has been reduced, high staff turnover) that will impact the time allocated to each audit.
- There is an unclear definition of roles and responsibilities for the audit team that will impact audit deliverables.
- The audit report must be discussed with so many people that it will take over 30 days once approved by the chief audit director and head of audit.
- Auditors usually share findings too late; which may impact the audit report publication date, during the reporting phase.
- The business did not agree with a few issues; multiple meetings were held with the business before proving the management corrective actions. This impacted also the audit report publication date.
- The business monitoring activities and risk assessments are too vague to understand the auditable entities, so auditors learn the key risks and high-risk processes during the planning phase. Thus, it takes six or seven weeks (too many) to finalize the audit scope.
- Insufficient training (e.g. IA methodology, data analytics, stakeholders' engagement, SME audit programmes, time management and agile approach) was delivered to new hires; they are still learning how to document audit testing, so much re-work was necessary to fix comments provided by the audit manager, senior audit manager and audit director.
- A new audit management system was implemented or is about to be released; the audit team is learning how to prepare and document the audit testing and results.
- Nobody is tracking or monitoring key audit deliverables; no IA metrics exist, so audits are taking longer than expected.
- The audit scope included so many high-risk processes and key controls (over 30 controls) that it was impossible to complete the audit in 90 days.
- The auditable entity was too big to cover all key risks and high-risk processes in one audit. This was the first audit conducted with the new IA methodology.
- Data analytics was not leveraged (data is underused) due to a lack of capacity and skills.
- There are no rules of engagement among the audit team and between the audit and the business.
- It takes too much time to close the audit database as audit managers and senior audit managers review most of the working papers during the fieldwork and reporting phases adding comments that must be addressed first.

Before sharing a few efficiency tips to help you with your audit, I want to highlight that auditors must meet CPE requirements ranging from 20 to 40 CPE credits (CIA). If you work for a financial institution, regulators constantly review audit reports, supporting documentation and conduct annual and regular reviews.

Auditors must request and review information, write and discuss potential findings with stakeholders; meet IA methodology requirements; and ensure the audit evidence supports problems raised. Auditors must complete a few tasks before publishing the audit report or closing the audit database in the audit management system. This is where "human" technical skills and planning skills get into play, such as auditor and stakeholders' styles and personalities, company culture, organizational structure, work styles and personnel involved that can impact the audit completion. Let's move to the audit efficiency tips that can help you to complete audits in 90 days or earlier.

Audit Efficiency Tips

- Have a more disciplinary approach during audit planning, fieldwork, and reporting phases, and consider one additional audit phase: the pre-planning phase. It would help if you started the pre-planning audit activities (five or six weeks earlier) before the planning kick-off meeting. The following pre-planning activities could be considered:

  - Allocated hours to the pre-planning activities (one audit manager and Senior Auditor) to ensure proper support.
  - Update the risk assessment (for the auditable entity under review) earlier during the last business monitoring activities or after completing issue validation activities to facilitate the preliminary audit scope definition.
  - Identify data analytics requirements. Always review prior audit working papers to identify data analytics completed earlier to save time.
  - Implement toll-gate meetings during pre-planning and before starting the fieldwork. Develop a standard tollgate template to track participation, feedback received from SMEs and audit scope agreement.
  - Prepare and send the document request list earlier.
  - Request all policies and procedures and review the business process mappings or MCAs.
  - Obtain all open issues that impact the auditable entity.

- Book audit resources in advance. Roll out a staff scheduling tool to manage the staff scheduling and deployment. Please pull together the team that completed the previous audit; however, I always recommend a strong audit manager (with prior experience auditing the area) and new team members. Experience always helps and is a plus. However, experienced personnel who also understand their roles and responsibilities are relevant to manage the audit successfully.

- Create an audit engagement checklist to track all tasks to be completed (pre-planning, planning, fieldwork, and reporting phases, including the business socialization time) with forward-looking dates, which will be determined based on the audit report publication date and time assigned to each activity. If key deliverables or target dates are at risk, escalation to audit director and above is highly recommended.
- Update the risk assessments timely. All information included in the audit planning memo should match what was highlighted in the risk assessment. High-risk drivers must be included in the audit scope; otherwise, scoping out decisions should be explained and discussed with IA SMEs owners to get their approvals.
- Define a smart audit scope by focusing on the highest risks and end-to-end processes (e.g. customer journeys [account opening, maintenance, and closure, customer complaints, contact centre, distribution, and sales], customer wire transfers or investment decisions) to have a broader and holistic view of key risks and controls. The RCM should cover no more than 15 key controls per audit. The audit manager should submit the audit scope to the tollgate meeting to get feedback from audit director, chief audit director and relevant IA SMEs. An agile approach could be leveraged to engage stakeholders earlier and through the audit. Always re-assess audit coverage versus audit resources to ensure that the audit scope is attainable, realistic and relevant during the audit engagement.
- Leverage the business monitoring activities to identify areas of concern and anomalies for further testing. Having robust business monitoring activities is desirable. For example, a few high-risk processes could be reviewed in preparation for the audits; data analytics tools could be leveraged to identify trends and outliers for further research (e.g. high volume of customer complaints, refunds, operational losses, large fraud losses, allegations, red flags with transactional data, material misstatements and mandatory training). Your data analytics champion should be involved during pre-planning activities to identify data requirements and sources, extract data (if possible) and complete data documentation requirements.
- Define and share the rules of engagement with the audit team and management. I want to share one example that you could leverage, but you may have others in mind as well:

  - Start pre-planning activities five or six weeks from the planning start date on the audit announcement letter sent to the stakeholders.

- Planning phase should be conducted in three or four weeks while fieldwork in three weeks, reporting in five weeks to complete audits in 90 days.
- The business should provide documentation requests in 48 hours; otherwise, the audit manager and senior audit manager will have to escalate this to the audit director (48 hours past initial agreement) and chief audit director (96 hours past initial agreement).
- IA issues must be reviewed and evaluated in 90 days or earlier, if possible (60 days). You could also consider reducing the time invested in issue validation activities for more complex issues such as 30 days.
- Regulatory issue validation activities must be completed in 90 or 60 days (if possible).
- Management corrective actions should be provided within 2–6 days; otherwise, the audit manager and senior audit manager will escalate to audit director (48 hours past initial agreement) and chief audit director (96 hours past initial agreement). It would be best if you shared the rules of the engagement with your stakeholders to get their support to complete audits in 90 days. Auditors must also review corrective management actions and provide management feedback within 24 hours.
- Audit report must be reviewed by chief audit director, other SMEs and QA team. They will have to check the audit report in 48 hours. Otherwise, escalation will occur (as listed earlier).
- Once the draft audit report is approved, socialization can start with the key stakeholders (1 week is provided before publishing the audit report). The stakeholders would like to review the audit report first.
- Close the audit folder in 2–6 days. All working papers must be reviewed by the audit manager, senior audit manager and audit director before submitting the draft audit report for review and, of course, before publishing the audit report. Ensure your files and working papers are organized and reviewed promptly through each phase. It would help if you did not move to fieldwork without reviewing all planning working papers (audit planning memo, walkthroughs and RCM).

- Create an audit delivery tracker (across the IA department) to track audit status, potential audit report ratings, key audit deliverables, and rationale for changing key milestones. The audit senior manager or audit director will be updating this tracker weekly.
- Design standard templates to complete the documentation requirements such as audit planning memo, DEA and OET, risk assessment, business monitoring and issue validation activities, among others. When auditors

document audit testing in a format they are used to, the audit process tends to go faster.

- Define how data should be shared to avoid multiple emails with stakeholders (e.g. SharePoint site). The audit manager could track the information requested and received so any missing documents could be discussed with the designed SPOC (business key contact).
- Look outside the box and ask the right questions. Do your homework before starting the audit. Proper preparation will significantly speed up the entire process. I want to share a few additional questions you might want to ask yourself or your stakeholders:

  - Are you focusing too much on things you would like to fix? Focus on what can go wrong, even if things look good. Does this make sense?
  - Why did the control change?
  - Why is the business not in compliance with new regulatory requirements?
  - Are there any maker and checker control in place? If you find an issue with procedure documents, try to go deeper and think about what else can go wrong. Should the business enhance this process or simplify the procedure document? Is the current process impacting the customer experience?
  - Can the business automate any key manual controls? Did you discuss this with your stakeholder?
  - Consider the procedure documents and see if all required steps are necessary and being followed consistently. Does it make sense to have ten steps to process a customer refund or a wire transaction? How was a wire transaction completed in 30 seconds, considering all steps required per procedure document? How was a customer refund processed in ten seconds? Use common sense.
  - Is there adequate segregation of duties or any toxic combinations? When was the last time the business reviewed user access? Did you audit this before?
  - Is there a backup for a sensitive position? Why not? Are there detailed procedure documents the explain how the fair value reconciliation is performed monthly?

- Embrace automation and innovate more. For example, you could create MIS reporting to track audits and issues, automate business monitoring activities, risk assessments, an audit report (if possible), and other audit documents (audit planning memo, DEA, OET, sample selection and issue validation activities). This also facilitates the review process, as well. An audit management system will improve the standardization process and save additional time.

- Use an audit management system to keep track of all activities that must be completed per audit phase so you can keep track of everything, including approvals required before closing the audit database.
- Embrace more technology to work remotely and to design and develop better data analytics tools to provide stronger assurance (e.g. customer wire transfers, payments, cash differences, red flags [AML, trade surveillance and account opening], customer's refunds) or to identify thematic concerns or risks (e.g. complaints, allegation, operational losses, fraud losses, transactional data and ATM). Identify key themes, trends, anomalies and new or emerging risks to facilitate the audit scope definition. If you want to identify sales practices concerns, data is key, but you will have to review all key data points together (e.g. customer complaints, allegations and operational losses).
- Review past audit findings and status. Plan the audit when most pending issues are ready for IA validation. You could include these issues in the audit scope and validate them all during the audit. However, if the organization has many open problems, it won't be easy to accomplish this, but at least a few could be considered during the audit engagement.
- Establish effective communication with your stakeholders. During the audit, stay in contact with your stakeholders to follow up on pending items and to share potential findings. It is okay to ask for missing documentation or additional documentation as needed. Schedule weekly meetings to share the audit status, especially when the audit team is already finding issues. Please pay attention to their reactions when sharing these findings and be prepared to provide additional details or request additional information to clarify their feedback.

To summarize the relevant key points here:

- Auditors need to manage each audit phase diligently.
- Resources must be identified, allocated or agreed upon with SMEs, if needed.
- Set clear and realistic deadlines considering the audit scope and resources available.
- Define a smart audit scope when planning audits. The majority of time should be allocated to the pre-planning and planning phase to identify high-risk processes and key controls. This could save time in the other audit phases.
- Have tollgate meetings with relevant SMEs (all required parties must approve the audit scope and high risks to be covered). Proper documentation should be developed and retained in the audit management system.

- Leverage data analytics, key reports and other innovation tools, if possible.
- Share and discuss the rules of the engagement with your stakeholders in advance and before starting each audit.
- Use the escalation process often during all audit phases to facilitate and resolve any bottlenecks or challenges; always leverage the agile approach.
- Coordinate better with the first and second lines of defence to minimize the volume of audits and reviews scheduled simultaneously. The business cannot manage well so many audits or reviews at the same time.
- Review the document request list in advance to avoid requesting information that is not necessary.
- Identify issues that could be reviewed during the audit engagement to save time and effort.
- Review all working papers through the audit to avoid surprises.
- Leverage the agile approach, if possible.
- Plan smart, execute diligently and share and report issues timely.

You need to bring valuable experience to the table to be more efficient. If you already have an audit team with enough knowledge to review the business or processes, these tips will provide valuable ideas to complete audits in 90 days. If you do not have enough experience, you need to focus on this first and how to develop the auditor of the future (e.g. coaching, mentoring, training). How can you bring additional expertise? As organizations progress from the pandemic, IA functions must transform and improve things faster. To achieve excellence and to add value to your stakeholders, audit leaders need to help IA teams to be where they need in terms of technical and soft skills. They need to help them succeed by providing the right tools and support and encouraging them to take on new challenges, look outside the box, be flexible and be curious to understand the unique business direction and risks.

I will cover how to build and recognize a first-class audit team in the next chapter; this is a great topic.

Chapter 15

First-Class Internal Audit Team

Personnel selection is a critical element in building a strong IA function. It requires time and effort to find the right talent. Nowadays, an IA function requires people with technical, soft, digital and data analytical skills. We need more auditors willing to add more value to their stakeholders. Technical skills are fundamental, but you can always find a candidate who may not be an expert but has an open mind to build their skills in the field.

I remember when I had to build an IA function in Mexico City. I had to interview many candidates to hire around 40 people who had to speak and write in English well and have IA experience in the financial sector. It took me a while because I wanted to find the right skills. However, I took the risk of hiring a few candidates that never audited a bank; I noticed that they had important skills such as curiosity, attitude and motivation to learn more. Sometimes we must avoid looking for the perfect candidate or relying on a machine to select the perfect resume.

Human nature is relevant and important. Audit leaders need to be more open to that. I built the strongest audit team that an audit leader could imagine. They added excellent value to the organization and drove the bank's transformation. Of course, you will always encounter challenges when managing people. Still, only good things can happen when you visualize what you want to accomplish, work hard, and feel confident about yourself and your audit team.

What are the most critical qualities you should look for to improve the IA transformation?

- Motivation to learn
- Curiosity to explore
- Discipline to meet expectations
- Attitude to be the best for stakeholders and customers
- Flexibility to adapt to all changes
- Desire to continue learning

DOI: 10.4324/9781003431893-16

- Discipline to engage with stakeholders
- Experience with the agile approach
- Good team players
- Diversity and inclusion
- Other relevant qualities

The audit skills can be taught if someone possesses other qualities (like those mentioned below).

Motivation to Learn

Motivation to learn different things even if they do not have all answers or experience. You can get enough experience in the field when you have the right attitude and you are not scared of taking challenging assignments. I remember when I got to the United States and started my career at Ernst and Young LLP in New York City, I was determined to learn as much as possible. I took challenging assignments when I was not even familiar with the processes or topics to be covered. I always had an open mind to learn from others, read many things, do additional research to get the answers and prepare myself for critical meetings. That attitude helped me to succeed in other complex projects and assignments locally and internationally. You have no limits and can accomplish everything you want; your confidence and determination can make a dramatic difference and impact others around you.

I have many years of consulting and audit experience; I always believe that you should learn something new every day and never be afraid to ask a single question or make a mistake. We need to grow every day to take on new challenges and challenge others with respect. COVID-19 has changed everything, and we need to challenge ourselves to explore different options by being more flexible, adaptable and open to new challenges.

Curiosity to Explore

To be an auditor, you need to look outside the box and figure out what could go wrong. You may need to figure out if the candidate in front of you has this ability through an interview process. Curiosity is accessible and depends on every individual. Motivate your employees to be curious, ask questions and make mistakes. They will learn from every single mistake they make. Reward them for their curiosity and the value added to the team and stakeholders.

I want to ask you: are you curious enough at work? What would you do differently starting now to encourage others to be more interested? Set the example. I am curious about things and always try to go deeper when interviewing stakeholders. I love asking the right questions, but you must prepare well for each meeting. Knowledge and curiosity go together.

Discipline to Meet Expectations

Internal auditors will have a variety of tasks to manage, including audits, issue validation, business monitoring activities, interactions with stakeholders, last minute requests from top management, business, regulators or other areas. Discipline is relevant when tasks must be completed on time and with the required quality. For example, audit directors have weekly, monthly, and annual deadlines to meet the annual audit plan. Indeed, if you work in an IA department, you will realize how important it is to meet the key milestones and, of course, the IA scorecard metrics (if any).

Managers must be able to guide the team, coach the team to meet all expectations, deliverables, complete audits in 90 days, complete issue validation activities on time and required training hours, among others. Having a disciplined approach with clear roles and responsibilities can help a lot.

Attitude to Be the Best for Stakeholders and Customers

The world is changing so fast, and so is the IA function. Data mining, analytics and digital experts are required more than ever. Innovation is the key to providing the best value to customers and stakeholders. We must always consider what can be done to improve our relationship with our stakeholders and how we could provide better services. Look always outside the box, even when planning the audit scope, always consider this tip.

Having continuous auditing tools can improve testing and efficiency. Having more frequent auditing is decisive for your stakeholders. Thus, when looking for candidates, these skills are always a plus. If your team is not proficient on this topic, find options so they can be trained (internal or external training options should be available). They need to build their curriculum to support the audit team.

Flexibility to Adapt to All Changes

Auditors need to be flexible at work and adapt to changes in the IA methodology and changes to the control environment, organizational structure, policies, procedures and local or global regulatory requirements, among others. Auditors never work with the same audit team members (conducting audits, issuing validation activities or interacting with other local or global audit teams), so they need to be more flexible to adapt to unique styles.

I was fortunate to collaborate with people from diverse backgrounds and cultures. I cannot express how wonderful these experiences have been for me and continue. Audit leaders must listen carefully, coach and develop others, and share their experiences more often with their teams; this could profoundly impact your audit team and stakeholders. Be transparent, be more yourself and lead from your uniqueness.

Desire for Continuous Learning

Internal auditors must keep informed of changes in the control environment, news, policies, procedures, and regulatory requirements. Globalization and, now, COVID-19 have changed the way businesses are conducted. Companies are adapting to the new normal, transforming the business, and investing more in customer journeys and digital solutions. We need auditors with diverse backgrounds, different perspectives, different soft skills and better emotional intelligence willing to add more value and share their points of view.

Continuous learning and education are critical for the success of the IA function in any organization. On average internal auditors must receive between 20 and 40 hours of training annually. Having a certification in IA, fraud or compliance such as CIA, CFE, CAMS or CISA is relevant. In addition, identifying opportunities for the team to work on other local or global assignments can also add terrific value to team members. As IA leaders, we must encourage team members to take additional training to enhance their skills.

Auditors never stop learning. We always need to set an example for our teams and colleagues, and leaders need to find better opportunities to develop audit teams. In an era of digitalization, providing challenging assignments and the opportunity to work with SMEs or other colleagues will help them reach the next level. You can learn so much from surrounding yourself with people that are better than you at something that they can easily lift you in ways you never imagined.

Discipline to Engage With Stakeholders

Collaborating closely with stakeholders is relevant to understanding business needs, current concerns or constraints, and new or emerging risks. To develop smart audits, auditors must be familiar with the businesses, local regulations, business policies, and procedures. Auditors need to build good relationships with their stakeholders, become trusted advisors, and understand where the business is going. Effective partnering also requires sharing points of view and best practices to enhance the control environment during audits, business monitoring activities and issue validation activities.

Collaborating closely with stakeholders can benefit the business and IA teams. Active communication with stakeholders throughout the audit process or issue validation activities in the pre-planning phase are essential to minimize re-open issues. Of course, this requires many hours of collaborating closely with stakeholders but saves time during audits or issue validation activities. When auditors understand the business, they can easily articulate the business strategy and focus on what matters to senior management. Thus, auditors must be service-oriented and keep current with the business.

In addition, how could we be the best for your stakeholders? Of course, having effective mechanisms for more issue tracking and escalation to senior management and board of directors, requesting feedback and planning effective meetings. Be transparent and agile when managing each key relationship. Audit leaders need to embrace innovation and drive more change to bring practical insight and add value to the entire organization.

Working as a consultant in financial services in different countries and leading critical projects gave me the flavour to understand how well we must collaborate with stakeholders to get the best of them, even when we need to deliver a difficult audit report. Auditors need to continue learning the business under their umbrella to build stronger relationships and provide better value and insight. They must also work well with the first and second lines of defence to strengthen the control environment.

Experience With the Agile Approach

In the era of agile, we also need project managers. Agile is transforming the way audits should be conducted. Thus, auditors need to be trained in the agile approach. This does not necessarily need to impact the IA methodology. Agile engagement with stakeholders and IA team members is required more than ever.

Audit managers are encouraged to take ownership of the audits and guide team members to meet expectations during sprints. Engaging stakeholders during the process is relevant to perform more effective audits and delivering audit reports earlier in the process.

Tools such as regular conference calls or meetings and recreational discussion threads can be helpful to create more effective teamwork and improve relationships and transparency with stakeholders. Agile allows audits to be more flexible and adapt to changes in business perspectives or as the audit progresses.

Good Team Players

Auditors must enjoy collaborating with their colleagues. Looking for good team players who can take the lead, coach team members, and manage integrated audits is crucial for your team's success. As a senior consultant, I remember how critical this topic was in my performance evaluations and how much emphasis managers and partners put on it. I appreciate their feedback and emphasis on this topic, which planted in my mind to always focus on developing influential team members. Finding the right talent who enjoys working with integrated audit teams and has the right soft skills to manage and collaborate with internal auditors and stakeholders is important.

Audit managers and senior audit managers need emotional intelligence more than ever to lead teams, influence others, including their stakeholders, and easily understand other points of view by putting themselves in their shoes.

Diversity and Inclusion

Globalization has added another important quality, diversity and inclusion. Organizations must pay more attention to managing talent, including staff wellbeing and diversity challenges. For example, internal auditors could be in Argentina and reporting to a chief audit director in Asia or having conversations with other regulators in the United States. Integrated audits constantly require the participation of different team members who do not need to be in the same country or location.

Nowadays, companies are paying more attention to diversity and inclusion. Auditors need to think globally and leverage the information within the organization to conduct smarter audits. This brings more challenges to internal auditors as they need to be familiar with diverse cultures and regulators and be open to considering how global issues may impact local audits. We need a more multidisciplinary team where we can exchange ideas and learn from others. Developing diversity competencies is critical nowadays and will become more relevant.

The diversity challenge can also be addressed with IA help. For example, audits can be added to the annual audit plan to review HR practices to ensure staff's fair treatment and representation or to conduct a diversity hiring audit. IA can give the board/audit committee an impartial view of how the organization meets its diversity goals. As a woman leader in this field, I encourage IA leaders to focus on diversity and inclusion, bring more diverse candidates, and support and develop employees. Audit directors, chief audit directors, and heads of audits need to contribute to an inclusive culture; they need to support more women, especially minorities, in leadership positions.

Other actions can be taken to support minorities:

- Train women for top positions, coach them and assign mentors. Coach and mentor with compassion and dedication. Compromised and inspired leaders make an enormous difference in this process.

- Support an IA diversity team that will focus on supporting diversity and inclusion (D&I) initiatives.
- Identify talent and provide development opportunities.
- Define and share D&I employee goals.
- Select a metric to improve diversity hiring (e.g. increase the number of women in the IA department and increase the percentage of qualified females in leadership positions [chief audit directors and head of audits]).
- Auditors can assess the methods used to monitor, measure, and report on the D&I programme. If metrics are reported, auditors can evaluate all for completeness and accuracy. This will show senior management what initiatives are working and the ones that must be re-evaluated. It will also help to hold them accountable for meeting their long-term goals.
- Review employee surveys to ensure they were designed adequately (relevant questions were asked and minorities were included). Auditors can evaluate whether follow-up actions were taken to address any concerns.
- Auditors can also evaluate exit interviews, layoffs and resignations; they may offer insights into whether D&I was a common theme.

Conducting a D&I audit could be beneficial for your organization to assess where your organization is on its diversity and inclusion journey. Finding the right resource to perform this audit could be a challenge as SMEs need to combine expertise and knowledge, including data analytics, to understand the talent selection, hiring, and retention process; compensation and rewards; training and development opportunities; survey results; key metrics; and D&I culture. It is also important to collect and analyse data related to employee engagement surveys, demographics, employment trends for the industry, and recruitment and selection criteria. Additional internal research could be conducted through other surveys, interviews and observations to understand employees' feedback and challenges.

Auditors can also assess areas of the business in which discrimination can exist. Company policies and procedures and how issues are managed could be a good starting point. Employees leave organizations mainly due to poor employee treatment, unrealistic performance objectives, and unfortunate interactions with their bosses.

Here are a few questions for audit leaders:

- Are you satisfied with the current efforts to hire, develop, and retain a diverse audit team?
- Do you have enough women, Black, Hispanic, Latinx, Asian and Veterans in your team, especially in leadership roles? Why not?
- Do you know how diverse your employees and leadership team are?
- Do you have metrics to measure progress? And do you share these metrics with your team?

- Are you meeting your goals?
- Are you willing to invest more efforts to improve these results? How?
- Have you included a D&I audit in your audit plan?
- Are you too focused on the audit plan delivery?
- Are you truly aware of minorities' challenges at work? How?

D&I is especially important; more organizations need to take this step to assess where they truly are. With this audit, the board and senior management can take only the first step to developing a more profound and impactful strategy to support the D&I efforts strongly. If you do not have the best talent, you will not be able to succeed or attract more talent. Attracting the best talents does not happen immediately and will not happen without improving D&I in our workplace and IA departments.

We need more transparency in the recruitment processes; there are still companies that leverage software to discard good candidates. We should not be hiring resumes or focusing on keywords on resumes to select candidates for the first interview. We need human intervention to select the most diversified pool. When you rely on systems with specific algorithms and keywords, there is room for imperfection, discrimination and manipulation. All these things should be carefully audited if we want more transparency, diversity, equity and inclusion. I want to be clear here; machines do not select the best candidates unless there is human intervention.

As Latina working in the corporate world, organizations must do many things to reach the point minorities deserve. Latinx is such a small minority that it needs much more support and auditors need to conduct smarter audits to help organizations identify and resolve the gaps. Companies do not fix things by going to the media, drafting a helpful article, or donating more money to make a better world. We genuinely need to look inside before going outside; leaders need to realize the small steps they need to take to help their employees first and all minorities at the workplace and worldwide. Companies need to create an entire culture that is equitable, inclusive, and consistent across the board. If you do not audit this, you will never be able to identify all potential gaps. We cannot resolve this by making assumptions or taking smaller steps; this is bigger than that.

Other Relevant Qualities

Nowadays, team members need multidisciplinary knowledge of the business and critical topics such as digital transformation, cybersecurity, third-party vendors, data management, data analytics, regulatory requirements, sales practices and fraud. Companies must be on top of this and invest in good learning programmes to keep personnel updated. Auditors need additional training and coaching to set their own annual goals.

Roles and responsibilities must be clear, and guidance should be provided. Meaningful conversations with direct reports can accelerate their career and personal development. Few organizations have implemented mentor programmes to promote communication and network building and increase engagement and retention of team members. A mentor could be assigned to team members (internal or external mentors) to provide support. The conversation between mentor and mentee must be confidential.

In addition, developing exchange programmes where you can give your audit team global exposure or exposure to other audit teams is critical for the success of an IA function. Your team will appreciate this opportunity, and this will enhance team performance.

Building a world-class IA function requires the right talent, leadership, stronger IA practices, innovative tools, and courage to change and challenge things. We need to develop internal talent and empower auditors to take the lead, learn and be more curious, flexible, cooperative, creative and adaptable to perform at their best. We must also provide them with adequate and relevant training and better technology tools.

I want to end this chapter by leaving a few questions:

- Does your team have the skills required? If the answer is "no," what is your commitment to your team to develop them and build a top IA function?
- What are you doing to improve stakeholders' perception of the IA role continually?
- Is there sufficient training to help auditors excel in relevant soft skills such as negotiation, communication, collaboration, including stakeholder engagement? How about data analytics, report writing and agile approach?

Automation is taking over, and auditors need to be prepared to audit the company's business strategies, culture, and D&I and find new ways to add more value. Thus, we must promote a culture of continuous learning and development. If you are an auditor, you need to learn something every day. Although I have a busy schedule, I have the discipline to take a training online or read an article daily. I also love reading books and read at least one book every month. Audit leaders must inspire change, lead with passion and have an excellent attitude to impact others. The more knowledge and experience we have, the better we will be able to assist and advise our audit teams and management in the future. Thus, audit training and development are critical, and I will cover this topic in the next chapter.

Chapter 16

Audit Team Training and Development

Audit leaders need to focus on the IA team formation and development since it impacts the value delivered to stakeholders, the reputation of the IA function, talent retention and career development. Forming audit teams based on specialization improves audit effectiveness and the advisory services that could be provided to the organization.

An IA function that encourages adequate and continuous training will impact the development of identified skills gaps, enhancing team effectiveness and adding value to stakeholders. While it may be impracticable to train audit teams before each audit engagement or project, audit team training should be developed on the basis of skills gaps. Internal auditors need to enhance their knowledge, skills and other competencies through continuing professional development (CPD). This will help them to remain competent in the growing and dynamic profession of IA.

Auditors must meet mandatory CPE credit annually. Tracking for compliance should be done until all personnel meet the expectations. For example, the Institute of Internal Auditors (IIA) encourages certified individuals to obtain training related to the Standards. At a minimum, certified individuals must review the standards annually, determine whether they perform internal audit services by the Standards and report their conformance or nonconformance to the IIA. There must be documented evidence of successful completion of the required training.

Before developing the training schedule for the entire year, an IA function needs to define and discuss expectations for each position (e.g. senior auditor, audit manager, senior audit manager). Guidance should be developed, shared with the team and considered when preparing job posting descriptions. For example, IA managers must supervise auditors and assist in the planning, testing, and executing of IA activities. A bachelor's degree and five to eight years of related experience are usually required.

Internal auditors must be trained to conduct audits and to develop an effective audit programme. Individual development needs can also be

DOI: 10.4324/9781003431893-17

addressed by coaching team members on the job, sharing best practices, mentoring, and developing additional courses. The training set and offered should meet the complexity of the industry and areas to be audited, including business and systems knowledge. IA members could subscribe and take mandatory training available for the business and prepare themselves before conducting the audits.

The company can train auditors with the required frequency if it decides to develop its courses. For example, IA methodology and others (e.g. IA system and stakeholder engagement and IA testing programmes) can quickly be delivered by the most experienced internal auditors and SMEs with the help of the QA team. SMEs can provide specific audit programme training.

Specific courses should also be developed and delivered to IA teams at least annually related to the following topics:

- IA methodology
- Business monitoring activities and risk assessment process
- Issue validation activities
- Stakeholders' engagement
- IA testing programmes (e.g. compliance, fraud, fiduciary, third-party vendors, continuity of business and culture)
- Regulatory changes
- Information security, including cybersecurity and data privacy
- Third-party management
- Fraud management
- Financial crimes
- Data governance and data management
- Digital banking and digital transformation
- Risk culture and decision making
- Updates on local regulatory requirements or key company policies, procedures
- Conduct risks and ethics
- Data analytics and innovation
- Diversity and inclusion
- Soft skills (e.g. leadership and audit management, communication, negotiation and presentation skills, feedback delivery, staff wellbeing, talent management, stakeholder engagement audit report writing).

Regarding communication skills, auditors must be tactful, flexible, curious and transparent (keep people informed of their findings). They must listen carefully to their stakeholders and use accessible language or local terminology. In addition, a solid ethical foundation is critical to avoid the temptation to let it go when the analysis reveals an open or fraudulent event.

Thus, they need to keep absorbing new technical skills throughout their careers. If the auditor is not current with the latest regulation, they could miss critical risks and issue an inadequate audit opinion.

Good auditors also must possess the following additional characteristics:

- Integrity. Auditors must do the right thing and encourage the rest of the team to behave accordingly. Audit leaders need to select individuals with solid work ethics. You can train specific skills, but you cannot teach integrity.
- Vision and good instinct. Instinctively aware of and able to understand situations. Sometimes, apparent things are not seen as we focus so much on finishing the testing and ensuring that the supporting documentation is obtained. Always ask yourself if the trend analysis or account balances make sense even though the sample selected was okay or all the documentation was provided. For example, during the pandemic, there has been increased risk related to hackers trying to take advantage of this situation and access customer accounts by phishing frauds related to the coronavirus. Thus, fraud should be considered in each audit even if fraud has not been identified.
- Ability to problem-solving and conclude on raw data.
- Critical and analytical thinking. Consider the accuracy, completeness, relevance and reliability of documentation obtained while working remotely.
- Observant. Actively observing physical surroundings and activities while performing walkthroughs or visiting business facilities.
- Able to always look outside the box, see the big picture and what can go wrong.
- People skills. Keep people informed of what you are finding. Even if you are dealing with complex stakeholders' styles, try to understand your stakeholders and put yourself in their shoes for a moment to empathize from their perspective. With adequate training and practice, this skill can be developed with time.
- Soft skills (e.g. communication, leadership, creativity and teamwork). Stakeholders want to talk always with auditors who understand their points of view. Effective communication facilitates audits or even bad results when sharing audit findings. Achieving this is not easy, but it will differentiate those auditors from the rest of the audit team members.
- Written communication skills. Issues and the audit report must be clear and professionally written.
- Be prepared for permanent change and adaptability. COVID-19 has changed the way companies manage their business. Everyone is going to do business differently during and after the pandemic. This also impacted

the audit work arrangements and how audits are managed (remote testing), so I think discussions must be held on all levels to plan for the short- and long-term testing strategies.

- Managing audit team interactions in a virtual environment. Team members may be in separate locations and may be impacted by different time zones. They may be working from home while children are at home from school, so scheduling time together cannot be easy, but with proper planning and considerations, it can be easily accomplished. Few team members may need more flexibility to manage specific family needs.
- Proper audit leadership to ask relevant questions and support the audit team. Henry Ford said, "Don't find fault; find a remedy." Leaders are trusted advisors who focus on finding agreement and solutions and always want to help. Leadership must be earned day in and day out.

A bachelor's or master's degree is required for any audit level. Few companies may encourage obtaining the CFE, CIA and CPA. Other valuable designations include the CISA or Certified Government Auditing Professional (CGAP).

In others, personal development plans (PDP) are a normal part of the staff performance evaluation and development process as they focus on developing personnel skills and helping them achieve their goals. A clear career path is crucial for the success of personnel and the IA transformation process. For staff who wish to progress to the next level, CPD should be planned to improve their competencies and demonstrate the skills required for the position (through more exposure and by taking more complex audits or projects).

A CPD may include the following activities:

- Formal audit training courses (particularly those which address new developments in the practice of IA)
- Developing additional skills relevant to the business under review (e.g. digital banking, data management, and risk management)
- Taking additional certifications (e.g. CIA, CFE, CPA, CISA and CAMS)
- Attending conferences or seminars on fraud, AML, cybersecurity, data management and cryptocurrencies
- Taking mandatory training for the business so the auditors can learn more about the business, specific operations, policies, procedures and regulatory requirements
- Learning new skills through other integrated audits by working with other audit teams
- Providing mentoring programmes
- Rotation programmes

A mentoring programme can be beneficial for IA teams. Companies can develop official mentoring programmes where employees can register and assign a mentor. Also, in the past, I implemented a programme where mentors were assigned to audit team members. It worked very well. The positive thing about an official mentoring programme is that the mentors do not belong to the same team, and IA team members could feel more comfortable speaking with them. While working as a consultant, having a mentor throughout your career is an excellent practice. Thus, the objective of this programme is to promote communication and networking among team members and to create another communication channel for listening and helping others achieve their professional goals.

Diversity is also important; audit teams with individuals whose talents and skills complement one another. Working with other local or global IA teams helps audit team members to participate in other audits (e.g. fraud, compliance, operational, technology, AML audits) and to develop additional skills (exchange programmes).

The skills developed by internal auditors will be reflected in other aspects of their work, better analysis, better engagement with stakeholders, and better abilities to provide more value to the organization. Skilful internal auditors can suggest areas for improvement without giving a solution.

What Are the Main Skills Gaps?

Specific skills are in high demand, such as data analytics, innovation, experience auditing IT platforms, data management, model risk, cybersecurity, digital banking, fraud, third-party vendors and culture. Developing these skills further will help the IA function add value to stakeholders and respond effectively to top-priority areas and new or emerging risks. A key differentiator of those who thrive in the audit profession is the ability to analyse information, arrive at clear and concise conclusions, and effectively communicate those conclusions.

A gap analysis can be done by hiring a third-party vendor (based on a survey report). Another way is by preparing an inventory of skills, experience and certification for your team so the skills gaps can be easily identified internally and addressed.

Few IA functions are investing in data analytics; however, sometimes, they are not advanced enough or do not have too many continuous auditing tools to conduct testing. For example, IA teams have used data analytics during business monitoring activities or fieldwork. Still, it must be more extensive, even during planning to direct the audit scope and improve the allocation of audit resources. We need more data and predictive analytics. Thus, IA must innovate and spend more resources on better predictive tools.

So why are IA teams not using too much data? At the top of the list are the gap in skills, headcount and lack of approved hours to develop more analytical tools. Thus, IA functions need to bring additional resources and train more personnel. However, there are alternative options, such as outsourcing. In addition, there is sometimes poor data quality that does not help to develop adequate tools.

There is an increased need to evaluate strategic planning processes and risk management functions considering globalization and turbulent markets. IA functions need the skills to understand investment strategies, customer journeys and services, and predictive models to define sales or investment strategies. IA needs to review risk models and risk management processes. The audit should ascertain that those processes are sufficiently robust, particularly in an expected disruption and change suffered during black swan events.

Targeted resources may be available through alternatives such as co-sourcing and rotation programmes. Given the complexity of stakeholders' needs and emerging risks in cyber threat management, data governance and fraud, it makes sense to explore such alternatives.

Increased investment in data analytics brings increased efficiencies and more value to the entire organization. IA should play a leading role in assessing and identifying proactively opportunities to provide additional value during black swan events. Advising stakeholders on leading practices or sharing issues earlier in critical areas (e.g. data management, fraud management, regulatory compliance, technology, cybersecurity, digital banking, digital solutions and third-party vendors) is a growing expectation for internal audit leaders. Overall, the pandemic has been a time of significant innovation and growth, with the audit profession demonstrating flexibility and agility to adapt quickly to the new normal. In the next chapter, I will share a few additional tips to manage and motivate the audit team.

Chapter 17

Tips to Manage and Motivate the Audit Team

The globalization of businesses, black swan events, technology changes, digitalization, regulatory scrutiny and increased attention of stakeholders and shareholders and increased demands from senior management and the audit committee require effective management of audit engagements and other tasks (e.g. IA and regulatory issue validation activities).

IA departments sometimes suffer high staff turnover. Remember, people join organizations but leave bosses, so I would like to share a few tips to manage and motivate audit teams in this turbulent environment. I always advise my team and others around to be the audit manager, senior audit manager, audit director or chief audit director that people want to work for. It is important to focus on people and manage resources more effectively. We need stronger IA teams to manage and assess the turbulent control environment promptly and effectively.

Many organizations underestimate the power of good leadership in increasing team morale, motivation, and retention. I have had more bad bosses than good ones, but I always cared for my team. My team was always my top priority. Organizations recognize the importance of loyal and motivated employees but sometimes fail to hold managers accountable for bad decisions.

Organizations must invest more in talent retention, management selection, coaching, and development. Audit leaders make all the difference. There are a few reasons why your team members might lack the motivation they need; they could be feeling unappreciated, bored with their responsibilities or unhappy with the high volume of changes that happen every week, including lack of transparency, communication, unclear goals and lack of flexibility offered to them. They may not trust audit leaders. They do not feel supported by them. Why?

Audit leaders must be honest, transparent, ethical, courageous and kind to help others discover their full potential. If your team grows, you grow with them. This takes empathy, self-awareness, honesty and authenticity.

DOI: 10.4324/9781003431893-18

I always lead with my heart. I teach to serve others, not myself. Your ability to impact others is not based on your skills, expertise, title or degree; it is based on your emotional intelligence and ability to connect with others and treat everyone with respect and passion. It is based on the trust, integrity, and commitment you deliver to them every day. It would help if you always did the right thing. Right is right, and wrong is wrong; always choose the right thing.

The following tips outline how you can manage and motivate audit teams:

- I firmly believe that *project management skills*, adequate *audit direction, and supervision* are critical to completing audit tasks successfully and on time; these are critical drivers of quality audits. Audit managers and senior audit managers must monitor audits and issue validation activities actively and proactively to minimize unexpected delays. Also, timely supervision and review by audit directors are important to ensure high quality of work; they must challenge the audit scope and the testing approach, be involved and collaborate closely with their teams.
- Audit teams *need clear goals*. They must create, share and discuss their strategic priorities and audit goals with their direct reports. Every year the audit priorities can change and should be communicated effectively and included in team goals. Also, auditors must define and align their personal goals with the IA department and organizational strategic goals. For example, "improve efficiencies when conducting audits and issue validation activities" by completing these activities in 90 days, managing the approved budget, minimizing travel expenses when there are different business locations, and leveraging more data analytics to conduct audit testing. Each team member must understand the part they need to play to achieve the IA department and personal goals. They must own these goals to achieve reliable results.
- It is not enough to define a goal; we also need to *monitor performance and deliver timely and constructive feedback.* Everyone loves to know how they perform during an audit, how they manage a meeting with key stakeholders, and how they are evaluated; this significantly improves employee satisfaction and morale. If you are a manager, make this a priority, and find opportunities to share feedback timely with your direct reports. Do not wait until the annual performance review to share your feedback. Remember that employees do not leave companies; they leave bad bosses. Look always for new opportunities to make a positive learning experience for everyone by focusing on how to make things better.
- *Accountability* is also an essential aspect. Each team member must be accountable for the quality of work and understand how it impacts the

audit team. Auditors are responsible for their performance and audit testing results. They must understand the interdependencies of their roles; if someone cannot complete the work on time due to unexpected events (e.g. vacation time and temporary leave), they should be able to support the team in completing the remaining tasks. Your team needs to work as a team; every individual plays a critical role in the success of the entire IA department. We all win together and make mistakes together, but of course, we always learn from that.

- Audit leaders must *empower people* by trusting them and providing them with the right technology tools and opportunities to discover the best in themselves and others. When team members feel supported, they are open to discussing more perceived problems or relevant topics, bringing more ideas to the table and asking more questions. Supportive leaders develop more substantial teams, they can easily identify talent and they support them strongly to build their skills. They encourage them to ask more questions; questions genuinely empower them.

- One of the most powerful ways to impact those you lead is to *ask them how you can improve as their leader*. You can leverage the one-on-one meetings with your direct report or monthly team meetings. You may not get too many ideas at first, but you can ask the next time or second time; this shows your team that this topic is relevant and you want to get their feedback. When you get their feedback, take their feedback seriously to improve things. This shows commitment, respect and professionalism to build trust among team members and stakeholders. Involve them in the solution, as well. Look for opportunities to encourage all to work together to find better solutions and add more value.

- Schedule *regular meetings* with your direct report to track audit progress, issue validation activities or share ideas. This improves communication, builds trust, increases efficiency, improves team morale and resolves or minimizes any challenges that they may be experiencing. It helps to build better relationships with your team. Although every IA department is different, find a way to schedule a zoom meeting or a conference call as this will help you to improve employee satisfaction. This could also lead your team to even more excellent results. Audit leaders must be available for their team members; this conveys that team members are valued and important. Thus, be always available to speak to them informally.

- Have all *staff meetings* monthly via zoom or phone call. Prepare an agenda where relevant topics are shared and discussed, such as organization changes, IA methodology changes, new QA findings or training opportunities and team celebrations (e.g. birthdays and anniversaries). This is an effective way to inspire and unify a message leaving little room for confusion. You can clarify any questions they may have. Clear communication is relevant, and audit leaders play a huge role here.

- *Celebrate* someone's birthday, team achievements and anniversaries, and schedule frequent team activities (e.g. happy hours). Celebrations should often occur in an organization. This makes work fun, releases stress, builds trust, and brings people closer. If performance is not good, I highly recommend creating smaller or easier goals so you can still celebrate and have fun with your team. You can be spontaneous; you do not need any formality to appreciate team members. This will enhance team morale and connectivity among team members.
- *Write thank you notes often.* People want to be appreciated and recognized. This can significantly impact your team and your reputation as an audit leader. Thank you notes not only change the person who receives the recognition but also change your attitude as a leader. Saying thank you makes me feel happier and more fulfilled. Gratitude has the power to change our life and the way people interact and connect. Great leaders realize how important it is to build trust; they are not afraid to show it or recognize it. Always recognize team efforts, be honest and transparent, and lead with your heart. Employee recognition should be tailored to each employer and organization. No one likes to feel undervalued, but when leaders are authentic and honest, they are fully recognized and admired by their employees and others. Employees are your greatest assets, but loyal employees are a significant asset for your team and your biggest competitive advantage.
- Conduct *satisfaction surveys*. Employee satisfaction surveys provide anonymous feedback and focus areas on improving the employee experience. A few of the best organizations I worked for conducted quarterly employee surveys. Everyone should be included. Avoid selecting only a few team members to participate in the survey; this will not be perceived as suitable by the team and could increase low morale; share the survey results with transparency and ensure actions are taken to address the audit findings identified. Audit leaders should discuss the survey results with their teams and explore options to address the concerns together to involve them in the solution.
- Assign *experienced personnel* to audits or issue validation activities, where possible. New hires should have adequate support to get familiar with the audit team, IA methodology, and the business. Also, assign top talent to more complex assignments to help their growth individually and collectively; they can develop their skills so much that they could be ready for the next promotion. Ensure they have a clear path to build their skills to move to the next level. Audit leaders must share their experiences, challenge the team, and share tips and best practices to help them adapt quickly to the organization and inevitable organizational and IA changes. Audit teams must look outside the box and find new ways to assess things differently.

- Audit leaders must always find time to *mentor* direct reports and others. They must be there for the audit team. Investing in people, training, coaching and mentoring your team is critical. Develop an approach based on positive and constructive conversations where you can coach, teach, challenge, and encourage your direct reports and others.

Audit leaders (the most experienced ones) can easily see key risks or problems where others do not and suggest ways to assess key processes or controls; they find solutions that others cannot see. They can influence others, manage conflict well, are very flexible, ask relevant questions during the meeting, challenge the team and the business with passion, bring fresh ideas to the table, and support staff thoughts and actions. Great experienced audit leaders are a competitive advantage for an IA department; they drive change wherever they go. They can develop the audit team quickly, retain talent and attack great candidates. They can easily inspire, motivate others and improve team performance.

- Discuss the staff's potential *career paths* in or outside the IA department. Great leaders always support their teams and others and are remembered for their outstanding accomplishments and passion for helping others. Caring creates trust and loyalty. Loyalty is what makes people stay and take care of the audit team. When conducting performance assessments, focus on leadership and innovation skills; this could be an opportunity to motivate your team with new goal settings and improvement. Reward individuals for doing different things that contribute to the whole team's performance and the organization.
- *Retain talent.* It is important to identify talent so you can help them to develop additional skills and move to other positions faster. The best way to identify talent is to collaborate closely with your team members, whether you are an audit director or chief audit director, to learn their preferences by listening and getting to know them personally. Through regular discussions, audit leaders can understand how to guide them to succeed. Another way to help them is to create a rotation programme to develop or enhance new and desired skills, including their leadership and emotional intelligence skills. Talent retention is key to developing strong audit teams and supporting the IA transformation. However, additional technical skills will also be required as the control environment changes. Thus, try to find a loyal employer who takes care of employees, appreciates their efforts and contributions and gives audit team members additional opportunities to succeed honestly.
- Discuss *new black swan events, challenges* and how you can help them. Maintain personalized connection with your team members. Be open and transparent so they can trust you and tell you to want they need to be

more successful. Also, leverage flexible work schedules for team members whom a stressful event has directly or indirectly impacted. Audit leaders must keep the team informed about what is going on, adjust expectations, and provide coaching and feedback to inspire team members. Use Zoom meetings, if possible, to create a personal connection with your team. Successful virtual teams have few things in common: more flexibility, effective communication, closer collaboration, and happier and more engaged employees. Of course, all this happens with only good leadership.

- *Be flexible* in adjusting your audit plan. If you do not have enough resources to complete the audit plan, do not force the audit plan to be completed without making any adjustments, this could impact your team's commitment and hurt team morale deeply. Considering the current scenario, define what is possible for your team and plan accordingly. The audit plan must be flexible to incorporate new or emerging risks and adapt quickly to new or unexpected black swan events.
- *Do not fear change.* Change can be good or bad, but do not fear it. The business changes constantly, and the IA methodology needs to be enhanced too. You may experience many changes weekly, and some team members may feel exhausted or overwhelmed. Embrace change and be clear and transparent when a new change is coming, significantly impacting IA teams or the IA methodology. Audit leaders must share their experiences and provide good examples to facilitate the discussions. For example, announcing a significant audit change or employee departure the same day or the same afternoon, or a few minutes earlier than a big IA call is scheduled, is upsetting. Thus, audit leaders must be very transparent when IA is going through many changes, as audit team members may request additional clarifications to process those changes.
- *Support innovation and relevant training.* Your team wants to learn and grow. Audit leaders must inspire creativity and change. They need to take risks, but supporting their teams is especially important. Audit leaders should support professional development through adequate and relevant training workshops, conferences and seminars. Auditors can then share the lessons learnt and best practices to add more value to the rest of the team members and stakeholders.

Also, encourage brainstorming, collaboration, constructive criticism and welcome mistakes. How can you inspire innovation if you do not allow failure? Allowing trial and error encourages team members to keep trying and stimulates collaboration. You open the door to innovation and creativity when your team is free to raise hands and share ideas and concerns. Audit leaders promote innovation, creativity and flexibility at work.

Your team needs to be organized to promote innovation and critical thinking. Allow time for critical thinking and innovation; this should be a top priority. How can your team innovate if there is not enough capacity and time? How can your team innovate when there are other key audit priorities? How can your team innovate if there is a small budget for these activities? Some companies have "innovation days" or brainstorming sessions to promote creativity at work. For example, Google gets closer to data and the real need of users. Google's famous "20% rule" encourages employees to dedicate 20% of their time to projects that interest them.

Your aim as a leader is to inspire, lead, serve and provide your team with training and better tools for growth. You also encourage growth and innovation by surrounding yourself with a diversified team with skills and experience that complement yours. You cannot do this alone, but you can accomplish marvellous things with others. A motivated workforce is a competitive advantage for any IA department.

Audit leaders must have the vision to continue seeking new opportunities constantly, to ensure audits are planned holistically, and more data is leveraged (e.g. customer complaints, operational losses, transactional data, fraud losses, technology incidents) to add more value to the entire organization. We need to adapt quickly to the new reality, the new digital and business transformation. We need to take a dynamic and more impactful approach to stay relevant. Innovation is an ongoing event, and it can only become better and better. Audit leaders should look for creativity, imagination and critical thinking when recruiting new talent. Additionally, they should encourage D&I to build even stronger audit teams.

- *Stand by your team.* The stakeholders may challenge your audit findings, but you must protect your team. They need to know you trust them and protect them from anything that happens. Audit leaders understand how to manage conflict, negotiate audit findings, and support their teams during difficult conversations. They must show empathy and respect for others even when they disagree with the challenge; however, they know how to manage each situation positively. They build respect and are recognized by the team and stakeholders for their professionalism, dedication, and passion for driving change.
- Take care of your health and mind. Keep yourself physically fit through good exercise and diet. Mental health is important for your attitude and productivity. It is important to take care of your health every day. It would help if you led yourself well to be a successful leader. A leader caring for himself can provide reliable guidance, adapt quickly to changes, and have an open mind. If you do not take care of yourself, you are telling yourself that everyone else is more important than you and teaching this

to others too. This doesn't seem right; you must lead your team by providing a good example. Lead yourself better to be a better leader.

Exercise is a great "reset switch," and here are a few additional tips:

- Make it a priority, a non-negotiable part of life.
- Make it a habit – even if you run for a few minutes, you will never regret that. It would help if you were disciplined to do something every day, even when tired. I have my routine to work out twice a day; I go for a walk for at least an hour, listen to music and then work on the treadmill for 40 minutes.
- Choose something you enjoy (e.g. meditation, yoga, reiki, reading or listening to an optimistic book, keeping a gratitude journal and spending time in nature).
- Take breaks to recharge batteries!
- Get enough sleep; rest is crucial for your body and mind!
- Eat healthily and drink lots of water.
- Spend time away from the office with your family and great friends.
- Learn when to disconnect to focus on yourself.
- Compete with yourself to be the best version of yourself. Do not compete with anyone. Focus on yourself. That's it!

We all want a work-life balance, but we are fully responsible for that. Many people do not know how to set boundaries and do not recognize when they are doing too much. I am a breast cancer survivor, and I got to a point where I had to fight for my life twice and realized how important it is to take care of myself every day. I learnt the lesson! Never take your life for granted. If you have good health, you have everything you need to be successful. Also, avoid a toxic workplace as this will not be suitable for your personal development and health. Set boundaries and work accordingly. If you are looking for a good advice now, the answer is self-care.

I want to end this chapter by leaving a few questions:

- Are you applying these tips at work?
- How can you describe your team morale? Is the staff turnover high? If the answer is yes, what is your commitment to identifying the root cause, developing, retaining talent and supporting your team?
- How do you drive team motivation?
- Are you taking care of yourself and your team?
- What helps you restore your energy and renew your soul every day?

What motivates you? Self-awareness matters. Who we are is how we lead our teams. Daring audit leaders must care for and be connected to the teams they lead. Motivate your team and see the benefits. The rest will come. Do not underestimate this topic's importance in developing stronger audit teams, especially during a pandemic or black swan events.

Can you become a better audit leader? Can you serve others better? The technical skills are not enough to motivate employees and build stronger audit teams. It would help if you had more than that; it is about connecting with your team, listening to them, allowing them to succeed, and empowering them to communicate and collaborate better. Compromised employees are more engaged, add more ideas and stay with a company longer. Do not forget to look to your team for inspiration. Pay attention to things that have worked in the past and always be open to new things, learn from others, but always do your best to motivate and inspire others. Also, do not forget an important task: take care of yourself always to serve better. Remember, your growth is a result of your self-care.

Chapter 18

How to Recognize a World-Class Internal Audit Function?

I love the topic we will cover now, how to build and recognize a world-class IA function. If you work for an IA department, are you part of a world-class IA department? Why? Please write down your answers so we can review your answers later. If you are not working for an IA department, what are the key attributes you are looking for, or how could you recognize a world-class IA function?

I am an executive audit director with over 26 years of experience in the financial sector leading complex and large projects, a few related to audits and some more focused on other key business areas or initiatives. I had the fortune to work for a world-class IA function too. My audit team was recognized for valuable insights, contributions, outstanding audit reports and the advisory role. My team was on top of everything and involved in all relevant initiatives and projects to add value or provide timely feedback to stakeholders. I built trust and reputation among peers for identifying relevant risks and providing great value to my team and other stakeholders.

Also, I developed my team so much that all stakeholders recognized the level of expertise and knowledge they had to execute audits or complete issue validation activities. The team truly felt proud of belonging to a well-recognized audit team. I had a dedicated team, a diversified team that supported each other. Our risk assessments were detailed and robust to identify our stakeholders' new, emerging or relevant risks. Our business monitoring activities were so detailed that they helped us to identify issues, anomalies or areas of concern. We did not have gaps in coverage as we did not waste our time on irrelevant topics or low-risk areas; we defined smart audit scopes and knew each corner of the business. We led the IA transformations; everything changed and improved.

As I mentioned earlier, organizations that can achieve the "World-Class" distinction have a competitive advantage, better reputation among stakeholders, more confident shareholders and board, more detailed and robust risk management, IA methodology, and stronger teams with lower attrition rate and better team morale.

DOI: 10.4324/9781003431893-19

I am going to share here a few of the main attributes to build and recognize a "World-Class" audit function:

- A *wonderful place to work*; team morale is high. Audit team members want to stay, learn and develop their skills further. They understand that this is the career path they want to take, and they benefit from a diversified mix of skills and experience. There is a strong succession plan, a detailed and relevant skills gap analysis (in skills and competencies), and stronger recruiting and training. The IA department invests so much in training and development that it is easier to attack, retain and develop talent. We are giving employees reasons to stay. Also, IA has the board of directors support as it understands how important the third line of defence is in the organization.
- The *department people want to get resources from*. The IA function is so well positioned in the organization that they wish specific resources to fill the most senior-level positions. However, recruiting them is difficult as they do not want to leave the IA department. I am a firm believer that the best auditor are the ones that have relevant experience, excellent emotional intelligence skills and can put themselves in their stakeholders' shoes. Those who understand the business well, challenge things, communicate effectively and drive positive change are viewed as business partners and sources of quality challenges.

Another sign of a "World-Class" function is when the business or second line of defence reaches out to audit directors or above for guidance or best practices. They are always busy to attend business requests. I have always supported team members to move to the business as this is another way to develop talent and add more value to the entire organization.

Many organizations suffer from a negative IA reputation due to high staff turnover, low morale, focus on irrelevant issues, and lack of value added to the business. People want to leave as soon as possible, and team members find better positions outside the department or the company. The last one cannot be considered a "World-Class" audit function; things must be done by audit leaders very quickly and diligently. Talent Management is vital to hiring, retaining, developing and attracting the best talent.

Audit leaders must ask themselves:

- How do stakeholders and audit team members view the IA function?
- Is the IA department involved in the most relevant initiatives, projects, and control forums? How is IA adding value to the organization or during meetings?
- Why are IA resources leaving heavily?

- Does IA have a strong relationship with stakeholders?
- Are you supporting team members moving to the business?

- *Rapport building.* It is important to build solid and lasting relationships with your stakeholders. We need to communicate effectively and understand the business; we must put ourselves in their stakeholders' shoes. Auditors must be ready for difficult conversations, mainly when discussing complex findings; both parties must understand that they are acting in the organization's best interest.
- *Great reputation.* Audit built such a good reputation that even challenging audit reports were well recognized and supported by senior management. Auditors question the business and may also receive many challenges due to the complexity of audit reports. However, audit directors and above strongly support the audit team even if highly challenged by the first or second line of defence. Audit teams are not intimidated by business partners; they are experienced enough to manage difficult conversations and drive change.

Integrity and ethical behaviour are key to an IA department's success. Leaders must empower teams to have difficult conversations with management but need to support them. If you are working for an IA department where you feel alone when presenting complex audit reports or findings, this is not good; specific work must be done, and audit leaders need to pay more attention to this as this contributes enormously to low satisfaction and low team morale. A difficult conversation with stakeholders is necessary and is not a mistake.

Experienced audit leaders, including chief audit directors, who understand stakeholder expectations, address business concerns and cover critical risks, including strategic business risks, can also encourage stronger advisory relationships with their stakeholders. Auditors need to educate stakeholders about risks, share best practices, and discuss new emerging risks and mitigation strategies. Also, they need to coordinate the coverage with the second line of defence to minimize duplication of efforts and testing gaps.

Audit leaders must ask themselves:

- How do the stakeholders view the IA function?
- Are you supporting your team during difficult conversations?
- Have you developed your audit team to manage difficult conversations?
- What leadership practices do you want to implement to improve IA's reputation in your organization?
- What kind of example will you set?

- What can be done to make innovation easier for everyone?
- Are you ready to encourage innovation in your organization? Is this a top priority for you?

- Constantly *striving to enhance the testing approach.* Innovation is part of the IA DNA. IA is continuously improving audit efficiencies through additional technology tools and data analysis. We cannot drive change if we do not leverage relevant or more data. Innovation is key for the IA department, but data analytics or continuous auditing tools have been implemented already. Stakeholders have experienced the value added through these innovative ideas, and audit teams have shared relevant findings and outstanding audit reports.

  The IA department has proved that efficiencies are obtained by leveraging more continuous auditing techniques during business monitoring, issue validation, and audits. The audit department is not still in the process of identifying efficiencies or is in the initial stages. Auditors understand the value of data and know how to review and analyse data or use smart data analytics tools. They have access to better technology even when conducting testing. For example, an ideal scenario is to provide auditors with tablets to conduct audits in branches or complete additional testing when visiting third-party facilities. Auditors need to look for ways to leverage more technology to be more effective and efficient; for example, notes can be taken during walkthroughs or when counting cash in the branches. Also, auditors can leverage key reports or dashboards developed or used by management during business monitoring activities. Audit leaders must embrace change and empower their teams to look outside the box to leverage better technologies and data during audit activities. Thus, we need to innovate more every day.

  Audit leaders must ask themselves:

- Is your team leveraging data? How much?
- Does your team have the right skills and knowledge to analyse data?
- Are you leveraging key management reports for business monitoring activities and other activities (e.g. risk assessments and issue validation activities)?
- Have you been effective and efficient during the last audits?
- Have you implemented any continuous auditing tools? Why not?
- Have you identified any relevant issues recently or last year by leveraging more data? Why not?
- Have you automated risk assessments, business monitoring activities, and audit reports? Why not?
- Are you truly ready to be a change agent in your organization?
- Are there any innovation champions in your audit department?

- Do you understand the value of innovation? Does your team understand it?
- Can you automate any key controls or testing to enhance assurance activities?

I am a firm believer that the best audits are the ones that leverage and use sound and relevant data. I have seen audits not conducted efficiently and effectively when reviewing previous working papers; to my surprise, data was not leveraged effectively or used. We must deliver value to our stakeholders through audits, issue validation, and business monitoring activities. Risk assessments must be more flexible to adapt quickly to organizational changes and effective in identifying new or emerging risks. IA departments need to evolve and elevate the IA function faster; we need to be more flexible and innovative to provide more value to the entire organization. We need better technologies and tools to provide smart assurance even during remote testing.

Transformation processes and strategies using digital technology can potentially improve processes and services positively. Digital transformation also requires the support of the right culture, technology and people. Companies are accelerating the digital transformation, and due to COVID-19 is becoming more relevant. Thus, auditors must explore the potential for conducting or testing things differently to add better value to stakeholders. Audit leaders need to support or create a team that can maximize relevant technology for monitoring and testing purposes.

- *Forward thinkers.* Auditors must be able to anticipate risks and audit relevant and emerging risks; they need to identify smart audit scopes to perform better audits. We cannot focus only on operational or compliance risks or leverage prior audit testing programmes. Experience matters and matters a lot! It is important and relevant to bring external auditors who have relevant experience, strong technical skills (auditing and accounting), industry knowledge, negotiation skills (getting your point across), marketing (push the visibility of your department), and SMEs (e.g. Compliance, AML, Fraud, Technology, Third-Party vendors, Cybersecurity). They may have seen the same situation in another company; they can add so much value to your testing approach that it will enhance your stakeholder's satisfaction after delivering the final audit report. Innovative ideas and suggestions for testing different areas or improving business processes and practices come from people who have experienced much in audit work.

We cannot evaluate the same risks repeatedly; we need to look outside the box and identify what can go wrong in the current environment and scenario. We cannot understand the business by reading only the policies and procedures, training, looking at prior audit work, following a checklist or testing knowledge checks because we have been doing that for a long time. I have sad news for you: you are not doing a fantastic job; you are not truly auditing your business. Audit leaders must empower team members to evaluate things differently; welcome innovative ideas; and use their imagination, creativity and common sense more when planning and conducting audits.

I am detailed oriented and always look outside the box; I never buy the first idea or approach. I have seen and experienced a lot in life and during my consulting and audit work. I am passionate about coaching my team, challenging them, and trying to teach them the best testing approach. I wouldn't say I like standard audit testing programmes; every testing approach or programme should start from scratch. We are not facing the same risks when conducting similar audits; things change constantly and even more in the business environment with more innovative technologies, new regulatory requirements, new emerging risks, and black swan events. We need more out-of-the-box thinkers in this century, more auditors willing to innovate, leverage more data, ask the right questions and challenge the business harder.

- *Management recognizes audit as a competitive advantage.* Stakeholders perceive value; they welcome audits and auditors' feedback. The board of directors or regulators may request the IA team to review key areas or processes because they trust the IA department over other options. When the audit reaches this status, others, such as the compliance and operational risk teams, will follow. The audit raised the bar, and others need to improve by default.
- *Diverse staff skills/background. We need* diversity in an IA department. We need CPAs, CFEs, CIAs, CAMs, CISAs, SMEs, people with experience and knowledge, everything that gives diverse perspectives to any audits or audit work. We need to move from traditional audits to audits that can add value to the business and the entire organization, where innovation and innovative ideas are welcome and encouraged. We need to conduct more atypical audits that consider an end-to-end process, such as the ones that focus on customer journeys, customer experience, process improvements in general, governance processes, data management, fraud management, risk management and business strategies.
- *Strong* and *robust IA methodology* to conduct end-to-end process reviews, develop strong risk assessments for all auditable entities and conduct stronger business monitoring activities to identify relevant risks. We also need adequate audit technology to facilitate the entire audit process, from staffing and resourcing, documentation of testing and findings, including tracking, monitoring, and resolution. The risk-based audit must be added to the annual audit plan based on the most current risk assessment results. Business monitoring activities are critical to constantly review the key relevant risks and processes and to have appropriate risk assessments and flexible audit plans.

Audit teams must be familiar with the IA methodology, and there should be more practical training to understand key changes that impact the audit approach. Additional training is required when changes occur too often, including effective channels or people (SMEs or QA team), to quickly answer the audit team's questions.

The IA methodology should not be changing too often. Otherwise, this does not facilitate efficiencies during the audit and could jeopardize audit consistency and compliance with the most recent changes. If the IA methodology is solid and transparent, auditors can perform better during audit engagements. When there is a "World-class" audit function, you get valuable feedback from management as you help them to sleep better at night. An audit can identify the most relevant risks; its approach is more agile and flexible to evaluate process changes, regulatory changes or emerging risks. Thus, the audit approach must evolve as the business faces new daily risks.

Audit leaders must ask themselves:

- What keeps you up at night? What could go wrong?
- What is on the agenda of the board of directors?
- What is relevant for your stakeholders?
- How often do you update your audit plan? Why?
- Is your approach dynamic, agile and flexible?
- Are your risk assessments flexible?

- *The audit directors and chief audit directors are never satisfied.* Once you get the "World-Class" designation and recognition from your stakeholders and others, your work does not end there. You will have to work more to ensure that your testing approach remains relevant and continues adding value to the entire organization. They need to be familiar with the best practices, learn from others and reach out to other organizations or colleagues to understand how they are evolving. Strong leadership is required; more innovative leaders must focus on key business initiatives, strategies and digital transformation.

The "World-Class" status attracts more high-quality individuals, more significant support from senior management, and broader acceptance within the organization. Leaders need to get accustomed to not only thinking out of the box but never getting into the box at all. This is a powerful concept. Never feel comfortable when auditing. Challenge yourself and your team nicely, so they understand that everything is dynamic; you will never find all the answers inside the box. Do not limit yourself; you need to expand your knowledge and understanding of the business but look outside the box to figure out the best testing approach.

If you go back to your initial thoughts about the "World-Class" audit, how many were on your initial list? Well, if not too many, much work must be done. How about your IA department? Can you consider your

IA department a "World-Class" now? For many organizations, getting into the IA transformation will require much work, such as additional investment in resources, technology and data analytics tools, and understanding the current stage and gaps between the current state and the desirable stage. It takes time to develop a "World-Class" audit department and maintain and continue developing it through various stages of the IA modernization process. Auditors must constantly adapt to business challenges, changes and regulatory requirements. Also, we need to allocate more time to deliver strategic audits and design and have more data analytics tools to provide relevant and faster feedback to stakeholders.

Building a "World-Class" audit function requires exemplary leadership and reputation, proper talent management practices, more experienced personnel, practical training, stronger IA practices, and significant partnerships with key stakeholders. Innovation and data analytics also play a key role in a successful IA transformation. Data analysis is still underused, so more will be required. Thus, any audit functions that can achieve these elements together should be considered a "World-Class" function.

Chapter 19

Top Internal Audit Risks and Hot Topics

The pandemic has impacted the entire world dramatically. It has had an unprecedented impact on the economy, the world of work and our mental and physical wellbeing. Companies are facing new risks; few had to shut down or reduced activities in specific locations or countries. Thus, auditors need to be familiar with new and emerging risks and understand the company strategy, operations, safety of their employees, third-party vendors' role, and other challenges. Not all companies experimented with the same risks or problems; however, we are going to cover here some key risks and hot topics as listed here:

- Fraud and other financial crime
- Cybersecurity and data security due to more remote work
- Digital transformation
- Project management
- Business continuity and crisis response
- Outsourcing and managing third-party relationships
- Effective talent management
- Health and safety of employees
- Technology risk
- Regulatory change and compliance
- Government intervention and legislation such as Coronavirus Aid, Relief, and Economic Security (CARES) Act
- Changes in policies and procedures to attend to customers' needs (change management)
- Corporate governance and reporting (data management)

Companies must consider the effectiveness of old and new controls due to changes in policies and procedures to meet customers' needs or new regulatory requirements. Suppose few controls cannot be executed due to social distancing or remote work. In that case, management needs to identify those cases, evaluate control deficiencies and design and implement

DOI: 10.4324/9781003431893-20

new monitoring mechanisms to minimize additional risks. Self-assurance activities must take over, and other monitoring strategies should be implemented to mitigate other risks. More automated controls are required, and smarter monitoring tools should be available to identify concerns or emerging risks promptly.

Although new processes or controls could be temporary, it is important to track all those changes, including the new monitoring controls implemented by Management. Approvals should be obtained from senior management; the first, second and third lines of defence must also be involved to challenge recent changes in the control environment to ensure compliance with policies, procedures, and regulatory requirements. There should be an appropriate governance framework to manage all temporarily implemented modifications. During this process, auditors need to work closely with management to understand key business priorities and changes in policies and procedures to determine the impact on the audit plan. New audits may be required to assess new customers' needs, changes in policies and procedures, and continuity of business plans, among others.

In addition, the shift to a digital world is causing additional risks such as authorized push payment fraud, which can be exploited by organized criminals. Crypto will continue to gain momentum. Remote banking fraud and cybercrime will continue to raise. Organizations need better screening and transaction monitoring tools to prevent and detect these activities, minimize risk, and provide customers with additional information. Organizations need better screening processes to evaluate customers' activities across different channels (online banking, branch banking, contact centres and ATMs), verify customers' addresses, and identify fraud activities with previous products, relationships or connections with other companies. Organized crime is sophisticated and has excellent tools and knowledge to facilitate fraud activities. Monitoring tools are highly required while organizations fine-tune their risk-based approach.

Fintechs will continue to drive innovation to manage AML and CFT (combating the financing of terrorism) risks. Some fintechs will also embrace 360 degrees surveillance on customers to better understand and identify suspicious activities. Fintechs will continue to adopt biometrics to identify customers and manage user authentication to prevent financial crime.

Here are a few key questions for management:

- Are there enough practical monitoring tools to assess additional risks or the implementation of new controls?
- How are Management tracking and sharing results of self-assurance activities and actions taken?
- Is data being leveraged for monitoring purposes or self-assurance activities?

- Is Management considering biometric authentication and blockchain technology?
- How will Management enhance transaction monitoring or customer screening?
- Does Management have a robust contingency plan for long-term remote work?
- How does the business intend to attract, retain and develop the skills required for new projects and initiatives?
- Are any areas needing additional resources to meet customers' needs or implement new processes or controls?
- Has management assessed the impact of changes in policies and procedures?
- How is management tracking changes in policies and procedures?
- Has management identified concerns with a third-party vendor?
- Has management identified key themes such as increased operational losses, fraud events or cash differences in branches, other locations? Has a root cause analysis been performed and shared with senior management?
- What information (e.g. KPIs and metrics) is being leveraged to understand how black swan events impact the business results, business strategies and third-party vendors?
- Have any key projects been held due to resource constraints or budget limitations?
- Is management investing in other technologies?
- Is management raising staff awareness of relevant cyber threats? How?
- Are security patches on personal devices being updated timely and managed adequately?
- Is there governance around key technology projects or initiatives?
- Is the project governance aligned with the approved project framework?
- Does the company have an adequate system of records to track innovation projects, budgets, progress, challenges or issues?
- Is the first line of defence paying attention to compliance requirements? How?
- Has the compliance function been impacted by black swan events?
- Have long-term liquidity risks been assessed and addressed? How?
- How effective was the company in adapting to black swan events?
- Are there any lessons learnt reports available? And how has management been monitoring corrective actions (e.g. key management reports and monitoring tools)?

Cyber risk has increased in size and sophistication as more people work remotely. The more people online, the more security is required. Cybersecurity impacts the population more often; it is not just an isolated event.

Auditors must assess cyber risk and inform the audit committee of any additional risks, corrective actions or enhancements implemented, including the effective use of user access controls and the management of PII. More frequent meetings with the audit committee may be required to explain how IA is assessing emerging risks and testing cyber risks.

In addition, IA must audit the information security functions to ensure proper controls over remote access, PII, and enterprise patch management. All means of digital communication, not just emails, must be secure from organized crime or intruders (e.g. phishing or malware infection). Also, staff awareness and understanding of information security risks are particularly important; additional training must be provided to personnel frequently. Auditors must assess this risk and include audits in the annual audit plan that considers third-party vendors' impact. Many third-party vendors may not have robust security policies and are more vulnerable to these events.

How IA can add value:

- Assess if cybersecurity awareness is adequate or if enhancements are required to provide additional information or training to personnel working remotely. For example, during training, employees should learn a few tips to enhance security at home (e.g. PII away from other members of the household, do not take pictures or save any images on your phone, design a safe and private workspace, keep children away from PII or computers during work hours, and close all browsers and applications when not working).
- Perform risk assessment of the organization's cybersecurity programme, including key risks and processes, and compare testing results with leading practice industry standards (e.g. use multifactor authentication, biometrics, do not use default passwords, revoke access immediately upon terminations, monitor privilege users, and protect home office).
- Assess the implementation of current cybersecurity models such as enhanced security breach detection and data encryption methods and access management policies and procedures to comply with the corporate's cyber-risk appetite.
- Conduct penetration testing of key systems to identify control weaknesses.
- Evaluate the ability of third-party security vendors to mitigate cybersecurity risks, including contract agreements and monitoring tools (data penetration testing with vendors). Also, ensure there is an agreement with third-party vendors to report any cyber breach that has occurred in a timely manner and in compliance with regulatory requirements. Auditors could also evaluate the incident response, if a cyberattack impacts a third-party vendor.
- Assess and monitor the security team's management strategies for increased cyber threats, including off-boarding personnel and contractors, mobile device management, phishing activity, user access and data sharing.

It is essential to train employees in cybersecurity as more events will happen. Companies must implement security awareness training, and auditors must be familiar with cyber risk to conduct smart audits. Adding real-life examples (during the training) can be extremely helpful. Training is an important ingredient of a cyber fraud prevention strategy. Cybercrime is a well-organized business; hackers are improving how they commit these crimes; they evolve fast. We need to understand how cybercriminals operate and how fraudsters and hackers interact on the internet (as both figures work together). Thus, early detection strategies or tools should be available to minimize risks.

Digitalization typically has a few goals: to enhance operations, improve transparency and facilitate business strategy and transformation. From an operational standpoint, technologies (e.g. artificial intelligence and automation) improve processes, increase customer satisfaction, reduce costs over the long term, and minimize manual risks. Companies need to be more competitive and obtain and retain more customers. During the pandemic, we realized the relevance of digital technologies to facilitate the purchase of products and services online. Most customers did not want to go to retail branches, in-store branches or other locations. The pandemic has dramatically accelerated the digital environment, product and process simplifications, and automation as an increased number of people are working remotely, and customers value security, safety and convenience. With more digitalization comes higher frauds too. Digital copy is growing across the globe. For example, in the financial sector, identity theft, account takeovers (unauthorized account access) and new accounts fraud (unauthorized use of customers' identities or information to open new accounts) are increasing dramatically.

How IA can add value:

- Review audit changes in policies and procedures and evaluate the design and effectiveness of new key controls.
- Challenge complex products, services and procedures that are not efficient at all or require many steps to process a customer transaction. Auditors need to think freely and challenge management to simplify products, services, and procedures faster.
- Assess how organizations leverage key data for strategic decisions (e.g. customer complaints and behaviours, competitors' products and services). Data access, including accuracy and completeness of data, is relevant for building stronger and more effective monitoring tools.
- Review the governance and control frameworks over digital processes, systems and data management to conclude the effectiveness of key controls and oversight activities.
- Review the change management and risk transformation processes to identify areas of opportunities, enhancements or concerns. Nowadays, we have more significant governance challenges when sensitive data

(in terms of privacy, confidentiality, consistency and other factors) is distributed across the cloud and handled during remote work.

- Identify opportunities for process automation (e.g. customer authentication, customer consent, disclosures, daily cash balancing requirements, checker controls over customer wire transfers or during the account opening process, third-party vendor payments and GL reconciliations).
- Identify common themes, concerns, and red flags raised in audit reports to identify additional opportunities for process automation or a holistic resolution.
- Assess recent technology solutions, artificial intelligence or machine learning utilized by the company to identify red flags (e.g. unusual activities that do not match with customer's behaviour, a spike in password reset requests coming from a particular IP address, the study of customer's unique behaviour or movements when processing transactions or validate access in front of a computer).

Organizations need to improve *operational efficiencies* to reduce operating losses and be more efficient when executing customer requests or transactions and opening new accounts. During a pandemic or other black swan event, cost savings may include more layoffs, freezing pay raises or promotions, closing additional branches, cancelling specific locations by not renewing office leases, and putting some key projects or initiatives on hold. Other environmental factors influencing organizational processes may include remote work, reduction in staff, organizational changes, new regulatory requirements, new mergers and acquisitions and higher fraud events.

Management must assess key processes and the most expensive ones to reduce costs. Without a periodic review of key operational processes, inefficiencies may develop over time. However, changes will always occur; controls will be simplified or removed, and additional risks could happen, too; thus, IA needs to be aware of all relevant changes and assess and evaluate the revised key controls (or new ones).

How IA can add value:

- Review high-risk processes and key controls to identify improvement opportunities.
- Leverage more data analytics tools to identify common themes and anomalies across the enterprise with a significant focus on key data points (e.g. customer complaints, allegations, operations losses, significant fraud losses and customer refunds) to identify control breaks or other opportunities for enhancement.
- Design and implement more automated auditing tools to identify new or emerging risks, concerns, outliers, anomalies and key risk indicators that could trigger certain events.

- Facilitate workshops with employees to discuss high risks and IA-leading practices to support consistent compliance with policies, procedures and regulatory requirements. Process and product simplifications should be addressed too.
- Assess the effectiveness of monitoring tools or key management reports, including self-assurance activities, to identify issues timely.
- Assess policies and procedures regarding data analytics functions, proper storage, and key controls over data repositories, change management and data access.

IA needs to identify the *key technology projects and business initiatives, project delays (if any),* and why they are still important to meet corporate strategies and goals. Auditors should assess the governance of key projects, accountability, change management process, regulatory requirements, the second line of defence involvement and challenges provided, resource capacity and budget constraints, among others. IA needs to sit at the Steering Committee table to challenge initiatives and share IA-leading best practices. Also, IA can review these key projects or initiatives earlier. For example, suppose new products or promotions are launched. In that case, IA should also attend the product approval committees to provide feedback and ensure key risks, controls and open IA issues (that may impact the initiatives) are also considered.

How IA can add value:

- Monitor key initiatives to ensure adequate execution based on business objectives and priorities.
- Provide independent assurance over project governance and strategy, including project management and monitoring mechanisms (e.g. return on investment [ROI], budget, resources, issue escalation, monitoring and resolution), regulatory requirements, third-party vendors involved (e.g. contract agreements, service-level agreements, resource capacity and potential constraints and open issues), governance forums (e.g. steering committee meetings or other operating forums/committees including the second line of defence credible challenges provided to management) and customer journeys (if defined).
- Review the QA process, including user acceptance testing (UAT).
- For those technology programmes that were put on hold (due to the pandemic or other black swan events), auditors should evaluate how management is managing risks across the areas involved, assess additional key technology solutions, review resource capacity, budget constraints, open issues and compliance with policies, procedures and regulatory requirements, including the third-party vendors, involved.

Also, one of the most important lessons from this pandemic was the importance of crisis management. Companies had basic *Business Continuity Plans (BCPs) and crisis response* plans as they were unprepared for such a complex and lengthy pandemic. We need to consider these scenarios more often in the future. Companies had to update, re-write and enhance their BCPs or develop new ones.

How IA can add value:

- Assess BCP awareness by key personnel and if enhancements are required to provide additional training. Assess the leadership's readiness for crises by surveying to determine the level of understanding and preparation to manage complex scenarios.
- Assess the safety of employees that still need to go to the office (while others are working from home). Social distancing requirements and protocols were followed in retail bank branches, in-store branches and contact centres.
- Review the ongoing programme to monitor potential outbreaks and communicate and coordinate with critical third-party vendors. Ensure the business impact analysis is robust enough and contemplates employee absenteeism, third-party disruptions and remote-control projections.
- Confirm that the business has conducted a post-mortem review to identify lessons learnt and if the BCP and crisis response were updated timely.
- Conduct an independent review of the entire crisis management system, key processes and key controls, including governance, communication and incident resolution.
- Assess the adequacy of policies and procedures and the company strategy to manage complex scenarios. A comprehensive framework should ensure the continuance of critical operations, minimizes customer and staff contact, and provides customer support (e.g. redirecting customers to electronic banking services, ATMs or contact centres).

Organizations were also impacted by *third-party vendors* that could not meet the business demand due to reduced personnel, broader restrictions and a lack of supplies. However, the pandemic increased the organization's exposure to new risks and potential compliance failures that may result in additional fines, lawsuits or reputational damage. Organizations had to re-assess the supply chain, vendors' capacity and solvency; increase management oversight activities; add, or remove a few vendors from their pipelines; or improve the contract agreements.

How IA can add value:

- Assess the vendor strategy, selection and due diligence process, including the exit strategy/termination process.

- Review key contract agreements (including the right to audit clause), ongoing monitoring activities and their capacity to meet demands or services.
- Evaluate the third-party risk assessments for high-risk vendors to remain current and relevant, especially when facing additional risks or challenges.
- Review third-party compliance with companies' information security standards, privacy and regulatory requirements.
- Conduct testing on-site (e.g. visiting vendor facilities where customer data is used to assess how PII is managed and protected and comparing third-party procedures to the organization's corporate requirements).

Another important topic is *talent management*. The pandemic has changed the rules. Few organizations laid off personnel, and more people are looking for new opportunities. During the pandemic, people needed more flexibility as their responsibilities increased at home. The search for future talents and highly skilled SMEs has been a challenge. Organizations must invest heavily in retention programmes to develop, retain and motivate personnel.

Before the pandemic, there was a strong preference for hiring employees that lived in proximity to an office. They may have worked from home once or twice weekly, but most of the time, the expectation was to be in the office. Now, they can hire people anywhere in separate locations or countries to support the business.

A few key factors contributing to a possible high staff turnover include stress, lack of flexibility, no promotions or recognition, inadequate leadership, poor communication and collaboration between management and staff, and resource gaps.

How IA can add value:

- Assess the talent pool's design and effectiveness, skill gaps, and development programmes.
- Audit the recruiting, hiring, and retention process.
- Assess the maturity of the organization's succession plan for managerial staff and technical roles.
- Audit the internal communication process, employee surveys, and results, including actions taken by management.
- Assess the performance evaluation process and exit interviews.
- Assess the wellbeing programmes available and consider employee feedback.
- Assess the corporate talent management system against leading practices (including using metrics such as incentives, remuneration, staff turnover, development programmes and training).

Leaders should have frequent conversations with their employees to help them overcome challenges. They must build stronger relationships with team members to build trust and transparency, so employees feel more secure and supported. Also, to maintain employee engagement, they can hold daily touch points, provide more flexibility to manage their schedules and provide timely feedback. Talent management is critical, and leaders must pay attention to hiring, retaining and developing promising talent.

Let's move now to the *technology risk*. Most of the workforce has moved to a remote working environment, adding new challenges. Many companies experimented with network capacity issues, VPN access and licensing. Organizations did not plan for this scenario; they had to request additional access, computers, laptops and monitors to work remotely, which took time, especially for large organizations. Organizations had to ensure network/VPN could support the remote work and employees could still execute the critical transaction.

How IA can add value:

- Review use control access for adequacy, including proper segregation of duties for current or new controls. Also, auditors can review the third-party vendors to identify potential toxic combinations that could increase fraud risk.
- Identify additional areas for enhancements that can facilitate better automated controls and self-assurance activities.
- Assess high-risk automated controls for appropriateness; leverage data analytics tools to assess process execution consistency and compliance with corporate policies, procedures and regulatory requirements (e.g. customer authentication requirements and disclosures, and privileged access).
- Identify if a few controls may be relaxed or bypassed by employees due to pressures, productivity concerns or potential sales practices; strengthening third-party vendors' monitoring activities is relevant. Also, auditors need to assess compliance with regulatory requirements (e.g. SOX compliance, and privacy and regulatory requirements).
- Leverage more data analytics as auditors can look at large amounts of data and relationships and higher-risk transactions (e.g. customer authentication, customer signatures, transactions over certain limits that require secondary approval or processed before and after business hours) to identify control breaks.
- Identify additional tools or metrics to measure workforce productivity.
- Share IA leading practices to maximize technology capabilities and capacity planning and to develop a support model to address employee issues or concerns.
- Review new digital tools deployed, ensuring a full assessment of security controls (e.g. new mobile devices, cloud solutions or additional automation deployed) and compliance with corporate policies, procedures and regulatory requirements.

Regarding *regulatory change and compliance*, federal financial services regulators are focused on the efforts of supervised entities to execute on business continuity and pandemic plans.

The Federal Financial Institutions Examination Council (FFIEC – comprising the Federal Reserve Board (FRB), Office of the Comptroller of the Currency (OCC), Federal Deposit Insurance Corporation (FDIC), National Credit Union Administration (NCUA) and Consumer Financial Protection Bureau (CFPB), released additional guidance to minimize the effects of a pandemic. Government approved $5 trillion in aid packages to help those affected by the pandemic opening new opportunities for fraud activities not just from SBA programmes but across agencies. Since the start of the pandemic, the Office of the Inspector General (OIG) has opened many complaints and investigations relating to unemployment insurance benefits paid under the CARES Act. The level of fraud has been huge (Office of Inspector General – U.S. Department of Labor – About OIG).

What have we learnt? Well, better guidance is always required before distributing funding and a robust control environment (e.g. better checker controls such as customer authentication requirements, better data analytics tools to identify red flags [e.g. customers with the same business address, phone number, IP address, and bank account number; several account applications requested for the same business account, same PO Box number or same Social Security number; IDs or business start date or registrations date not verified; suspicious email addresses that do not match the customer name or devices associated with prior fraud events). Fraud involving identity theft is the biggest complaint on hotlines. Thus, financial institutions need to reinforce customer authentication requirements to minimize risk; for example, processing transactions without proper customer authentication (IDs, biometrics) is not acceptable anymore. This is not about making the customer experience easier but always protecting customers.

Identity thieves applied for SBA loans primarily Economic Injury Disaster (EIDL) and paycheck protection programme (PPP) loans using stolen Social Security numbers and business Employer Identification numbers (EINs). Also, scammers always target consumers through phishing schemes to steal their Social Security numbers and other personal information needed to commit SBA loan identity fraud. Considering all the data breaches and privacy concerns we have seen, organizations should be more concerned about security and protect sensitive customer data across the enterprise and other key channels (e.g. retail branches, online banking, mobile, and contact centres).

SBA loan identity fraud increased in 2020 and 2021. The Federal Trade Commission (FTC) says that in 2019, they received 43,920 reports of fraud involving business or personal loans; the number more than doubled in 2020 as the FTC had 99,650 reports.

FTC pointed out that social media was a "Gold Mine" for Scammers in 2021According to the FTC (Federal Trade Commission), social media scams have increased dramatically, accounting for about US$770 million in reported losses in 2021. The FTC had more than 95,000 reports of fraud initiated on social media in 2021 across a variety of categories, including investment scams, online shopping scams, and romance scams. Fraud is a hot topic that must be considered more in future audits, especially if you are auditing financial institutions.

How IA can add value:

- Conduct an independent review of all new key controls or regulatory requirements to meet customer needs (e.g. customer communications, key management reports, monitoring activities and customer complaints).
- Assess monitoring activities over fee waivers, the extension of repayment terms and delays in payments, and confirm if management is leveraging additional data points to identify concerns or red flags.
- Assess fraud management programmes, business monitoring activities or metrics to ensure operational losses (fraud) are within threshold limits or to identify trends, concerns, anomalies or other potential fraudulent indicators (e.g. new customer applications will have to pass fraud checks and other safeguards).
- Conduct data analytics to identify non-compliance with fee waivers, customer refunds, customer authentication requirements, and account funding requirements (during the account opening process), among others.
- Review and challenge customer authentication requirements to protect and educate customers, and share best practices (e.g. to implement or expand biometrics [fingerprint and facial recognition], non-biometrics through mobile apps in branches, and online transactions).

Auditors need to be familiar with the newly emerging internal and external fraud types (e.g. healthcare-related fraud, furlough fraud, vacation fraud where fraudsters send fake links to get customers' information, identity theft, charity scams, digital copy and check fraud [it refers to any fraudulent effort to obtain money illegally by using bad paper or digital checks]). Companies need to leverage more preventive data tools to identify red flags sooner and to reduce operational losses. They must also feel comfortable with data sources, governance and critical controls to ensure the data is available, accurate, complete and effectively protected.

Before finishing this chapter, I would like to share a few tips that financial institutions could consider, enhance or implement to minimize internal and external fraud:

- Monitoring controls to ensure that key controls are being executed consistently and comply with corporate policies, procedures and regulatory requirements (e.g. customer authentication requirements, manager's approvals or secondary reviews during account opening, maintenance, and closing [maker and checker controls], customer wire transfer requests, customer's refunds, fee waivers and third-party vendor's payments). Customer signatures should be validated against IDs and other signatures on file.

- Monitoring controls over cash to ensure that daily cash reconciliations are executed and documented and daily cash differences are cleared promptly. Data analytics is important here to identify and analyse any significant cash differences in retail branches, ATMs, or bankers and assess if teller's thresholds effectively minimize operational losses. If branches are closed due to the pandemic, monitoring controls should also be implemented over cash in closed branches. Also, dual controls must be assessed, and if a higher volume of exceptions is noted across the branch network, monitoring controls must be in place.
- Monitoring controls to identify structured transactions and controls to minimize risks (e.g. employees avoiding additional authorization requirements).
- Review if mandatory training requirements (e.g. sales practices, fraud management, data management, cybersecurity, compliance requirements) are met, and proper monitoring controls are in place to identify non-compliance.
- Periodic user access reviews to confirm adequate segregation of duties exist and to minimize any toxic combinations (e.g. maker and checker controls, dual controls by different individuals, independent QA validations). One individual should not manage an entire transaction, activity or controls from beginning to end (e.g. wire transfer, customer manual payments, third-party vendors payments, bank reconciliations and GL accounting).
- Monitoring controls over all types of exceptions processed to ensure compliance with corporate policies and procedures. Maker/checker controls should be in place to minimize risks (e.g. customer requests transactions but not present in a retail branch, incomplete customer authentication requirements, account opened but not funded, accounts opened but not screened and several debit cards requested).
- Dormant accounts review (e.g. customers' accounts that did not have recent transactions but deposits over $100,000) to minimize internal manipulation. It is also important to consider sensitive data queries by bankers who do not manage specific customer accounts (potential red flag).
- Review the volume of check deposits. For example, a high volume of check deposits (through AMTs and retail branches) with immediate withdrawals or transfers to other accounts must be diligently monitored. Check-kiting takes form in two ways: issuing or altering a check or bank

draft for insufficient funds or misrepresenting the value of a financial instrument to extend credit obligations or increase financial leverage. For example, fraudsters can write themselves a check from bank account X for $5,000, even though they only have $50 in that account, then deposit it into bank account Y. They can then withdraw that money immediately from bank account Y before the bank can even verify their account X, to begin with. This is a widespread practice that generates significant operational losses to financial institutions. Better preventive controls should be in place here.

- Organizations need to look for fraud risks to protect customers proactively. If organizations believe fraud cannot occur internally or externally or only occur externally, they are not considering the ecosystem; we are all being impacted by organized crime and fraudsters. If we do not look for fraud, we cannot prevent this timely. We will continue reacting to what we know, but other things may happen without being noticed. Fraud happens often. We need more counter-fraud practices such as training and education, anonymous and secure whistleblowers' reporting mechanisms, more fraud experts that can assess fraud risk in every critical and high-risk area, better due diligence over employee background checks including contractors and third-party vendors, code of ethics with zero tolerance to fraud and a clear message from the top.
- Conduct more surprise reviews (e.g. in retail branches, third-party vendors locations [e.g. PII and handling of records]), leverage more data analytics and video surveillance.
- Reduce factors that could increase fraud, such as removing key controls or key fraud monitoring controls and minimize employee layoffs by implementing more innovative strategies to reduce costs (e.g. analyse operational losses to identify root causes, control breaks, and opportunities to reduce operating losses, voluntary reduction in paid leaves, lend employees to other companies or areas, analyse building space rented or used to reduce it [retail branch locations or other buildings], furloughs, provide additional flexibility to work from home to save on rent and other utilities or extra costs, and renegotiate contracts with third-party vendors to get better deals, to go paperless [switching to a VoIP phone system and generally opting for technology that saves money and increases productivity]).
- Monitoring controls over high-risk transactions through online banking, ATMs, and customer wire transfers across border locations (the United States and Mexico) or to high-risk countries due to potential AML risk and fraud activities. Particular attention should be placed on customer wire transfers processed (e.g. late in the day or changes to instructions, aggressive or impatient customers or urgent transfers, customer's signature that does not match the ID or information on file, wires to remove

the entire balance on the account every time a deposit is made, high volume of check deposits and immediate transfers, structured transactions [several ATM withdrawals or in branches including additional wires transferred to mother accounts or their accounts] or other unusual activities).

- Design and implement additional monitoring controls or independent reviews over manual high-risk controls to minimize errors and potential fraud (e.g. teller's decisions when processing a transaction [no formal Manager approval], verbal approvals from management when reviewing a high critical account).
- Leverage more data analytics or more data analytics tools when designing monitoring strategies. Data is key to identifying relevant fraud, AML, compliance and operational risks. For example, when reviewing account opening in general (e.g. debit and credit cards, deposit products, personal loans and mortgage loans), always check the following data points, correlations, anomalies or trends:

    - New accounts opened but cancelled immediately (high volume)
    - Accounts opened but not funded after 60 or 90 days
    - Accounts opened before or after branch business hours
    - Exceptions processed around customer's authentication, documentation or screening requirements (either small business or personal accounts), but the new account was processed (e.g. the customer was not in a retail branch, but the account was opened)
    - Several accounts opened with the same information (e.g. business address, phone number, PO BOX address and bank account number)
    - Several applications requested for the same business account
    - Customer address not verified, PO Box numbers or international addresses used.

    The business needs to design and implement more effective continuous monitoring tools or self-assurance activities to monitor, identify and follow up on red flags as banking accounts are opened daily. All lines of defence need to be more creative, proactive and realistic when designing and selecting the best approach to review key controls with relevant data. Sampling techniques will never be enough to identify red flags.

- Always leverage operational losses, fraud events or fraud losses to learn how things happened and how fraudsters knew and identified the control breaks. Suppose you also add another important topic to the equation, such as customer complaints data, allegations and NPS results. In that case, you could identify common themes, topics, anomalies, sales practices or areas of concern for further testing or to identify new issues. Thus, try to connect the dots when leveraging different data points in general; I always do this.

- Design and conduct better or smarter fraud audits, or self-assurance activities to include potential fraud risk. Fraud risk should be included in the PRCs, MCAs and RCMs, especially if the area under review is exposed to higher risk.
- Care about staff wellbeing by supporting their needs and more flexible requests.

Auditors need to add more value, sit at the table and understand the new risks and mitigating controls, especially fraud-related ones. The pandemic has dramatically changed the stakes and increased both internal and external threats. Hence, it is essential to have a more robust control environment, better technology and data analytical tools to update risk assessments and conduct more innovative audits. Reactive, post-fraud discovery investigations are costly, and fraud can dramatically impact the organization's reputation and customer experience. Prevention, creativity and innovation are critical ingredients for the three lines of defence.

The world is changing fast, and future audits will require additional expertise and more fraud experts. IA departments must prioritize critical thinking skills and encourage their teams to use more data when performing business monitoring activities, updating risk assessments, completing issue validation activities and conducting audit engagements. From a risk assessment perspective, we were not ready for such a complex pandemic; we did not even consider that something like this could happen.

If audit reports are clean or, no issues are found, audit leaders need to reassess if their teams are auditing high-risk areas, leveraging enough relevant data and having the right technology tools and skills to define the audit scope. Data analytics is essential to conduct business monitoring activities, finalize risk assessments, complete issue validation activities and conduct more brilliant audit engagements. Auditors should have an important goal in future years: leverage more data to review all key controls listed in the RCM; they should move away from sampling techniques sooner than later.

Organizations have to disclose risks and uncertainties related to the pandemic, as it impacted significant estimates (e.g. market and geographical concentrations in an area and in the volume of business with third-party vendors and customers). They must continue sharing assumptions that impact the audit committee timely. Thus, auditors must also assess the appropriateness of disclosures, assumptions, and projections.

Also, audit leaders must enhance the audit testing approach, staff skills, and supervision. Remote work may be challenging for new hires and junior audit staff. Audit leaders must be more involved in supervising their teams and work even more closely with their business partners. For example, auditors should be on higher alert for potential fraud risks. Suppose auditors noticed that the organization laid off key personnel or high-risk third-party vendors (e.g. retail branches, operations area and technology support). In that case, higher emphasis must be placed on designing the proper testing approach as internal controls could be broken due to insufficient resource capacity. Going to third-party locations could be a good option to evaluate the control environment.

In a turbulent environment and knowing the high fraud losses mentioned earlier, auditors need to adjust their audit programmes, review the risk assessments and their testing approach, and leverage more data to identify and review new risks or emerging risks. Creativity has the power to change everything; thus, we need to innovate more when assessing and reviewing key controls that may have potential fraud risk exposure. We need to understand and review fraud risk better.

Creativity is an attitude, so we need to try new ways to review a key process; we need to look outside the box and quickly identify trends, and anomalies to understand what's happening. Thus, creativity is taking risks, making mistakes and having fun with the goal of improving the way we assess things. Creativity is an attitude that auditors need to have to add more value to their stakeholders. In the next chapter, we will spend more time on the IA role in the fraud assessment process.

References

Federal Financial Institutions Examination Council (FFIEC), *Interagency Statement on Pandemic Planning*, FDIC, FIL, Washington, DC, March 6, 2020.

Federal Trade Commission, *Identity Theft Awareness Week Starts Today*, Federal Trade Commission, Washington, DC, February 1, 2021, www.ftc.gov.

Federal Trade Commission, *Social Media a Gold Mine for Scammers in 2021*, Federal Trade Commission, Washington, DC, January 25, 2022, www.ftc.gov.

Federal Trade Commission, *FTC Finds Huge Surge in Consumer Reports About Losing Money to Scams Initiated Through Social Media*, Federal Trade Commission, Washington, DC, January 27, 2022.

Office of Inspector General – U.S. Department of Labor – About OIG, *Significant Concerns*, U.S. Department of Labor, Washington, DC, September 20, 2020, www.dol.gov.

Chapter 20

Internal Audit Role in Fraud Assessments

The pandemic was brutal, and no one was prepared for that; however, fraudsters quickly took advantage of this. At the start of the pandemic outbreak, we were all reactive; we did not know how to manage the situation initially; the financial institutions and other organizations had to implement new processes and controls quickly, but now and in the future, we need to be more flexible to identify unknown risks or emerging risks. Thus, organizations need more preventive controls to identify, discuss and implement additional measures to minimize fraud risk.

Organizations need to enhance the fraud management programmes (FRM) as fraud will increase over the following years. Auditors need to understand the current fraud risk management programme and consider the following questions when completing the assessment:

- Is the organization flexible in its antifraud posture?
- Is the FRM robust?
- What are the key fraud risk drivers?
- Has the organization completed the fraud risk assessments across business areas? Is the organization incorporating key relevant data and lessons learnt into these risk assessments?
- Has the organization allocated resources to the highest priorities and high-risk processes?
- Has the organization leveraged or considered peer practices?
- Is your organization leveraging data for monitoring or self-assurance activities?
- What are the key fraud management reports?
- What information or metrics are available to detect misconduct?
- What are the key areas of concern or control breaks regarding operational losses? What could controls have prevented or detected fraud events?

DOI: 10.4324/9781003431893-21

- Has the IA department reviewed the FRM and compliance programmes related to conduct risk or misconduct?
- Does the organization identify fraud red flags or fraud trade alerts regularly? Who is responsible for reviewing this information, and how is reported to senior management?

Auditors also need to have a basic understanding of both fraud and cybersecurity risks. Can you imagine the impact of cybersecurity and fraud risk together? Additionally, professional scepticism is key; looking outside the box, asking the right questions, challenging the business and assessing fraud and cybersecurity risks are much more relevant nowadays. The pandemic has created a new set of fraud activities, so it is time to holistically review the organization's strategy, FRM and long-term goals. The FRM must be flexible to adapt to new regulatory changes, organizational and technology changes, and political landscape results of FRM activities, fraud risk assessments, fraud monitoring activities and fraud investigation results.

The responsibilities of an auditor related to fraud are to appropriately identify, assess and respond to fraud risks with due care and professional scepticism. The auditor plays a key role in determining potential fraud risk and identifying the best audit testing approach. This discretionary aspect is tied to the requirement that the auditor maintains an attitude of professional scepticism when conducting an audit. However, detecting fraud is not the auditor's primary responsibility, so they do not need to be an expert. The primary responsibility to detect fraud is on management, but if management does not disclose that to the audit team, it will be harder to detect fraud.

The gaps of misunderstanding among management, the public and auditors about the roles of internal audit-related to fraud risk still exist. For example, when there is fraud in an organization, shareholders and senior management will challenge the IA team: why did the audit not detect the fraud event? What did IA review in the past? Or the worst-case scenario, the entire IA team is changed due to the magnitude of the fraud event identified. The reputation of the IA department can be highly questioned.

IA should have enough knowledge of fraud to:

- identify red flags indicating fraud may occur and determine whether further actions would be required or an investigation should be recommended.
- evaluate the design and effectiveness of key controls to prevent or detect fraud.

However, what exactly is fraud? Fraud refers to a deception that is intentional and caused by an employee or organization for personal gain. To meet the legal definition of fraud, we need to see the damage, usually money, to the victim. For example, a teller who takes cash and submits a cash difference is committing fraud. The organization is absorbing the operational losses. Another example of a third-party vendor is billing duplicate invoices for services never provided to the organization; thus, the third-party vendor is committing fraud.

Under the common law, fraud must be proved by showing that the defendant's actions involved five separate elements: (1) a false statement of a material fact, (2) knowledge on the part of the defendant that the statement is untrue, (3) intent on the part of the defendant to deceive the alleged victim, (4) justifiable reliance by the alleged victim on the statement and (5) injury to the alleged victim as a result.

Government regulatory authorities, such as the Securities and Exchange Commission (SEC) in the United States, use laws and regulations to prevent and detect corporate fraud. The Sarbanes-Oxley Act of 2002 (U.S. PL 107–204) was established after significant fraud events committed by Enron and WorldCom. Sarbanes-Oxley required more frequent disclosure by public companies to prevent fraud. It also enhanced the SEC's power to monitor and investigate compliance with securities laws, adding stiff penalties for fraudulent behaviour by corporations, their officers and their accountants. This has increased the role of internal and external auditors and audit committees.

One of the more recent corporate fraud cases is that of Wirecard, a payment transfer and processing company in Germany. In early 2020, auditors discovered a $2 billion discrepancy between the company's books and the actual money it held. Wirecard had been cooking its books for several years. German authorities arrested the CEO, and the company filed for insolvency on June 25, 2020.

The IA function must be more flexible and innovative to identify and proactively detect fraud risks. Companies need more data analytics to identify potential fraud events or assess fraud risk. Thus, auditors need to consider key topics when conducting business monitoring activities, validating issues and conducting audit engagements as listed below:

- Use better data analytics tools and technology solutions to identify common themes and anomalies that may highlight potential fraud events (e.g. higher cash differences, more significant or unclear operational losses, higher third-party vendor payments, an excessive number of exceptions processed, high volume of customer complaints). Does management have proactive data monitoring tools or key management reports to identify, track and analyse red flags?

- Hire auditors with fraud expertise, such as CFEs, who can assess and evaluate potential fraud risk over high-risk processes (e.g. during the risk assessment construction, business monitoring activities, issue validation activities and audit engagements).
- Assess the appropriateness of fraud risk assessments for each business area, including anti-fraud policy, code of conduct, key policies and procedures, and technology tools to ensure consistency and transparency across the organization. Does the organization have a fraud response plan, an anti-fraud policy and key policies and procedures? Does the organization identify the anti-fraud controls in the PRCs or MCAs? Auditors should review the design and effectiveness of anti-fraud controls (e.g. management reviews, maker and checker controls, controls over employee override decisions, key automated controls, mandatory absence, user access, hotlines, allegations, background checks and pro-active data monitoring tools such as trade surveillance alerts).
- Assess cybersecurity and fraud risks together. We need to review cyber more holistically by considering potential fraud risks such as identity theft, anonymous payments or red flags.
- Review if the organization has an independent fraud investigation department that reviews and investigates fraud cases (internal and external fraud cases); thus, assess the skills and capacity of the team, quality of fraud reports, challenges provided to management and corrective actions requested (if required).
- Review business continuous monitoring tools, self-assurance activities, key management reports, escalation protocols and key forums (e.g. independent audit committee and ethics committee) where fraud concerns are reported, discussed, analysed and corrective actions are discussed (if required).
- Review the fraud training for employees and if delivered to key personnel such as those who manage cash, customer PII or book entries in the GL (e.g. tellers and bankers, contact centre, treasury, operations, finance departments). Is fraud training delivered to managers and executives? What's the training completion rate?
- Review employee support programmes, job rotation, mandatory absence and hotlines. Accordingly, to the "Occupational fraud 2022: a report to the nations" (published by the ACFE, 2022), organizations with hotlines detect fraud faster and have lower losses than organizations without hotlines. However, whistleblowers used more emails and web-based/online reporting than telephone hotlines.
- Assess if organizations have implemented an independent and robust whistleblowing programme to promote transparency and discourage retaliation.

- Review the disposition of the whistleblower complaints (during business monitoring activities) and determine if additional testing is necessary. Also, auditors should consider operational loss data and customer complaints data to identify potential fraud risk concerns (e.g. in the retail branch network, store branches, ATMs including online banking, insurance claims and third-party vendors).
- Assess if management conducts post-mortem reviews to identify lessons learnt, control breaks, root causes and corrective actions (if required). Did management modify the anti-fraud controls or implement additional control following a fraud?
- Identify red flags when interviewing personnel such as employees that:
  - live beyond their means,
  - do not cooperate with audit requests or others, so they are too defensive when discussing audit issues or other topics,
  - do not want to share controls,
  - have unusual close associations or relationships with customers or key third-party vendors,
  - do not take vacation time and,
  - have financial difficulties or family problems.

Auditors must educate management about fraud risk and audit role when identifying red flags. Suppose management does not want to buy an issue or challenges auditors hard. In that case, auditors will need to provide additional information and metrics and share leading best practices to ensure management understands the issue's impact. When auditors suspect that a fraud event has been happening for a long time (after conducting additional testing), audit leaders need to encourage senior management to request an internal investigation.

Management needs to understand when fraud could occur, and what relevant controls and monitoring strategies must be in place to minimize fraud risk. Adequate and robust fraud awareness programmes must be designed, developed and implemented to reduce fraud risk. Suitable people must be involved in identifying potential fraud risks, key controls and monitoring tools in each area of the organization.

Compliance and IA teams should be involved in fraud awareness processes to share best practices and challenge the business. Auditors can add value during this exercise; the advisory role is critical. Auditors can participate as facilitators, advisors and educators by delivering adequate training, participating in brainstorming sessions and challenging fraud risk assessments. In one of my past audits, I identified a global fraud risk issue that required additional conversations with the international fraud team; the global fraud programme had to be enhanced as more effective fraud investigations were needed. The audit team added outstanding value to the organization by sharing valuable leading best practices. However, I never gave up despite the challenges I received when I started sharing this finding. Auditors must be courageous and determined to challenge things and drive positive organizational changes.

Thus, IA departments must emphasize having adequate fraud skills when conducting audits in general. We cannot challenge a fraud risk assessment performed by the business without having the right skills and understanding of the key processes and key controls. We need to evaluate potential fraud risks in high-risk processes and assess the design of key controls. I encourage my team to take additional certifications, especially the CFE, as it provides auditors with the knowledge and skills required to evaluate key processes and controls better. Unfortunately, fraud has always been with us, and it has intensified during the pandemic and will grow.

After detecting a fraud, internal auditors should notify the legal or fraud investigation department or the fraud risk management unit (FRMU). Thus, a fraud investigation is a next step; the investigation team must investigate the event. The board of directors and senior management must be notified immediately if internal fraud is suspected. The audit committee needs to ensure that internal and external auditors fulfil their responsibilities related to potential fraud events. Most audit committees will want to obtain additional information about the control break, impact, root cause and management corrective actions, including lessons learnt (despite an investigation being in progress).

A fraud assessment or evaluation is different from a fraud investigation. Audit leaders must establish the right approach and expectation for when, how and why they should be involved in a fraud investigation if required. Specific IA departments have an IA fraud team that supports fraud investigations in conjunction with the corporate investigation team; others prefer not to be involved. In addition, an investigation must follow additional protocols regarding interviews conducted, confidentiality, retention of evidence and documentation requirements and fraud report.

If auditors need to participate in fraud investigations, the following topics should be considered:

- The audit chapter must identify audit responsibilities related to fraud investigations.
- Resource capacity to manage the investigations as a dedicated team is desirable, knowing that greater fraud skills are required. The CAE must ensure that the assigned unit or individuals have adequate knowledge, expertise and reputation to manage the fraud investigation. If the audit lacks expertise, the CAE must evaluate the approach and whether an external investigator is needed.
- Approval from the audit committee as a budget and resources are required to conduct fraud investigations successfully.

- An IA contact (IA general counsel) who will authorize the IA participation in the investigation upon request. Before assigning any IA personnel, the conflict of interest and independence must be assessed diligently.
- If an internal legal counsel is required, additional protocols must be implemented to manage the communication, evidence, documentation and further interactions during and after a fraud investigation. Also, it is important to assess if others must be involved (e.g. HR, more qualified fraud experts or CFEs, forensic accounting consultants and third-party vendors that can extract or analyse data relevant to the investigation).
- Communicate the approach to follow when fraud cases are identified during audits.
- Design and implement adequate protocols and procedures (to manage the interviews, confidentiality, evidence retention, escalation protocols and final report).
- Define the data analytics approach to use relevant data during the fraud investigation.
- Keep the fraud investigation confidential.
- Exercise professional scepticism.
- Define a reasonable timeline and a plan to conduct the investigation and deliver the report timely.
- Comply with the policies and procedures that govern fraud investigations at the corporate level.

A fraud investigation is not typically an IA responsibility; fraud investigations are best managed by more experienced personnel outside the IA department. Organizations should not expect IA to conduct fraud investigations; however, IA can review if key controls are implemented by management to minimize fraud risk and detect and prevent fraud.

Fraud Risk Testing and Examples

We are going to cover here additional tips and examples to facilitate the fraud assessment and testing of fraud risk for financial institutions:

- Develop continuous auditing tools to assess fraud risk for each auditable entity, especially if the fraud risk driver is rated high or critical.
- Improve access to the news and social media information that could highlight situations or events that may have impacted your organization or your customers. I always search the internet for new fraud events that affect the financial industry globally or those related to specific hot topics (e.g. branches, ATMs, safe deposit boxes and third-party vendors, including armoured services). Always search online for additional information or events if you are auditing a specific topic or area.

- Develop a fraud risk assessment guideline to ensure consistency across all auditable entities in terms of quality or quantitative measurements (e.g. transactional data, operational losses and fraud losses, customer complaints regarding fraud, staff turnover, open issues, policies and procedures, and fraud training programme).
- Although some auditors may be using more data analytics to identify unusual transactions and trends, more analytical tools or key reports are required during business monitoring activities, issue validation activities and audits; auditors need to be very agile to assess potential fraud risk. They should access significant fraud events, including operational losses, allegations and customer complaints. If you review the data, what does the data tell you:
  - higher cash differences or operational losses in certain retail branches, ATMs in specific locations or in-store branches and online banking.
  - higher volume of exceptions in specific branch locations, or processed by bankers or tellers, employees.
  - higher operational losses, fraud events, allegations, customer complaints and refunds. These are a few examples, but they may require additional research, testing and further analysis to conclude.
  - Payments made to third-party vendors that do not exist or customers who weren't supposed to receive those payments.
- Develop an IA mandatory fraud training for all auditors that incorporates real case examples. Annual training (e.g. fraud awareness, red flags and ethics) is excellent, but it is also essential to have training that is continual and in motion when new events occur.

Let's focus now on a few exciting areas for further testing in financial institutions:

- Auditors should review the incentives provided to key personnel (e.g. branches, wealth management offices, third-party vendors). They should be able to assess opportunities, pressures and rationalization to commit fraud when updating risk assessments, conducting audits (e.g. branch visits, team member experience with performance evaluations, incentives calculations), interviewing personnel and reviewing key management reports. Also, it is essential to assess if incentive plans were approved at least by the HR and finance departments. Auditors should also review customer complaints data to identify themes, trends or concerns.
- Third-party vendors are now an essential inclusion in an anti-fraud programme, the more complex the organization, the more extensive the third-party vendor inventory and risks. The most common fraud events are fictitious billing (fictitious vendors), duplicate payments, overbilling,

bribery or extortion and poor vendor vetting. Auditors should review the following:

- Vendor's address (a PO Box number is a red flag).
- Vendor's emails: for example, general email addresses such as @gmail.com, @yahoo.com and @pp.com or lack of websites or details are a red flag.
- Disbursements to identify anomalies such as duplicate payments, rounded total payments (this is a red flag), fictitious invoices or sequential numbers (red flag). Also, it is essential to review the vendor database to identify additional anomalies, such as missing or same data across different vendors.
- Central price and supplier tracking system to review products, services, bids, prices, payments made and supporting documentation.
- Contractual clauses such as the right to audit, anti-corruption/anti-fraud clauses to facilitate audit mechanisms and punishment systems if defaults happen.
- Fees or incentives agreed (contract agreement) to minimize potential sales practices.
- Due diligence (background checks, screening) process and business monitoring activities to ensure compliance with contract agreements, SLAs, policies and procedures.
- Changes in risk assessments or third-party vendors' inventory for further research and analysis.
- Customer complaints and how these complaints were resolved by third-party vendors or management.
- Operational losses or fraud events, if any.
- Additional guidance developed by management regarding procurement strategies under a crisis.

Organizations need to enhance the vendor selection process, including the vendor vetting process, to ensure transparency and minimize employee collusion, unfair practices, fictitious invoices, duplicate payments and conflicts of interest. The vetting process needs to be effectively managed and well documented. This could include verifying the US federal tax identification numbers (FEIN) against the IRS website; screening to determine if vendors and officers are on sanction lists or have a criminal background or undisclosed relationships; and verifying vendors' addresses, phone numbers and references. Also, it is important to verify the age of a business (especially during the pandemic considering the fraudulent activities committed), review the filings with the secretary of state, and use data aggregation like TransUnion, LexisNexis and Thomson Reuters, among others. Having the correct data is critical to complete effective audit testing and identifying anomalies, trends or concerns (e.g. companies with the same email addresses, mailing addresses, phone numbers, fax numbers, internet protocol (IP) addresses, bank account information and recent company and subcontractors' changes and bid pricing patterns).

Let's move to additional examples regarding investments, deposit products and other products (e.g. debit and credit cards, personal loans, mortgage loans); auditors should review the design and effectiveness of key controls to minimize potential fraud risk as listed here:

- *User* access to ensure that there is adequate segregation of duties. For example, a banker should not control all transaction steps, so a maker and a checker control must be in place. A continuous auditing tool could be designed to monitor user access quarterly.
- *Mandatory absence* for sensitive positions; a minimum of two consecutive weeks of absence should be required in sensitive positions. Employees with electronic access to systems and records should not have access during this period for this policy to be effective. Thus, auditors must review mandatory absence to ensure compliance with policies and procedures. If exceptions are identified, auditors must confirm if the business conducted a look-back review and if an unusual activity was identified. If waivers are provided to specific personnel, adequate compensatory controls must be in place to monitor their actions during the waiver period. Proper approval and rationale should be obtained and documented. A continuous auditing tool could be designed to monitor mandatory absence quarterly.
- A *clean desk* during unannounced branch visits to identify any suspicious documents (e.g. blank forms signed by customers, customer's token, credit or debit cards inside banker's drawers, customer's complaints not entered in the system, and printed account statements when policy does not allow to print any). Auditors should consider this information a red flag and perform additional testing to ensure compliance with record retention and information security policies.
- *Net key delivery.* Auditors must review and test key controls in branches such as customer authentication, maker and checker key controls, mandatory documentation and customer presence through video surveillance (just to verify that the customer was present when a transaction was requested and processed).
- *Account statements.* Controls should be in place to manage customer PII. Financial institutions may not allow account statements printed in branches or only following specific key controls or protocols. Account statements should not be mailed to or from branches, so auditors need to check if some bank accounts have either a branch address or a PO

Box address. If bankers have account statements (during the clean desk testing), auditors need to understand if there are key controls in place to manage all until delivery or destruction.

Account statements can be modified, altered and used to perpetrate fraud; financial institutions have suffered internal fraud due to a lack of controls. Financial institutions may not even offer hold-all mail services to minimize fraud risk. A customer envelope must be stored in a secured location under dual control if sent to a branch location (red flag). Another continuous auditing tool could be designed and implemented here to identify accounts with branch locations or PO Box addresses (red flag).

- *Account maintenance.* Suppose bankers, tellers or other contact centre employees speak with the account holder. In that case, they will have to authenticate the customer and verify the customer's signature before processing any account maintenance changes (e.g. name, phone number, address, signatories, beneficiaries and PIN) to minimize the account takeover fraud. Customer authentication must be executed without exceptions to mitigate potential fraud risk. Additional changes to account information, such as beneficiaries, will require additional screening, authorizations and documentation requirements. Adequate checker controls or an independent verification team are highly recommended to meet customer authentication and documentation requirements (especially if accounts are opened through online banking).

  By generating a query or daily report of credit or debit card requests made within two to three days of address change requests, financial institutions could identify red flags before mailing cards to customers. Another analytical tool could be to create a list of all locations where fraud activities are more common across the United States (e.g. cross-border locations, California, Florida, Texas) and ask the data analytics team to pull address changes or new accounts opened against this file to identify red flags (monthly basis).

- *Customer wire transfer requests.* Wire fraud is a federal offense under U.S. law and refers to fraud committed using electronic communications such as telephone or computer. Wire fraud has been increasing globally and will become more challenging to detect as fraudsters leverage different channels (e.g. retail branches, ATMs and online banking), make check deposits and immediately withdraw or transfer funds to other accounts.

  Wire fraud patterns are shifting to higher-value luxury automobile and real estate transactions. Financial institutions need additional tools to monitor and flag those transactions across different channels. Auditors must conduct holistic audits to review customer behaviour, trade alerts and red flags across multiple products and channels. More continuous auditing tools will be required to audit high-risk processes and review key controls and regulatory requirements.

Auditors need to leverage more data and focus on significant concerns such as:

- Fraud losses are concentrated in specific locations.
- Customer's signatures that do not match the documentation on file.
- Customer's consents and disclosures not timely provided.
- Multiple wires process below $10,000 or additional signs of structured patterns.
- Inactive investment agreements or exceptions processed for a high volume of wires.
- Frequent changes to customer wire transfers or instructions.
- Wires to high-risk countries or business that is unreasonable.
- High volume of instructions after processing demographic changes (e.g. change in address and phone numbers).
- Many wires to remove the entire balance once a deposit is made.
- Customer wire transfer requests processed in a few seconds when the process should have taken longer by the procedure document. Maker and checker controls must be in place to authorize each transaction or transaction over specific amounts. Auditors must verify that the approval limits are reasonable, in compliance with the procedure document, and applied consistently across the retail branch network.
- Incomplete customer authentication requirements. Customer authentication requirements should be described in the wire policy and procedure document, and auditors should review the key controls to minimize fraud risk.

Wire fraud happens due to many factors such as poor customer authentication processes, no key controls in place (e.g. maker and checker controls), red flags or overrides decisions processed by tellers without proper supervision, callbacks not conducted over required limits or done to the wrong number. Auditors need to review the wire policy and evaluate the key controls to minimize potential fraud risk.

Automated controls must be in place to minimize fraud risk (e.g. maker and checker approvals, exceptions or red flags should be approved by a manager or above, and callbacks may be required [over specific amounts] to comply with the wire policy and procedure documents). However, the initiation and processing of wire transfers should not be executed solely by automated systems. All wire transfers must be processed using dual controls. There should be human intervention, where two or more high-level managers review and approve the transaction (checker controls). Also, the wire agreement should be amended if the parties to the wire transfers have changed.

For large transactions or frequent wires processed in branches, I highly recommend leveraging video surveillance to confirm that the customer authorized those transactions. Also, auditors should review user access (tellers and bankers) to ensure that all approval limits correspond with their roles and responsibilities. Risks associated with wire transfer controls should be taken seriously as fraud events could also increase the company's reputational risk. Thus, wires should be evaluated continuously if the organization process a high volume of transactions.

- *Customer complaints.* Fraud complaints must be analysed, who managed the complaints and how all were resolved. This can provide additional details of control breaks. Adequate segregation of duties is necessary to ensure customer complaints are resolved timely and by independent personnel.

  Let's discuss one example here:

  - A banker has been committing a particular fraud. He opened a customer investment account, accessed the customer's online account, moved funds without the customer's consent and sent the account statements directly to his branch location.
  - The customer trusts the banker so much that he always calls the banker to confirm the balance; the banker helps the customer immediately, even with customer complaints.
  - The same banker has resolved customer complaints. However, one day something happened. The customer went to another branch to request his account statement and realized that something happened with his investments. Numbers do not match with prior account statements.
  - This is a good example; it could happen without proper controls. Thus, I always prefer having key controls in branches, such as adequate segregation of duties to open, monitor and resolve customer complaints (independent team). Also, account statements should be sent to customers, not branch locations.
  - Thus, complaint data should be analysed with operational losses, fraud events and staff turnover to identify trends, concerns or control breaks. Also, user access should be reviewed frequently to minimize potential fraud risk. Of course, if you have a good, automated tool to complete user access testing, it will facilitate the identification of toxic combinations. These ideas could be considered during business monitoring, issue validation activities and audit engagements.

- *Account opening process.* New account fraud typically happens within the first 90 days a bank account is open, so financial institutions must watch new accounts diligently for suspicious activities. Additional monitoring must be in place to identify red flags. Also, most fraudsters will start making small deposits and withdrawals in the first month. A maker and independent checker control must be in place (in branches or outside branches) to ensure compliance with screening and documentation requirements (e.g. customer authentication, signature verification, customer consent and disclosures).

Let's review a few additional red flags or trends to watch for:

- Many new account fraud perpetrators will make deposits on a Friday or Saturday before a banking holiday to have additional time to withdraw the funds before other financial institutions return checks due to forged, stolen and counterfeit checks. Check fraud occurs due to weak controls or lack of controls such as no check holds placed, immediate availability of check funds, weak customer authentication and check reviews (e.g. forged, altered, counterfeit checks not noticed by tellers). Then, the checks are returned later (by other financial institutions), but unfortunately, the money is already gone. The bank will have to recognize an operational loss if the money cannot be recovered.

- Fraudsters can easily open new accounts with information on the internet, so always look for unestablished businesses or those with little or no information online. Moreover, business accounts are often given additional privileges for being business accounts and more significant daily maximum withdrawal limits. For example, another red flag could be if the applicant's home or business address is not in the exact location where the account was opened.

- There are several fraud cases connected with accounts opened online as they do not require funding and can easily be opened through a contact centre or online banking. Auditors should develop more data analytical tools to identify red flags (e.g. many debit cards requested or accounts opened in different retail branches and online for the same customer, different customers with the same phone number, address or customers using mail drop instead of an actual address, expired IDs).

- Remote deposit frauds are happening very often due to the following control breaks:

  - no manual reviews conducted on all checks or over a certain threshold amount,
  - altered/stolen checks deposited through ATMs, so funds are available immediately,
  - duplicate checks services not used,
  - customer authentication is not required,
  - check images not reviewed,
  - no fraud monitoring tools implemented by the business to identify red flags (e.g. same account and routing number involved in prior fraud events but not noticed).

- *During* the pandemic, organizations implemented *new products, services and changed processes* to serve customers better. When there are significant changes, auditors need to assess how the new way to interact with customers brings additional fraud risk. For example, when we add cybersecurity to fraud risk, there is a more significant concern here as this is another sophisticated way to commit fraud. Criminals are interacting with companies through different channels and products, so auditors need to assess how fraud could be committed and leverage relevant data to identify those anomalies. We should not underestimate the power of modern technologies and innovative solutions when assessing fraud risk. Hackers are constantly identifying new ways or advanced ways to commit a crime. When companies can mitigate the risk or enhance additional controls, fraudsters will find another way to commit the same or more significant crimes. Fraudsters go to the dark web and ask for help from others to get into specific accounts. They ask for passwords, share information and are effective in committing fraud.
- *Fraudsters* also use call centres to change addresses and phone numbers; the new checks are mailed to revised addresses. They use dormant accounts, and sometimes they know the victims to get additional information from them quickly. *Dormant accounts* are deposit accounts that have been inactive for a period or for which contact with the account holder has been lost. Dormant accounts are extremely attractive to fraudsters due to the lack of customer activity and management oversight activities to notice unfamiliar transactions, trends or anomalies (lack of transaction monitoring tools).

   Let's review a few potential control breaks that can facilitate these fraudulent activities with dormant accounts:

   - There is no adequate oversight, monitoring activities, or even maker and checker controls over dormant accounts.
   - Returned emails managed by a team that reconciles or monitors these accounts.
   - There is no adequate communication or follow-up with customers before moving accounts to inactive status.
   - Employees have improper user access to these accounts; no adequate segregation of duties exists so they can process transactions without customer's requests or move funds to active and inactive status very frequently without proper supervisory approvals.
   - There are no adequate controls in branches when customers want to withdraw money or transfer to other accounts (e.g. no proper policies or procedures, no customer authentication protocols followed before processing customer requests).

Auditors should consider the following testing procedures:

- Perform monthly trend analysis to identify concerns, anomalies or red flags; the business should have effective monitoring reports so auditors can leverage this information for monitoring purposes.
- Conduct a look-back analysis on dormant accounts and reconcile the monthly dollar amount to identify unusual activities by considering additions, transfers or withdrawals shortly before and after the account hits dormancy.
- Review user access (e.g. adequate segregation of duties, maker and checker controls should be in place) to minimize fraud risk.
- Review all related policies and procedures to ensure key controls are noted (e.g. customer authentication and documentation requirements, manager's approvals over customer withdrawal or when accounts are moved to an active status, and user access).
- Review customers' addresses to identify unusual transactions such as account maintenance activities before or in dormant status (changes in addresses or phone numbers).
- Returned emails are overseen by a department other than branch personnel, contact centres and third-party vendors (segregation of duties).
- Auditors could develop and implement additional continuous monitoring or auditing tools to enhance business monitoring activities and testing during audit engagements.

- *Safe deposit boxes.* Unfortunately, safe deposit box fraud still occurs in financial institutions across the United States. There are few frauds on the news as customers' items are lost or stolen. The number of bank branches in the United States has been declining, and sometimes, safe deposit boxes are misplaced or impacted by hurricanes. No federal or state laws limit what customers can store in a safe deposit box. The Federal Deposit Insurance Corporation does not insure it.

  Also, during the pandemic, banks have reduced operating hours or temporarily closed a few branches with safe deposit boxes limiting customer access. Others may require just an appointment to access their safe deposit boxes. Thus, auditors need to assess the following key controls or processes:

  - Account opening and customer authentication procedures. For example, customer authentication protocols are followed in retail branches before granting access to customers or third-party vendors. Also, safe deposit boxes should be offered to customers with a transactional history with the bank to minimize AML risk.

- Customer authentication requirements. For example, account maintenance requests should be processed after completing customer authentication requirements.
- Dual controls over third-party vendors engaged in the safe deposit box drill-opens. Records of all entries retained and documented, including a description of items found.
- Segregation of duties; for example, maker and checker controls during the account opening process (e.g. customer screening, customer agreement and disclosures, manager's approvals).
- Customer's contract agreements signed timely or amended, if requested.
- Inventory of keys; this inventory should be maintained and reconciled (e.g. rented and non-rented keys kept under dual controls).
- Training available. Bankers must receive specialized training to identify suspicious behaviour. If the number of safe deposit box visits does not match the system that electronically monitors all transactions, it may be a red flag. Also, the customer has a few safe deposit box visits or safe deposit boxes in separate locations but no activity on their other bank accounts or where they live. Thus, auditors could design additional continuous monitoring tools to leverage more data and be able to identify these or other anomalies.

I want to discuss another important topic related to cash management in a branch network, especially during a pandemic or another black swan event. Cash could be manipulated and stolen due to control breaks, lack of management oversight activities (e.g. no maker or checker controls in place, no automated controls to process key transactions [e.g. user access, screening process, resolution of red flags sent to branch personnel], no daily cash reconciliations performed by branch personnel, no key cash management reports to identify and follow up on cash differences).

Management should develop policies and procedures to manage cash and set or modify teller's thresholds (if required) to manage the identification, escalation and investigation of irregularities noticed, including cash reconciliations or cash shortages. Usually, when the inherent risk for cash is high, auditors need to assess if the key controls are adequate to mitigate the fraud risk. However, fraud risk is higher during the pandemic, considering the inherent risk associated with cash.

Adequate segregation of duties (e.g. maker [teller] and checker controls [manager or above]), detailed policies and procedures, daily cash reconciliations [e.g. surprise cash counts of cash, foreign currency, vault and ATMs to the system of records], reasonable teller cash limits (they should not be too high) or cash differences [thresholds]) are usually the most critical internal controls over cash. Are cash thresholds adequate or too high to minimize operational losses? All cash differences must be identified, tracked, monitored, followed up and cleared timely.

Although management should be responsible for designing and implementing key controls in a branch network, cash differences must be reviewed by an independent unit (it is better to rely on a separate team outside branches and within the operations area) to minimize fraud risk. This independent unit could also request corrective actions when those differences are over the approved thresholds or escalate concerns to the investigation department (due to significant cash trends identified or unexplained cash differences). I recommend developing additional continuous monitoring tools to review key cash controls quarterly. Cash is a high-risk area, especially in an extensive branch network.

I love assessing fraud risk when conducting audits; I read articles about internal fraud cases or external frauds. Not many fraud cases go public, but there is much information online to leverage or educate us better. Another important thing is networking with SMEs, CFEs and other professionals. I enjoy educating others but also learning from others.

To minimize internal fraud, it is essential to understand the company culture. Several examples and corporate scandals at companies have shown the negative impact of a poor ethical culture. Thus, IA should also review the organizational culture and conduct a culture audit; let's move to this important topic now.

References

ACFE, *Occupational Fraud 2022: A Report of the Nations,* March 2022, https://acfepublic.s3.us-west-2.amazonaws.com/2022+Report+to+the+Nations.pdf.

US Department of Labor, *Sarbanes-Oxley Act of 2002, Public Law 107–204,* US Department of Labor, Washington, DC, www. dol.gov.

Chapter 21

Internal Audit Role in Auditing Culture

The corporate culture reflects the behaviour of managers and employees, how they interact with each other, how they interact with the second and third lines of defence, regulators and external auditors, and how they resolve issues. Are stakeholders challenging auditors too hard? Can they stand constructive criticism? Is senior management too worried about getting a bad audit rating report rather than fixing the issues identified? Are they willing to share relevant information timely or to cooperate with auditors? Can you speak openly with senior management? Does the organization have a good reputation? Ethical behaviour is a critical ingredient of good corporate governance.

An organization cannot build or enhance the culture in a month, during training or during key meetings with senior management. It takes time to educate everyone, promote open dialogue, empower employees to react or escalate things further and compromise to the highest standards possible, even during difficult times or under pressure. The financial crises of 2007 and 2008 left lessons, but the main one was that a robust risk culture should permeate all levels of the organization. The corporate culture impacts everyone in the organization; we are all part of an ecosystem, and everyone is responsible for raising hands, challenging others and doing the right thing.

High-profile scandals such as those at Toshiba and FIFA have demonstrated the impact of a poor corporate culture. For example, Toshiba overstated its earnings by more than $1.9 billion for years. Toshiba's toxic ethical tone at the top was the primary cause of its improper accounting practices. Regarding the FIFA scandal, the investigation revealed a toxic culture of unethical behaviour, non-compliance and corruption that started from the top and trickled down to every facet of the organization. A poor culture that promotes unethical behaviour and facilitates corruption dramatically impacts the entire organization and its reputation and loses customers' trust forever.

Corporate culture matters and must be a top priority for senior leaders, the board of directors and the company; an aligned corporate culture

DOI: 10.4324/9781003431893-22

improves performance, employee satisfaction, retention and morale. A misaligned corporate culture disempowers employees and encourages unethical and unhealthy behaviours such as sales. The CAE should understand the style of key senior leaders to manage the relationship adequately and identify instances of lack of management actions, accountability and insufficient oversight activities. High staff turnover in certain areas or key roles could be a good sign that things need to change at the corporate level. The CAE must understand how the current environment impacts employee morale, performance, productivity and overall satisfaction. Does it relate to unhealthy incentives, high pressures, lack of communication, unrealistic goals, poor leadership, harsh working conditions and a weak control environment? Take a close look at your corporate culture. Can you honestly say that your culture is healthy, transparent and empowers employees to do the right thing?

An excellent corporate culture requires a clear code of ethics, conflict of interest declarations, good team morale, low staff turnover, higher employee engagement, better senior management accountability and engagement to resolve issues timely, excellent tone at the top, transparent communications, high corporate reputation among employees and customers, mature risk management and compliance frameworks, robust policies and procedures, fair rewards and incentive programmes for all employees (organization rewards the right kind of behaviour but penalize the wrong one), constant improvements and training opportunities. These good practices do not guarantee an excellent organizational culture; organizations must continue reinforcing zero tolerance and adequate behavioural, ethical and compliance standards. Have you audited the corporate culture in prior audit engagements? Did you consider a holistic audit? Are you considering culture risk in your risk assessments?

Organizations with a positive corporate culture have always had better opportunities for improvement and will positively impact the business transformation, improve customer services and feedback and enhance employee morale and engagement. There is never an ideal scenario, but corporate culture must constantly evolve to support leading best practices; this can be a tremendous competitive advantage for an organization. The foundation must be there, and the guidance and corporate standards must be clear. They must be available to everyone to support a healthier environment and the resolution of control gaps.

The Sarbanes-Oxley Act of 2002 resulted from the corporate financial scandals involving Enron, WorldCom and Global Crossing. Effective in 2006, all publicly traded companies must implement and report internal accounting controls to the SEC. In addition, specific provisions of Sarbanes-Oxley also apply to privately held companies. It also encourages the disclosure of corporate fraud by protecting whistleblower employees who report illegal activities. Section 806 of the Sarbanes-Oxley Act authorizes the U.S. Department of Labor to protect whistleblower complaints against employers who retaliate and further allows the Department of Justice to charge those responsible for the retaliation criminally (US Department of Labor).

Section 406 of the Sarbanes-Oxley Act (US Securities and Exchange Commission) requires reporting companies to disclose the following information:

- Whether a company has adopted a code of ethics for its principal executive officer, chief financial officer, principal accounting officer or controller, or persons performing similar functions.
- If a company has not adopted a code of ethics, the reasons must be provided.
- Any changes to, or waivers of, the code of ethics provisions.

A well-written, user-friendly code of ethics can create the foundation of integrity, trust and ethical behaviour promoted and supported by top management; a code of conduct describes why they are so important to the success and reputation of the organization. Also, it can provide the framework that employees can use and follow to execute their daily activities. Whenever employees have doubts about whether an action is ethical, they can use the guidance to make the right decision or to escalate concerns further.

Some organizations may have tremendous or good signs of corporate culture, but others have questionable and dramatic cultures. I still remember the first time I tried to raise a cultural issue in an organization; I got many challenges, but I was determined to raise that issue. I challenged the business, presented the facts and socialized it with all key stakeholders. This generated many changes in the organization and a positive business transformation. Auditors are responsible for auditing culture, which is more required nowadays. Auditors must have the courage and passion for challenging and driving organizational changes. Difficult conversations are necessary with senior management; we all need to learn from this process, including the first and second lines of defence.

A culture audit will help assess where your organization is and whether senior management, employees and third-party vendors are all supporting the overall business strategies and company goals. It will help you assess the control environment's effectiveness, employee morale and engagement, adequacy of the code of ethics, mechanisms to escalate concerns, and internal and external communications, including policies and procedures. Few of the potential growth factors that contribute to the relevance of managing culture risk and ethics could be the followings:

- Emerging regulatory and compliance risks include dealing with new third-party vendors, mergers and acquisitions or a market expansion.

- Social media facilitates feedback or commentaries online (e.g. misconduct and fraud events), so companies and employees are more exposed when events happen.
- Reputational risk due to significant fraud events, technology incidents, cybersecurity and customer complaints may impact the customer experience, operational losses and compliance risk, among others.
- Higher auditor's expectations to have the right skills to review culture risk, unethical behaviours, potential sales practices, bribery management, organization's governance structure, risk management policies and procedures.
- Lack of data to proactively identify potential unethical behaviours. Thus, auditors should leverage more data to analyse customer complaints, allegations, operational losses and significant fraud events, including bribery and corruption risks.

The organizational culture is constantly changing with new leaders, new employees, new corporate enhancements, new regulatory requirements and the latest changes in the control environment. Audit leaders need to plan risk-based culture audits ahead and conduct these audits per risk assessment results or when new emerging risks arise. However, sometimes audits could be done more frequently or earlier due to organizational changes, new ethical concerns, internal significant fraud events or sales practices.

The CAE must determine the best approach and skills required to conduct these audits (e.g. local or external resources from other regions or co-sources). For example, during retail branch or wealth management audits, auditors and SMEs can develop a cultural questionnaire or employee survey to assess employee morale, their goals and expectations, performance concerns or incentive pressures, their understanding of code of conduct, escalation protocols, incentive programmes, policies and procedures.

Here are a few potential survey questions to consider during future audits:

- Do you understand your goals?
- Have you discussed your performance goals with management?
- Are expectations clear and effectively communicated?
- Did you experience any incentive pressures?
- How would you describe the organization's leadership style?
- Do you feel appreciated by the organization?
- Do you feel appreciated by your manager?
- Does your manager support your goals and career aspirations? How?
- Does your manager provide timely feedback?
- How are employees recognized and rewarded?
- How diverse is your team?
- Do you know how to raise concerns or escalate ethical or inadequate behaviours? How?

- Do you feel free to make decisions or need your manager's approval first?
- How are customer complaints or third-party vendor complaints identified and resolved?
- Does your business or team manage risk in compliance with the company's risk appetite?
- Did you complete your mandatory training?

To develop these questionnaires, auditors should consider senior management and the board's feedback to address specific concerns regarding incentive programmes, strategic business goals and potential sales practices. Auditors must be transparent with management when taking this testing approach, as auditors will interview their employees.

I want to share a few ideas and tips for future testing:

- Interview top executives to understand the tone at the top, and their leadership style in identifying, monitoring and resolving issues. The behaviour of top executives has a tremendous impact on the organizational culture; they should also promote the right culture at lower levels. Are they familiar with the MCAs, self-assurance activity results and open issues? Leading by example is important and influential, and they should support a zero-tolerance policy. If senior management promotes ethical behaviour, rewards integrity and promotes trust and transparency, others will naturally operate in a risk-minded way.
- Assess how management promotes a culture of risk awareness (e.g. delivering internal and external training, attending workshops with experts from the first, second and third lines of defence, and leading relevant forums or committees to independently analyse fraud and ethical events, employee involvement and actions taken). Training should be robust and conducted in person rather than online; relevant and accurate examples are discussed to promote discussions and lessons learnt. How is management tracking the risk awareness progress? Does the code of ethics exist? Is there an independent ethics committee to discuss sensitive and confidential cases?
- Review corporate policies and procedures to understand the tone at the top. Does management support D&I initiatives? Are guidelines specific, transparent, available and go beyond the equivalent of "if you see something, say something"?
- Review risk scorecards and metrics for each business line to identify areas of concern and understand business results, current risk appetite and tolerance. Are the thresholds reasonable and attainable? Management should share overall scores across the organization, quickly

motivating employees to improve and reach their goals. This will encourage employees to do the right thing; everyone is engaged.

- Review significant fraud events and actions taken by management, especially internal fraud events. Is there a zero-tolerance culture? Did management penalize employees for committing internal fraud? Are adequate policies and procedures to identify, track, analyse, escalate and resolve internal ethical concerns? Have lessons learnt been shared with employees to minimize any potential risks? Organizations must integrate lessons learnt into communications and future training opportunities to promote transparency, better employee expectations and performance results.
- Observe people's behaviour while visiting retail branches, third-party locations and other business locations, and interact with customers. Auditors can identify important red flags for further research and analysis. Do front-line managers play a role in risk oversight activities? Are adequate checker controls in place when managing cash, processing customer wire transfers or other transactions, screening customers or opening new customer accounts?
- Review the incentive programmes. Auditors should be able to review policies and procedures, incentive calculations, employee deductions due to penalties imposed for errors made (red flags), and compensation and performance metrics aligned with the organization's core values. Are the goals reasonable and attainable, or is the organization indirectly pressuring people to commit unethical behaviours? When Enron went bankrupt, it was clear that its goal-setting process and practices were at the heart of misconduct (challenging and specific employee performance goals were set).
- Review the compliance programmes; IA needs to review what truly works and what does not work at all. Is the compliance programme robust enough to identify unethical behaviour? Does it leverage sufficient data? Is it innovative?
- Review the hiring process, including employee screening, training and how HR assesses job candidates' moral development.
- Leverage relevant data (e.g. customer complaints, allegations, operational losses, internal fraud events and transactional data to identify trends, patterns and concerns) for further research, testing or conducting thematic reviews. HR should be able to share staff turnover rates by business, department, results of exit interviews, employee complaints and allegations and unethical cases. Auditors can also obtain additional information from whistleblower hotlines. For example, auditors should consider customer complaints regarding third-party vendors' performance or open issues as they may highlight other concerns for further consideration.

- Review and analyse customer feedback; always review online review platforms and Facebook, LinkedIn and Google to identify any potential concerns or signs of positive or negative culture. Does the company have a good reputation? Do customers trust the products and services offered? What's trending on the news now? Raising concerns based only on observations could be complicated; however, data analytics can facilitate discussions with senior management.
- Analyse how the pandemic or other events have impacted the corporate culture as employees work remotely. How are leaders engaging with their direct reports? How are they establishing genuine connections with them? How is the pandemic impacting team morale and productivity? COVID-19 changed everything and brought additional challenges to nurturing corporate values.

I highly recommend including culture in each audit engagement. We need to consider cultural risk in every risk assessment. The higher the risk score for this driver, the higher the need to review culture risk during the audit. Also, during each audit engagement, auditors have an invaluable opportunity to observe and document management reactions and leadership styles. "Trust your instincts" when you review something that may be related to an ethical concern or something that does not look right (still not confirmed, but you honestly believe something does not make sense). Sometimes stakeholders do not want to cooperate with audits or try to convince auditors not to review specific areas, their responses are not too convincing, or they do not respond to follow-up questions. Thus, experienced auditors can quickly notice that. Auditors need to use professional judgement as it is not easy to evaluate culture; they need to assess the results of interviews and observations carefully, understand the business and leverage relevant data to conclude testing.

Auditors need to go deeper and deeper when identifying initial concerns; they need to identify the root cause to determine whether an underlying cultural behaviour caused the issue. They should use critical thinking to challenge processes and current practices that are great at first but do not make sense anymore. They must ask questions, review the evidence carefully, understand assumptions and analyse basic concepts. Do employees have too much pressure to meet the sales goals? Is there a conflict of interest with a particular third-party vendor? Why was there a control break; why did management not penalize a few bank tellers for having higher cash differences (all over the authorized cash limit thresholds)? Why are policies and procedures too vague? Why did management not fire the employee who committed the fraud? Make sure you go deeper to identify the root cause of your initial concern. Thus, auditor leaders must discuss issues with senior management and the audit committee that may indicate a poor culture. If similar concerns are identified in multiple audits, audit leaders must escalate this further; this may require a holistic solution, quicker response and more oversight activities from senior management.

The CAE needs to take a lead role in assessing corporate culture risk across the enterprise and evaluate the staff skills and capacity to provide adequate input, transparent communication and constructive feedback to senior management, the board and the audit committee. The CEO, board and audit committee should welcome culture audits. The CAE will need to have proper conversations with key leaders to explain the purpose and value of each audit to gain additional support. This is an overly sensitive area, and you should expect challenges from management. Courage is another essential attribute to challenge ethical concerns once identified; auditors need to review things deeper and not be afraid to discuss sensitive topics. However, the CAE can be a fantastic leader to drive change and add value to the organization by embracing challenges and looking for additional opportunities to develop the audit team and more data analytics tools. It only requires one individual to challenge one thing and change how an organization or people behave.

Let's move now to another great topic: blockchain.

References

US Department of Labor, *Sarbanes-Oxley Act of 2002, Public Law 107–204, Section 806*, US Department of Labor, Washington, DC, www. dol.gov.

US Securities and Exchange Commission, *Final Rule: Disclosure Required by Sections 406 and 407 of the Sarbanes-Oxley Act of 2002, SEC Release Nos. 33-8177; 34-47235; File No. S7-40-02, RIN 3235-AI66*, US Securities and Exchange Commission, Washington, DC.

Chapter 22

Internal Audit Role in Auditing Blockchain

While blockchain is gaining popularity, audit leaders must prepare to help stakeholders and assess key risks related to this new transformational and innovative technology. It has impacted different industries and will transform the banking and financial industry. The adoption rate of blockchain technology may differ for each organization, country, third-party vendor and customer. IA has a marvellous opportunity to provide excellent value when assessing new or emerging risks and conducting smart audits. Of course, the advisory role will be relevant here too, and IA needs to start gaining additional skills and expertise as this technology continues gaining more momentum.

El Salvador has passed President Nayib Bukele's bill to make Bitcoin the legal tender in the country. Biden put out an executive order on cryptocurrencies (March 9, 2022), calling on the government to examine the risks and benefits of cryptocurrencies. The Biden administration also wants to explore a digital version of the dollar. Companies use cryptocurrencies, such as Microsoft, Starbucks, Subway and Burger King. Thus, blockchain will continue gaining momentum; new and more sophisticated risks will arise, including more cyber-attacks and fraud events, climate change and other potential pandemics. As more countries and organizations will consider using blockchain-based solutions, IA leaders need to consider the skills gaps and how to build stronger audit teams to meet the demand; they need to be prepared to advise management to minimize new or new emerging risks.

A blockchain is a distributed ledger that allows digital assets transactions in real-time; it is a shared database that records transactions made in bitcoin or another cryptocurrency. There are nearly 9,000 cryptocurrencies (February 2023), so users can transfer digital assets around the globe in exchange for good services and products and illicit transactions (e.g. to commit crime and support terrorism, to hide financial activities such as money laundering, tax and sanction evasions, and to commit theft

DOI: 10.4324/9781003431893-23

and fraud). Almost all cryptocurrencies, including Bitcoin, Ethereum, Bitcoin Cash and Litecoin, are secured via blockchain networks. If you enter a record, it will be permanent; thus, this technology is secure (using cryptography), and you will not be able to modify it. Other nodes on the network can also see this transaction. This adds more transparency and security to this process. Thus, a blockchain is a shared ledger distributed across several nodes in a network of computers. A blockchain network can be open to the public (Bitcoin and Ethereum) or private (Corda and Hyperledger). Anyone can read and write in a public network without explicit authorization and permission.

How blockchain technology can benefit users:

- Enhances security; blockchain technology uses advanced security technology, and each transaction is encrypted, confirmed and has a proper link to the old transaction using a hashing method. The confirmation indicates that the transaction has been recorded in the blockchain.
- Improves transparency; the supply chain becomes more transparent than ever.
- Improves efficiencies; the digital ledger provides a single place to store transactions, and the automation of processes reduces the time invested.
- Decentralized; no chances of one-point failure.
- No barrier to entry as there is no central authority to accept or reject users in the system.
- Reduces costs as intermediaries (third-party vendors) are not necessarily accelerating the clearing and settlement processes in security trading.
- Minimizes payment risk; identities are not linked with accounts or transactions.
- Minimizes fraudulent activities; the private key owner can only transfer digital funds. The private key ensures actual ownership of all digital assets as opposed to custodial access provided by banks.
- Smart contract-triggered financing; automated innovative contract protocols avoid disputes and fraudulent activities in transactions, settlements and claims processing.

With blockchain technology, banks can verify customer documents and confirm the genuineness of the sender and receiver, facilitating the onboarding process. It can also grant loans facilitating the customer verification process and the customer journey regarding account maintenance requests across all business areas. This technology can also process mortgage loans in a few days. Also, payments via blockchain can be more secure than a typical bank transaction. You do not need to share sensitive information when you make a Bitcoin payment.

Blockchains are used to explore medical research, in e-commerce (to track, send and receive products), in marketing campaigns or efforts, to improve the accuracy of healthcare records, compliance with BSA/AML regulations and so much more. Thus, everything will be tokenized at a certain point, so organizations need to start simplifying products, processes and procedures to facilitate blockchain implementation. The time is now.

We also need to consider the risks as they favour criminal activities. For example, cryptocurrencies can facilitate transactions on the dark web, including weapons, drugs, human trafficking and terrorism. This brings new challenges for the IA function, considering that this technology is used across different industries and countries. This raises a few questions for the audit profession:

- What are the main challenges for your IA department?
- Are you prepared (the first, second and third lines of defence)?
- Has IA developed adequate procedures or testing programmes to assess the performance of blockchain systems and other potential risks?
- Are there adequate business monitoring processes in place?
- What are the internal and external risks?
- How can IA add value when an organization is about to develop or implement blockchain?
- What would be the best engagement model?
- How can IA adapt to innovative technologies?
- What would be the IA's role as innovative technologies emerge?
- What are the skill gaps?
- How can IA leverage data analytics?

IA must be involved in every step when the organization adopts blockchain to provide valuable input related to corporate governance, data access, data maintenance, data storage, BCP, code management, change management, fraud management, AML, cybersecurity and third-party vendor risks, among others. IA involvement will vary, considering that the organization may develop its blockchain internally or implement one provided by third parties.

IA needs to build the expertise to be fully prepared when this happens. IA needs to hire auditors with stronger coding, cybersecurity, data analytics, AML, fraud, compliance and blockchain knowledge and expertise. As mentioned in previous chapters, hiring auditors with better analytical and critical thinking skills who can innovate, help others look outside the box and drive more value-added change is genuinely relevant.

When it comes to institutions such as banks, the following risks must be considered during the project development, implementation and user phases:

- *Project governance and implementation risk:* proper framework must be in place to manage the entire project and implementation. Policies and procedures must be developed to handle issues identified during and after implementation, adequate committee governance, structure and a formal charter (to take the project and ensure proper project oversight, budget, resources), procedures for adding or removing nodes, algorithm verification, network access and authentication protocols, change management, data security and storage, code design, testing, implementation and maintenance. Blockchain does not have proper standards considering its rapid growth. Thus, there is no standardization across the blockchain ecosystem.
- *Information security risk:* auditors need to assess the critical controls in place to protect customers' PII, including personal health and financial information. Data privacy is one of the essential issues regarding blockchain. Thus, existing corporate protection mechanisms must expand to blockchain or distributed ledger technology (e.g. adequate rules and protocols to comply with policies, procedures and regulatory requirements). For example, individuals holding private keys or information that controls access to digital assets could also be at risk of potential kidnap or extorsion, their credentials could be stolen or compromised, or hackers can attack their personal computers or mobile devices to get their keys.
- *User access risk:* one-way blockchain ensures the security of each transaction by using public and private keys. These keys are a series of characters that offers unique security properties and follow encryption protocols. If a user loses the private key, the user will lose access to their data. Each organization must define blockchain security and access protocols; thus, auditors must assess cybersecurity practices to validate permitted users and methods in developing smart contracts. How are companies granting access to keys or digital signatures?
- *Data storage and disaster recovery risk:* adequate controls must be in place to ensure data recovery in case of catastrophic events; thus, auditors need to review BCP. Also, expanding ledgers leads to a need for continuous enhancement of storage capacity. The processing power and storage capacity increase in a blockchain environment as every recordable transaction is verified. Thus, BCP will require a shorter recovery time.

- *Code:* the code used to write the blockchain software is another relevant area to review. Auditors need to evaluate cybersecurity risks and any potential exposures to bad actors who may want to impact the code during planning, development, implementation, maintenance and usage. Inadequate encryption protocols can expose the data stored on the network. Auditors need to validate the controls over the blockchain network, including smart contracts (code using the blockchain that allows parties to create a self-executing contract) to mitigate code and cryptography risk.
- *Malicious users can impact the blockchain network:* so organizations must design and implement critical controls to minimize cyberattacks. Management needs to consider this when developing and implementing this virtual technology. Continuous assessments and testing of critical controls are highly recommended. How secure is your company network? How about third-party vendors? How are companies mitigating the risk of phishing attacks?

  Phishing is a type of cyber-attack where a malicious actor poses as a reputable entity or business to collect customers' PII (e.g. credit or debit card details, username, password, customer's address). Phishing is used to steal digital currencies from users.
- IT operational risk: auditors need to consider any potential operational risks resulting from transactional and processing errors (human and system errors), handling fluctuation in clearing and settlement transactions and payments. A root cause analysis could facilitate identifying control breaks to enhance the control environment. Management should identify key reporting mechanisms, better monitoring controls and continuity of business and disaster recovery mechanisms to address any issues or concerns. Data analytics will play a relevant role in timely identifying trends, problems and anomalies for further research or testing.
- *Regulatory and legal risk:* although this innovative technology is gaining momentum, a global regulatory framework is not yet in place. All participants must agree on mutually acceptable terms and comply with current laws and regulations. A legal framework is highly recommended, but a standardized regulation on data privacy, jurisdiction and dispute resolution is necessary. Different jurisdictions have different laws and regulations, and this virtual technology will have other global implications.
- The Department of Justice's Cryptocurrency Enforcement Framework (published in October 2020) recognizes that cryptocurrencies play "a role in many of the most significant criminal and national security threats our nation faces." It also summarizes existing laws and regulations surrounding cryptocurrencies and discusses some of the primary regulators in the cryptocurrency space: the Department of the Treasury's Financial

Crimes Enforcement Network (FinCEN); Office of Foreign Assets Control (OFAC); Office of the Comptroller of the Currency (OCC); SEC; the Commodity Futures Trading Commission (CFTC), and the Internal Revenue Services (IRS) and Tax Enforcement.

- *Third-party vendor risk*: as blockchain becomes more adept, third-party risk will grow. Third-party vendors could provide solutions such as wallets, smart contracts and blockchain payment platforms. Nowadays, they are exposed to higher risks such as lack of proper controls, internal or external fraud events, cybercrime, employee errors, weak security protocols and harmful codes. They can face additional claims or litigations due to errors related to pricing valuations, reporting, administration of funds, trade execution and algorithm performance. The organization must review the contract agreements carefully to protect organizations against these events, especially during the development and implementation phases.

- *AML risk:* criminals are using and will continue using cryptocurrencies to support terrorism, hide financial activities and other suspicious activities to avoid detection and punishment. Organizations need more robust AML/CFT preventive and monitoring programmes and implement stronger account opening procedures for those that operate virtual currencies or operate virtual currency money services businesses. In addition, companies that process transactions at the global level must be aware of the registration and KYC requirements in other countries. IA department should have strong Federal Bank Secrecy Act (BSA) programmes.

- *Valuation risk:* poor valuation mechanism of cryptocurrencies and no stable prices. For example, bitcoin suppers many changes that are difficult to predict. Thus, investors do not have protection against their investments.

- *Fraud risk:* fraud losses are increasing globally, so companies need stronger fraud management frameworks, detailed fraud risk assessments, key controls and preventive and monitoring tools. The "Occupational fraud 2022: a report to the nations" (Association of Certified Fraud Examiners, ACFE) highlights that 8% of reported cases involved cryptocurrencies.

Cryptocurrency fraud and cryptocurrency scams are rising. Here are some common scams:

- Higher returns on investments offered to new crypto users. Once the new user sends the money to invest in new projects, scammers will disappear, losing the investments.

- Wrong address. User is tricked into sending their digital assets to the wrong address. This can happen when someone posts a fake address online or a typo in the address.
- Crypto theft. Hackers can hack investors' crypto wallets and steal bitcoin or other cryptocurrencies.
- Ponzi schemes. New adopters are required to give artificial returns to the early adopters. A high-yield investment programme (HYIP) is an example of a Ponzi scheme. This investment fraud offers a significant return on investment by convincing existing users to increase their capital with new buyers.
- Pump and dump schemes. Stock owners try to raise prices before selling off their holdings at an artificial peak.
- Initial coin offerings (ICO) scams. The SEC fined Floyd Mayweather and DJ Khaled for failing to disclose payments received for promoting investments in ICOs (Centra Tech). Here are some additional red flags to identify ICO scams: sky-high returns promised (Bitconnect), unclear technical white papers or copied from others and long-term roadmap, no digital token needed (Dentacoin), fraudulent, anonymous or nonexistent team members and background (Centra).
- Financial crimes. Crypto's instant transactions, portability and international reach mean that crypto can be used for money laundering, bribery and kickback payments, and tax avoidance.
- Conversion of misappropriated assets to cryptocurrency.
- Manipulation of reported cryptocurrencies assets on the financial statements.

Blockchain technology can potentially improve business processes in financial services, capital markets and other industries in the short and long term. Robust key controls, reporting and monitoring controls must be in place to identify red flags and minimize the risks discussed earlier. Auditors need detailed risk assessments, business monitoring activities, continuous auditing tools and smart audits to evaluate these potential and other emerging risks. Before an organization adopts this innovative technology, auditors should review high-risk processes and key controls to minimize these risks.

Let's focus on a few key testing areas for financial institutions as listed below:

- As customers record all transactions in a shared ledger so auditors can perform real-time audits with real-time data, IA teams can keep a read-only node on the blockchain to monitor transactions and leverage data analytics for further testing. Auditors could leverage the automated controls (if any) to design more continuous auditing tools. The business may develop additional reporting and tools; thus, auditors should validate all.

- Review intelligent contracts. The Blockchain system supports smart contracts, which could facilitate automated compliance testing. Auditors can save time by identifying the key controls and data sources for testing purposes. They should consider the following, too: user access, code changes, third-party assessments, and incident and change management processes, among others.
- Review key reconciliations and key controls to ensure accuracy and integrity of information recorded in the blockchain and the organization's financial and tax records. Auditors need to consider and review the tax implications, as well. Continuous auditing tools can be a perfect mechanism for identifying potential red flags.
- Test the blockchain governance framework, Steering committee role and engagement (e.g. budget, resources, issues identified), management oversight activities, compliance with policies, procedures (e.g. change management, data management and storage, fraud management and regulatory requirements), and regulatory requirements, the second line of defence engagement, issue management activities (e.g. tracking, monitoring and resolution) and third-party vendors (e.g. due diligence, business monitoring activities and terminations).
- Test user access, remote key management controls (key generation, storage, distribution, recovery), confidentially of the information and vulnerability assessment of code and blockchain system (to minimize cybersecurity attacks). Management needs to complete penetration testing; thus, auditors need to review the testing conducted, issues identified and resolution.
- Test continuity of business and disaster recovery plans considering the new blockchain implementation requirements. If required, verify and review updated policies and procedures, corresponding plan approvals and testing methodology approach, testing results and remediation plans.
- Review transaction agreements among all parties involved in the transactions to ensure compliance with laws and regulations. For example, blockchain technology can improve regulatory processes such as know your customer (KYC) rules, AML and data protection regulations. Thus, auditors must assess the regulatory requirements, the committee's governance, regulatory reporting mechanisms, management oversight activities and remediation plans. They must review the second line of defence model engagement, challenges provided and compliance testing programmes by reviewing presentation materials, meeting minutes and testing results.
- Validate the completeness and accuracy of data recorded in the blockchain database. Critical controls must be in place to access, archive and retrieve data without losing any information.

- Review the blockchain vendor selection process, due diligence, contract agreement, SLAs, third-party risk assessments, business monitoring activities and key reporting provided by blockchain vendors (e.g. performance metrics, issues identified and customer complaints). Auditors also need to audit high and critical third-party vendors and enhance business monitoring mechanisms to identify new or emerging risks and red flags proactively.
- Review the resource capacity. Is blockchain resource intensive? Is the organization experiencing resource capacity issues? How about oversight activities? Are there appropriate monitoring controls in place?
- Fraud management programme. Organizations must identify and design adequate preventive tools to minimize fraud and financial reporting risks. Auditors will have to review the anti-fraud controls such as code of conduct, policies, management certification of financial statements, hotlines, fraud training programmes, fraud risk assessments, management oversight activities including key fraud management reports, proactive data monitoring and data analysis.

Audit leaders must build teams with proper skills to audit blockchain technology and cryptocurrencies. SMEs, stronger IA testing programmes and more innovative tools will be required to monitor and review key controls. The technology will advance so much that new tools and enhanced protocols across industries will be a new reality. No single testing programme will be sufficient to audit blockchain and cryptocurrencies and must be adapted to each organization.

IA departments will need a significant level of technology and cybersecurity expertise, including data analytics and innovation skills; thus, audit leaders have an unprecedented opportunity to play a critical role here by helping organizations with blockchain and cryptocurrency assessments. Training opportunities should be in place and delivered to key personnel evaluating end-to-end processes. Auditors need to be familiar with organization policies, procedures, regulatory requirements and all risks to effectively assess the risk project governance framework, risk management activities, high-risk processes and key controls. They must also enhance their blockchain technology skills to play an effective advisory role. Thus, auditors need to get more familiar with this innovative technology and distributed ledgers that will continue to evolve.

The pandemic has changed everything; digitization will continue to gain momentum. Digital assessment will be the new paradigm; customers will want to access more and new online products, minimize interactions with different actors and pay fewer or no fees. Organizations will have to compete highly to provide better, more attractive, innovative products;

customer journeys will become more important to attract and retain customers. Blockchain can facilitate and transform things. Thus, auditors will need shorter audit engagements, better audit scopes and more continuous auditing to identify risks in real-time.

Again, think back to how the internet gained momentum and spread across the globe. Before global adoption, it existed for a long time; now, think about blockchain for a second. Blockchain will follow a similar approach and reach greater masses even faster. The marketplace still understands blockchain technology, its value and its usage, and there is a long way to go. All stakeholders need to understand these risks, control procedures and take steps to ensure all risks are minimized in the long term. Thus, audit leaders must define a plan to obtain and develop audit skills to provide better assurance and advisory activities. To add value to their stakeholders, they must stay abreast of leading guidance regarding governance, risk management, regulatory requirements, AML/CFT, third-party, technology, cybersecurity and fraud risk considerations.

Let's move to another important topic: the chief audit executive's role.

References

ACFE, *Occupational Fraud 2022: A Report of the Nations,* March 2022, https://acfepublic.s3.us-west-2.amazonaws.com/2022+Report+to+the+Nations.pdf.

US Department of Justice, *Report of the Attorney General's Cyber Digital Task Force,* US Department of Justice, Washington, DC, October 2020, https://www.justice.gov/archives/ag/page/file/1326061/download.

Chapter 23

Chief Audit Executive's Role

The purpose of leadership is to lead, influence, develop, motivate others and drive change in an organization. A leader has a strong vision that others may not see at the beginning but has the conviction and passion for picturing the future and actions that need to be taken to achieve better results. The chief audit executive's (CAE's) role is critical to the IA department's success. The CAE organizes the IA department; establishes the goals; executes the annual audit plan; requests the budget to conduct audit engagements and other audit activities; supports innovation and data analytics strategies; hires, retains and develops the audit teams; defines the audit performance metrics and team goals; and builds relationships with stakeholders.

The CAE needs to add more value to stakeholders; they will have to manage the audit plan and discuss relevant (high and critical issues) issues with senior management and the board of directors. The CAE leadership style can influence and impact the IA's effectiveness and reputation. A CAE may have a department with only nine, one hundred, or over one thousand people. The current CAE or new one wants to be a successful leader. However, different leaders have unique styles; few can be successful in specific organizations but struggle in others.

Considering the current environment, new challenges will arise, including additional pressures to improve efficiencies and add more value to the entire organization. Thus, the IA function should have a more impactful role by challenging senior management and auditing high-risk processes and high-risk technology projects, including strategic business areas by leveraging more data analytics and technology tools. Audit leaders must have the courage to challenge significant issues and lead themselves well to guide the IA function and impact others. A great leader is followed, respected, listened to, trusted and supported even when delivering sad news. The CAE must be a motivator and influencer to drive change and influence others. The role of the CAE has evolved in this century; leaders need to be closer to people; people demand more attention and human touch. Emotional

DOI: 10.4324/9781003431893-24

intelligence is critical; we follow visionary leaders who have the passion and hearts to make changes and influence others.

IA needs to be fully prepared to play the new game; we need more robust data analytics tools to anticipate risks and control breaks, identify opportunities for enhancements, identify emerging risks and communicate with stakeholders honestly, quicker and much better. Audit leaders must lead by example, stay engaged and serve others. Yes, audit leaders need to understand that they are in a privileged position to help their teams and stakeholders. They are in a unique position to direct, shape and positively influence change and impact the lives of others. To become more service-oriented, the CAE must understand stakeholders' needs, challenges and concerns and support his/her audit teams.

There is no better leadership style, but specific characteristics and characters benefit more than others, especially when managing people and interacting with different stakeholders. There are different CAE styles; there is no basic formula to becoming phenomenally successful, knowing that they can also be impacted by the organizational culture, internal politics, senior management desires and willingness to change, and maturity of the audit team. However, I would like to see more inspirational leaders in CAE roles. They should have the passion, courage, motivation and preparation to take an organization and audit team to the next level. We need more leaders to deliver first-class audit work and build stronger teams. This will not be easy, especially for new CAEs that must understand the organizational culture, business strategy and challenges, and also develop good relationships with stakeholders.

When considering a new CAE role or trying to find a new CAE for your organization, it is essential to understand the challenges faced by the audit team to position the IA function in a better place. Here are a few relevant questions to consider further through this process:

- *Has the CAE position experienced a high staff attrition rate?* – if the three is a high attrition rate, this is a red flag. If the company cannot retain a CAE or its direct reports for a long time, this will impact the department's ability to drive change and provide additional value. This could indicate how others value, respect and trust the IA function.
- *What is the IA team morale?* – if this is low, this is another red flag; how can we be more successful or drive change if we cannot retain talent? It will be challenging to conduct valuable audit engagement and other activities without the right audit skills. This is one of the most relevant topics a CAE needs to resolve; additional steps and corrective actions will be required. Underestimating this topic can have a devastating impact in short and long terms. Reputation is key to retaining good talent

and building trust; the reputation among team members spreads quickly outside the IA department.

- *Does IA have a suitable resource capacity?* – if not, the CAE needs to explore this deeper; why does the CAE not have the proper support to bring additional resources? This could be another indicator of IA recognition in the organization. If there is insufficient resource capacity, the CAE must escalate this to the audit committee. We cannot minimize the IA resource power if we want to add more value to the organization. Today's business world is one in which auditors are expected to work longer hours to absorb the work of others (positions are vacant or due to high turnover). CAEs and chief audit directors need suitable capacity and skills to meet the audit plan.
- *Are all chief audit directors working together?* – we need more holistic audits and review end-to-end processes, and all IA teams must work together. Do we genuinely need so many IA teams working in silos? It is time to rethink the way we conduct audits. We may need fewer IA teams, better data and smarter audit scopes to add more value to our stakeholders. An audit is an art; there are different artists and artwork but only one, Pablo Picasso. Auditors need better training; they need to know the business well, have more audit experts to identify audit findings and provide better value. We also need better leadership to guide, teach and challenge audit teams and stakeholders. No stakeholders will be happy with someone who plays politics or is only interested in just getting the paycheck.
- *What is the management style when sharing audit findings?* Do they respond timely? – this is especially important; if management challenges too much the audit findings (no apparent reason) and does not respond timely or tries to avoid IA feedback, the CAE will need to work more closely with senior management. However, they need to escalate this to the audit committee if things worsen.
- *What is your CAE style?* What was the prior CAE style? What CAE style are you looking for? An autocratic style is not good as impacts negatively the team morale. This style will never be beneficial during the IA transformation process. It will hurt the team deeply, and people will start moving out. This will result in a high or higher staff attrition rate. The transformational style will help but not all CAEs will bring that to the table. A transformational leader would benefit the IA function; the emotional skills to help others, add value and transform or improve things are relevant. However, these leaders are scarce.
- Here are a few additional questions to consider:

  - What is your leadership style?
  - What is your CAE or chief audit director style?

- For board members: do you pay attention to the soft skills or leadership style when hiring a new CAE?
- Do we need more transformational leaders? These leaders are scarce and are in high demand nowadays.
- What have worked well or have not worked at all?

Audit leaders must add more value to the organization and transform audit work. Thus, the CAE and chief audit directors (future CAEs) need to consider the following:

- We need stronger leaders who drive change without fear, understand the business, are familiar with IA leading best practices and are emotionally intelligent to manage challenges. I would like to see more audit leaders who support audit teams, are willing to be in front of the audience, can articulate audit findings and challenge management constructively. Audit leaders must have confidence, listen more and prepare themselves better when presenting critical concerns or supporting audit teams. Audit leaders know how to challenge things effectively and constructively and work hard for the change they seek; they love what they do and show passion and commitment to do the right things. When leaders demonstrate courage, their teams and others will sincerely follow and respect them.
- They must develop their teams and team members to be better leaders by coaching them, empowering them to make decisions, and influencing the business. Audit leaders need to create more leaders and build stronger and healthier teams. I firmly believe you have the privilege to serve others when you are in a leadership position. Everything starts with the basics. If you care about people, they will care too. The human touch and emotional connections are always important.
- CAEs need to build relationships with their stakeholders; they need to understand the key risks, business strategies, priorities, regulatory requirements, open issues and business monitoring activities, among others. They need to engage senior management, compliance, legal and other assurance functions to develop a more integrated assurance approach. CAEs and chief audit directors must constantly engage with audit teams and senior management to build trust and fully understand business needs and concerns.

  If CAEs hold a seat at the table, they will be able to understand business strategies, challenges, priorities, key technology initiatives and open issues. When IA understands the business strategy and the control environment, the result is smarter audits. Also, the CAE and the company's CEO need to have a common ground and agreement on key priorities for the IA function. Before starting the audit plan, both must meet to discuss the project, future audits and key priorities. CAEs must set aside time to grow positive relationships with the CEO, Chief Financial Officer (CFO) and other key stakeholders to establish trust and know them. They must also develop relationships with the HR department and improve communications with the audit committee chair.

By developing and empowering a strong audit team, the CAEs can focus on building healthier relationships by getting out of the office, picking up the phone and attending critical meetings. CAEs and chief audit directors need to be involved in important business meetings, forums and committee meetings to share IA best practices and feedback and to challenge things. We covered this topic earlier, and we have discussed the importance of identifying key stakeholders and how to build relationships with them.

They need to develop their networks with external partners to be familiar with new emerging risks, IA-leading best practices, industry trends and challenges, especially in the era of data analytics and innovation, including cybersecurity, technology, blockchain and fraud risk. They can learn from external auditors, consultants, third-party vendors and other CAEs.

- Great leaders influence, listen and consider feedback positively. CAEs must get regular input from stakeholders, especially when they attend meetings. Here are potential questions:

  - Is the audit team adding value?
  - Did IA find relevant issues during the last audit?
  - Does the audit team know stakeholders' needs and business priorities?
  - Which strategies can you leverage to influence your stakeholders?
  - Does IA consider the feedback received?

  CAEs must have a smart strategy to build robust and sustainable stakeholder relationships; they must be great communicators and negotiators and consider their feedback when planning audits or after audit engagements. I always trust my gut when discussing relevant topics, key processes or audit findings with my stakeholders. First impressions matter but experience matters, even more when defining an audit scope or selecting topics for further testing. This attribute inspires others when they see a true leader in action.

- CAEs must understand the organizational culture to manage politics adequately and how different pieces work together. Leaders need to be exceptionally skilled here to succeed. I highly recommend developing a plan to be successful within the organization's culture. For example, in specific organizations, CAEs and chief audit directors must discuss the audit report with several stakeholders before publishing it. It can be intense sometimes, but the CAE must go through different layers to ensure everyone is on the same page. Each organization is different; however, the CAE needs to be flexible, open, transparent and mature enough to adapt quickly and influence others.

- CAEs need to develop and retain good talent. The first step is often determining the organization's needs and skills gaps. No single CAE can be successful if he/she does not have a dedicated audit team or a clear vision of the future stage of the IA department. They must recognize and bind the best talent and retain and develop all to support the IA's goals.

  A high staff attrition rate is dramatic, costly, reduces team morale and impacts productivity even more. It is an issue for the IA department when it is so high. This is an accurate indicator of the quality of leadership and leadership style. The remaining employees feel hopeless and start looking outside, too; they start questioning why they should stay. CAEs need to know the root cause and fix this sooner than later. Emotionally intelligent leaders always put first the interest of their teams.

  Many companies have leveraged their audit skills and hired auditors for key business positions; they want IA to serve as a pool for future posts. IA can build its reputation by developing excellent talent for future leadership roles in the organization; this is key to improving the IA's reputation. Auditors need to learn new things constantly; there is high demand for cybersecurity, data analytical skills, fraud risk and technology risk. Audit leaders must focus on coaching, mentoring programmes and talent management and have the budget and flexibility to bring additional resources when required.

- CAEs must focus on innovation and data analytics to drive IA transformation. They should be able to share more value with more impactful data. They need to understand data sources and analytics used by other areas within the organization and identify more opportunities to leverage more data, if possible. They need to develop more effective audit reports, leverage more data and use more data analytics or visualization techniques to facilitate the dialogue with their stakeholders and the board of directors. They should be able to connect the dots and holistically explain how the audit findings impact the business and the organization.

  Stakeholders want more value, and they expect the CAE to provide timely insights on new emerging risks, concerns, themes and best practices. They may want to hear how an issue is addressed in other organizations; this could add considerable value to the entire organization. IA must play a relevant role in the data governance process by sharing best practices regarding data collection and quality, data management and protection across the organization.

Audit leaders need to ask:

- Is there a sound data governance process in the organization?
- Is data governance reviewed in coming technology audits?
- Have critical controls around data (e.g. user access reviews, information security and cybersecurity requirements, code security, cloud security, completeness and accuracy of key management reports) been reviewed?

Change is a fact; IA departments need to innovate more and provide more ideas and better automation to enhance testing and communication with stakeholders. CAEs must challenge the audit teams to improve efficiencies and deliver more excellent value during audit activities. The CAEs must think ahead and envision the future IA state two or three years from now. They must define transformational goals to provide better and more competitive value to stakeholders and the audit teams.

- Senior management appreciates shorter audit reports and audit committee decks so they can focus on matters, such as common themes or hot topics identified in different audits. Investing in better technologies and tools is perceived positively by management and improves IA's reputation.

Audit leaders need to ask:

- What should we start or stop doing?
- Could we automate the audit report?
- Could we enhance how the information is presented to senior management (e.g. better visualization techniques and shorter audit reports)?
- Are we feeding a culture of continuous improvement in our IA department?
- Are we empowering the audit team to drive change or to identify more relevant issues (e.g. compliance, fraud, third-party vendors, technology and AML)?
- Do we have the right tools to identify relevant risks that come with the new digital transformation?
- Are we considering regulatory changes throughout the year? Do we have the right technology to identify or assess those changes?

Thus, CAEs need to keep the technology transformation on the audit committee's agenda and request additional budget and support (e.g. advanced data analytics, machine learning, artificial intelligence and robotics) to improve audit efficiencies and to provide value to stakeholders.

- CAEs also need support to develop their skills through additional coaching and mentoring programmes. A coach could add terrific value (inside or outside the company). They must understand regulatory requirements and build relationships with external regulators and auditors.

- They need to be visible, interact with people and be available to the rest of the audit teams, not only their direct reports (chief audit directors). Leading by phone is not truly leading. They must show up not only in conference calls or town halls; they should be open to one-on-one meetings, mentoring opportunities and support of D&I initiatives. Please do it when you have the experience and power to help others. An open-door policy is required to inspire others to share more ideas and challenge things. Working remotely brings new challenges, but we can leverage the available technology more. Employees that feel listened to and supported are employees who perform even better and decide to stay.

    The chief audit director should attend the closing audit meeting, especially when a bad rating audit report is shared; however, the physical absence is not a good sign as they do not show support to the audit team. This is an excellent example of weak leadership. The audit team always pays attention to the chief audit director's behaviour, style and support; a positive and supportive leader can improve team morale and productivity. Emotional connections are essential to be a successful leader.

- Integrity is another attribute a great CAE must have. Integrity inspires confidence and support and builds trust and reputation among colleagues. They must do the right things. They must be consistent with words and actions. Always do the right thing even when you are getting challenges from stakeholders. Stand for yourself and your audit team when issues are raised or escalated further. I constantly challenge leaders and team members to lead with integrity and transparency. A peaceful mind is always healthier; a tree can be taller, but the root can be even deeper and more impressive. The root can only save the tree in extremely harsh weather conditions; when discussing a sensitive ethical issue, communicate honestly and consistently and never compromise your integrity and objectivity.

    When changes occur, CAEs must be there to support the audit teams to provide hope and guidance. A change is a reality in IA departments; audit leaders need to be transparent and give a clear message, not a confusing one. Change should be people-centred, not a last-minute announcement. Authentic leaders relate to people and care about how to deliver a message in all circumstances.

    Empowering people to accept and support the change is essential but challenging if not managed adequately. Audit leaders need to display integrity and empathy when delivering a message. Sending a last-minute email showing that "new changes are coming in a few minutes" is a terrible approach but having a chief audit director scheduling a last-minute call because the head of audit must announce something in ten minutes gives a dramatic message. The closer you collaborate with people and help them to go through the transition process or changes, the better you will be able to support and manage changes within your IA department.

- Audit leaders need to take care of themselves; a healthy mind and body are essential for the overall success of a leader. You cannot take care of people well if you cannot take care of yourself. When you are going up the ladder, stress is imminent. You need to eat healthily, exercise often and take rest. You need to set an example and encourage others to do the same. Adopting a healthy style improves your longevity as a leader. You can treat others better when you are happier, positive and healthier.

  When chaos arises, only balanced leaders (holistic leaders) manage the storm nicely, inspiring others to go through unprecedented times with a positive attitude. Thus, be positive and honest, and inspire others even more. Authentic leaders who care about their teams constantly look for ways to improve their mental, emotional and spiritual health. Holistic leaders know how to integrate values into their leadership to benefit their teams; they focus on body, mind and spirit, transparency, ethical behaviour and self-awareness. They leave a legacy in the minds and hearts of people; they lead from the inside out. They also take care of themselves while supporting their teams in self-care.

CAEs need to move the IA function to the next level; they need to transform the way audits are conducted; they need to define the future IA state and build a first-class audit team by:

- Starting and enhancing the audit transformation process faster (e.g. better audit automation through risk assessments, business monitoring activities, continuous auditing tools, audit management system, better audit skills and an agile audit approach). For example, a more flexible and agile approach is required at an accelerated speed. If data is used through the audit process, it can also change the way audits are conducted, or issues are identified. We cannot continue using the traditional sampling approach without leveraging data; it is no longer acceptable as we are taking many risks. Auditors need to access better data and have the right tools to conduct more successful audits.
- Incorporating more technology solutions (e.g. robotic process automation, artificial intelligence, advanced data analytics, machine learning). This will also allow a more flexible approach to deliver better feedback and support to your stakeholders. Innovation should be in the DNA of each auditor and embedded in the audit teams. I am not a big fan of having an independent innovation team separated from audit teams as they may not be familiar with the business needs, which could be a waste of time and effort.
- Challenging harder the lack of automation and effectiveness of manual or automated controls implemented by the business; can the company

enhance the customer experience, customer authentication process and the issuance of debit or credit cards?

- Conducting more holistic and targeted audits based on enhanced business monitoring, detailed/automated risk assessments and advanced data analytics tools with a significant focus on cybersecurity, customer experience, product and procedure simplifications and digital transformation, among others. Data analytics and innovation are key to gaining additional efficiencies and positioning the IA function as a strategic advisor.

  Audit leaders need to ask:

  - What can we automate to simplify the audit testing even more?
  - Is there an audit strategy to review cybersecurity risk across the organization?
  - Has cybersecurity been considered in future audits?
  - Do we have the right technology, tools and audit/technology resources to test cybersecurity?
  - Has IA conducted or is planning to conduct cyber-risk assessments of service organizations and third-party vendors?

- Simplifying the IA organizational structure by having fewer audit teams. We cannot audit compliance, AML or fraud independently anymore; it is time to innovate and define smarter audits; we also need the expertise to holistically audit end-to-end processes and the customer's behaviour and experience.

  Organized crime happens across various products and channels; customers have multiple products and access different channels (e.g. retail branches, ATMs and digital banking). Also, fraud occurs across other channels at the same time.

  Audit leaders need to ask:

  - How can we add more value to the business without looking at customers holistically?
  - Can we drive more efficiencies during audits (e.g. financial, AML, sale practices, fraud and compliance audits) by freeing up resources and focusing more on integrated audits and end-to-end processes?
  - Are we prepared for blockchain audits or digital banking audits?

- Considering climate change risks in each risk assessment and audit engagement. Industries more likely affected by climate change include, for example, financial services (including banks and insurance companies), transportation, construction and energy, among others. IA departments should not ignore climate change's impact. Understanding how climate change could impact each organization, including its third-party vendors, is essential.

Auditors could support the business by evaluating climate change risks' financial and strategic impact, including current policies, procedures, models and practical regulatory implications and requirements. IA should review the corporate risk management framework, strategies implemented and accounting assumptions. Auditors could also check the benchmarks, metrics, key performance indicators and leading best practices implemented by the company.

Thus, the CAE should encourage audit teams to enhance their skills and develop adequate risk assessment tools and testing programmes. The CAE should also consider incorporating this topic into annual financial audits going forward or operational audits. An innovative IA function will be incredibly influential in reviewing climate change risks as a partner in good governance.

- Having a flexible audit plan to add emerging risks, key themes and new regulatory requirements. Auditors need to keep up with business changes and understand the impact of those changes in the audit plan.
- Developing a more substantial pool of auditors to support audits and provide more advisory support to stakeholders. Are you hiring and developing the auditor of the future? Are you filling the skill gaps to innovate more?
- Working with the second line of defence to identify synergies or lack of coverage. Auditors must have good relationships with the second line of defence; they need to understand the enterprise risk management process, policies and procedures and be familiar with key risks, processes and controls. There should not be a disconnect; this will facilitate synergies and efficiencies when planning audits, ensuring that high-risk areas or functions (identified by the enterprise risk management team) are also considered.
- Completing audits faster, improving the audit report message and committee decks by focusing on high-risk areas, processes and control gaps.

We need better and emotionally intelligent audit leaders who can inspire others and have more empathy and passion for developing even stronger audit teams. Current business challenges demand higher expertise and better technology tools. To stay relevant and add value, IA needs to innovate and be more efficient and effective when conducting audits and providing practical advisory support to various stakeholders. True leaders are required; it is not enough to have leaders working on the surface or protecting their self-interest; we need great leaders who can drive change and inspire their stakeholders. Toxic leaders place organizations at significant risk through their behaviours and attitude toward others.

The time is now; it is time to transform the IA departments and deliver outstanding first-class audit work. To change the IA function, we need to transform ourselves first. What I love about my job is engaging in different areas of the organization's activities to provide the best value to my stakeholders and building stronger relationships and high-performing audit teams, including the level of cooperation required to drive positive and lasting changes. We also need to innovate more to reduce audit costs and to complete high-quality audit engagements faster and smarter audits (e.g. based on advanced technology tools and data analytics, continuous auditing and a better-integrated approach). Transforming an IA function comes with many challenges, but IA must transform itself quickly to catch the business transformation too. Audit teams and stakeholders deserve great audit leaders.

Bibliography

ACFE, *Occupational Fraud 2022: A Report of the Nations*, March 2022, https://acfepublic.s3.us-west-2.amazonaws.com/2022+Report+to+the+Nations.pdf.

Federal Financial Institutions Examination Council (FFIEC), *Interagency Statement on Pandemic Planning*, FDIC, FIL, Washington, DC, March 6, 2020.

Federal Trade Commission, *Identity Theft Awareness Week Starts Today*, Federal Trade Commission, Washington, DC, February 1, 2021, www.ftc.gov.

Federal Trade Commission, *Social Media a Gold Mine for Scammers in 2021*, Federal Trade Commission, Washington, DC, January 25, 2022, www.ftc.gov.

Federal Trade Commission, *FTC Finds Huge Surge in Consumer Reports About Losing Money to Scams Initiated Through Social Media*, Federal Trade Commission, Washington, DC, January 27, 2022.

Office of Inspector General – U.S. Department of Labor – About OIG, *Significant Concerns*, U.S. Department of Labor, Washington, DC, September 20, 2020, www.dol.gov.

US Department of Justice, *Report of the Attorney General's Cyber Digital Task Force*, US Department of Justice, Washington, DC, October 2020, https://www.justice.gov/archives/ag/page/file/1326061/download.

US Department of Labor, *Sarbanes-Oxley Act of 2002, Public Law 107–204, Section 806*, US Department of Labor, Washington, DC, www. dol.gov.

US Securities and Exchange Commission, *Final Rule: Disclosure Required by Sections 406 and 407 of the Sarbanes-Oxley Act of 2002, SEC Release Nos. 33-8177; 34-47235; File No. S7-40-02, RIN 3235-AI66*, US Securities and Exchange Commission, Washington, DC.

Index

Printed in the United States
by Baker & Taylor Publisher Services